EXPLORING ECOLOGICAL HERMENEUTICS

Society of Biblical Literature

Symposium Series

Victor H. Matthews
Series Editor

Number 46

EXPLORING ECOLOGICAL HERMENEUTICS

EXPLORING ECOLOGICAL HERMENEUTICS

Edited by
Norman C. Habel
and
Peter Trudinger

Society of Biblical Literature

Atlanta

EXPLORING ECOLOGICAL HERMENEUTICS

Library of Congress Cataloging-in-Publication Data

Exploring ecological hermeneutics / edited by Norman C. Habel and Peter Trudinger.
    p. cm. — (Society of Biblical Literature symposium series ; no. 46)
  Includes bibliographical references and index.
  ISBN 978-1-58983-346-3 (paper binding : alk. paper)
  1. Human ecology—Religious aspects—Christianity. 2. Human ecology in the Bible. 3. Bible—Criticism, interpretation, etc. I. Habel, Norman C. II. Trudinger, Peter L., 1953-
  BT695.5.E97 2008
  220.8'3042--dc22
                          2008003577

Printed in the United States of America on acid-free, recycled paper conforming to ANSI/NISO Z39.48-1992 (R1997) and ISO 9706:1994 standards for paper permanence.

CONTENTS

PREFACE

Norman C. Habel & Peter Trudinger

This volume is a representative selection of papers on the emerging field of ecological hermeneutics. These papers were first delivered at a series of Consultations on Ecological Hermeneutics held at the annual meeting of the Society of Biblical Literature in 2004, 2005, and 2006. Subsequently they were revised in the light of the hermeneutical principles outlined in the Introduction. Norman Habel and Peter Trudinger, the editors of this volume, are co-chairs of the ongoing SBL Section on Ecological Hermeneutics.

The introduction to this volume outlines the development of this new hermeneutic and the current steps for interpreting the biblical text. These steps—suspicion, identification, and retrieval—are employed by each of the writers in ways that reflect the concerns and context of the writers as they explore this new hermeneutical process.

Some have focused especially on a suspicion that either the authors or past interpreters of the text have been explicitly or unconsciously anthropocentric in their approach, thereby devaluing or dismissing Earth and Earth community. Others have extended this suspicion to focus on how a dualistic orientation has hindered readers from discerning a basic interconnectedness between humans and nature, or between the spiritual and the material.

Some have taken seriously the question of identification, recognizing that we humans are Earth creatures, an integral part of the fabric of Earth. As such, we have a choice to identify or empathize not only with human figures in the narrative, but also with other Earth creatures and domains of nature. Such identification is especially poignant when we discern the injustice done to nonhuman parts of creation—whether at the hands of God or humanity.

And some have explored the process of retrieval in a variety of ways, seeking to discern the neglected role of Earth in the narrative, to highlight voices of Earth that have been dismissed as mere poetry, or to uncover the suppressed character/role/voice of Earth within the narrative. Several writers have employed their creative imagination and formulated the interests of Earth implied by the narrative, thus enabling Earth to speak.

The diversity of the process employed by these writers illustrates that there is no "orthodox" ecological hermeneutical method. Rather, within the current environmental crisis, in dialog with the growing field of ecology, and in line with recent hermeneutical approaches such as feminist and postcolonial readings, ecological hermeneutics is a work in progress.

A number people have contributed to the preparation of this volume, in particular Joh Wurst, who functioned as the technical editor entrusted with formulating the text according to the sacred norms of the SBL.

The Charles Strong Memorial Trust, an Australian Trust committed to the study of world religions and religion and culture, provided the funding to enable this editing process. The contribution of the Trust to the development of ecological hermeneutics over the years in works such as The Earth Bible is greatly appreciated.

We also appreciate the expert advice of Victor H. Matthews, the series editor, and encouraging guidance of Bob Buller, SBL Editorial Director.

Abbreviations

2 En.	*2 Enoch*
AB	Anchor Bible
AcBib	Academia Biblica
ANET	*Ancient Near Eastern Texts Relating to the Old Testament.* Edited by J. B. Pritchard. 3d ed. Princeton, 1969
ATD	Das Alte Testament Deutsch
AUSS	*Andrews University Seminary Studies*
BDB	Brown, F., S. R. Driver, and C. A. Briggs. *A Hebrew and English Lexicon of the Old Testament.* Oxford, 1907
BHK	*Biblia Hebraica*
BHS	*Biblia Hebraica Stuttgartensia.* Edited by K. Elliger and W. Rudolph. Stuttgart, 1983
BI	*Biblical Illustrator*
Bib	*Biblica*
BibInt	*Biblical Interpretation*
BN	*Biblische Notizen*
BZAW	Beihefte zur Zeitschrift für die alttestamentliche Wissenschaft
BZNW	Beihefte zur Zeitschrift für die neutestamentliche Wissenschaft
CAT	Commentaire de l'Ancien Testament
CTA	*Corpus des tablettes en cunéiformes alphatétiques découvertes à Ras Shamra-Ugarit de 1929 à 1939.* Edited by A. Herdner. Mission de Ras Shamra 10. Paris, 1963
CTU	*The Cuneiform Alphabetic Texts from Ugarit, Ras Ibn Hani, and Other Places.* Edited by M. Dietrich, O. Loretz, and J. Sanmartín. Münster, 1995.
DCH	*Dictionary of Classical Hebrew.* Edited by D. J. A. Clines. Sheffield. 1993–
EKKNT	Evangelisch-katholischer Kommentar zum Neuen Testament
FOTL	Forms of the Old Testament Literature
GBS	Guides to Biblical Scholarship
Georg.	Virgil, *Georgica*
GKC	*Gesenius' Hebrew Grammar.* Edited by E. Kautzsch. Translated by A. E. Cowley. 2d. ed. Oxford, 1910

HALOT	Koehler, L., W. Baumgartner, and J. J. Stamm, *The Hebrew and Aramaic Lexicon of the Old Testament*. Translated and edited under the supervision of M. E. J. Richardson. 4 vols. Leiden, 1994–1999
HBT	*Horizons in Biblical Theology*
HKAT	Handkommentar zum Alten Testament
HS	*Hebrew Studies*
HTR	*Harvard Theological Review*
IBC	Interpretation: A Bible Commentary for Teaching and Preaching
Int	*Interpretation*
IRT	Issues in Religion and Theology
JANES	*Journal of the Ancient Near Eastern Society*
JBL	*Journal of Biblical Literature*
JBQ	*Jewish Bible Quarterly*
JETS	*Journal of the Evangelical Theological Society*
JJS	*Journal of Jewish Studies*
JPT	*Journal of Pentecostal Theology*
JR	*Journal of Religion*
JSNT	*Journal for the Study of the New Testament*
JSNTSup	Journal for the Study of the New Testament: Supplement Series
JSOT	*Journal for the Study of the Old Testament*
JSOTSup	Journal for the Study of the Old Testament: Supplement Series
JTS	*Journal of Theological Studies*
J. W.	Josephus, *Jewish War*
KEK	Kritisch-exegetischer Kommentar über das Neue Testament
L.A.E.	*Life of Adam and Eve*
MNTC	Moffatt New Testament Commentary
NCBC	New Century Bible Commentary
NIB	*The New Interpreter's Bible*
OBT	Overtures to Biblical Theology
OED	Oxford English Dictionary
OTL	Old Testament Library
OTM	Oxford Theological Monographs
OTS	Old Testament Studies
Ps.-Clem. Rec.	Pseudo-Clement, *Romance of Recognitions*
Resp.	Cicero, *De republica*
SAT	Studien zum Alten Testament
SBLDS	Society of Biblical Literature Dissertation Series
SBLRBS	Society of Biblical Literature Resources for Biblical Study
SJOT	*Scandinavian Journal of the Old Testament*
SJT	*Scottish Journal of Theology*
T. Adam	*Testament of Adam*

TDOT	*Theological Dictionary of the Old Testament.* Edited by G. J. Botterweck and H. Ringgren. Translated by J. T. Willis, G. W. Bromiley, and D. E. Green. 8 vols. Grand Rapids, 1974–
TFOTL	The Forms of the Old Testament Literature
UNP	*Ugaritic Narrative Poetry.* Edited by Simon B. Parker. SBLWAW 9. Atlanta, 1997
UT	*Ugaritic Textbook.* C. H. Gordon. AnOr 38. Rome, 1965
VT	*Vetus Testamentum*
VTSup	Vetus Testamentum Supplements
WBC	Word Bible Commentary
WMANT	Wissenschaftliche Monographien zum Alten und Neuen Testament
WUNT	Wissenschaftliche Untersuchungen zum Neuen Testament
WW	*Word and World*
WWSup	Word and World: Supplement Series
ZAW	Zeitschrift für die alttestamentliche Wissenschaft
ZTK	*Zeitschrift für Theologie und Kirche*

CONTRIBUTORS

Vicky Balabanski
Senior Lecturer in New Testament Studies
Flinders University
Adelaide, Australia

Laurie J. Braaten
Professor of Old Testament
Judson University
Elgin, Il, U.S.A.

Norman C. Habel
Professorial Fellow in Biblical Studies
Flinders University
Adelaide, South Australia

Ted Hiebert
Francis A. McGraw Professor
McCormick Theological Seminary
Chicago, U.S.A

Cameron Howard
Ph.D. Candidate in Hebrew Bible
Emory University,
Atlanta, U.S.A.

Hilary Marlow
Research Associate in Theology and the Environment
University of Cambridge
Cambridge, England

Susan Miller
Lecturer in New Testament Studies
University of Oxford
Oxford, England

Kristin M. Swenson
Assistant Professor of Religious Studies
Virginia Commonwealth University
Richmond, U.S.A.

Sigve K. Tonstad
Assistant Professor of Religion (Biblical Studies)
Assistant Professor of Medicine
Loma Linda University,
Loma Linda, Cal. U.S.A.

Peter Trudinger
Senior Lecturer in Biblical Studies
Flinders University
Adelaide, South Australia

Melissa Tubbs Loya
Ph.D. Candidate
Boston College,
Boston, U.S.A.

Marie Turner
Lecturer in Old Testament
Flinders University
Adelaide, South Australia

Elaine Wainwright
Professor and Head of School of Theology
University of Auckland
Auckland, New Zealand

Arthur Walker-Jones
Associate Professor of Biblical Studies
University of Winnipeg
Winnipeg, Canada

Introducing Ecological Hermeneutics

Norman C. Habel

In 2003 I published a detailed account of my personal role in the early development of what has come to be known as ecological hermeneutics.[1] Since that time there have been three consultations on ecological hermeneutics at the annual meetings of the SBL, in 2004, 2005, and 2006. As a result of these consultations, the hermeneutical process has been refined and given a more distinctive focus. In this introduction, I will highlight the major components of this hermeneutic as they are currently being explored by biblical exegetes.

1. The Earth Bible Principles

The current components of ecological hermeneutics explored at the recent SBL consultations are dependent on the ground-breaking work of the Earth Bible team and the writers in the Earth Bible project.[2] The aims of the Earth Bible project were to acknowledge, before reading the biblical text, that as Western interpreters we are heirs of a long anthropocentric, patriarchal, and androcentric approach to reading the text that has devalued the Earth and that continues to influence the way we read the text; to declare, before reading the text, that we are members of a human community that has exploited, oppressed, and endangered the existence of Earth community; to become progressively more conscious that we are also members of the endangered Earth community in dialogue with ancient texts; to recognize Earth as a subject in the text with which we seek to relate empathetically rather than as a topic to be analyzed rationally; to take up the cause of justice for Earth and to ascertain whether Earth and Earth community are oppressed, silenced, or liberated in the text; and to develop techniques of reading the text

---

1. Norman C. Habel, "The Origins and Challenges of an Ecojustice Hermeneutic," in *Relating to the Text: Interdisciplinary and Form-Critical Insights on the Bible* (ed. Timothy Sandoval and Carleen Mandolfo; London: T&T Clark, 2003), 141–59.

2. Norman C. Habel, ed., *Readings from the Perspective of Earth* (The Earth Bible 1; Sheffield: Sheffield Academic Press, 2000).

to discern and retrieve alternative traditions where the voice of Earth and Earth community has been suppressed.

To guide writers in achieving these aims, a set of ecojustice principles were articulated.[3] These principles were developed over a number of years in dialogue with ecologists such as Charles Birch.[4] The principles articulated below were refined in consultations and workshops concerned with ecology in general, and ecological concerns linked to theology and the Bible more specifically.

1. The principle of intrinsic worth: The universe, Earth and all its components have intrinsic worth/value.

2. The principle of interconnectedness: Earth is a community of interconnected living things that are mutually dependent on each other for life and survival.

3. The principle of voice: Earth is a subject capable of raising its voice in celebration and against injustice.

4. The principle of purpose: The universe, Earth and all its components are part of a dynamic cosmic design within which each piece has a place in the overall goal of that design.

5. The principle of mutual custodianship: Earth is a balanced and diverse domain where responsible custodians can function as partners with, rather than rulers over, Earth to sustain its balance and a diverse Earth community.

6. The principle of resistance: Earth and its components not only suffer from human injustices but actively resist them in the struggle for justice.

The writers of the Earth Bible project explored a given biblical passage focusing on one or more of the ecojustice principles enunciated above. The five volumes in that series provided the basis for the development of an ecological hermeneutic for reading the Scriptures and interpretative traditions.

When reading the text, an interpreter participating in the Earth Bible project, taking into account one or more of the above principles, asks critical questions to ascertain whether there is justice for Earth in the orientation, ideology, or focus of the text or its interpreters. Typical questions are: Is Earth viewed merely as a resource for humans or as a subject with intrinsic worth? Is Earth treated as a subject with a "voice" or as an object to be exploited?

These principles are not intended to be exhaustive or definitive. Ongoing dialogue with ecologists and those employing this approach have lead to further refinements of the hermeneutical process, such as the three-step model devel-

---

3. Norman C. Habel, "Guiding Ecojustice Principles," in Habel, *Readings from the Perspective of Earth*, 38–53.

4. Charles Birch, *On Purpose* (Sydney: University of New South Wales Press, 1990).

oped in connection with the SBL Consultation for Ecological Hermeneutics (2004–2006).

Ernst Conradie gave a valuable critique of this approach at the 2004 Consultation on Ecological Hermeneutics. This critique is based on a review of the Earth Bible project in *Scriptura* 85. He concludes:

> The Earth Bible project's description of a set of six ecojustice principles offers an innovative and resolute articulation of such a heuristic key. Its strength is its critique of the anthropocentrism underlying the production and reception of biblical texts. Such a critique remains insufficient for an ecological hermeneutic though.[5]

2. Ecological Hermeneutics

After consideration of the various critiques of the Earth Bible principles, dialogue within the Earth Bible team, and a robust analysis of so-called second-level hermeneutical approaches, such as feminism and postcolonial hermeneutics, a more precise set of steps was developed for testing and exploration as part of a Consultation on Ecological Hermeneutics at the annual meetings of the SBL.

A revised ecological hermeneutic requires a radical reorientation to the biblical text. The task before us is not an exploration of what a given text may say about creation, about nature, or about Earth. In this context, Earth is not a topos or theme for analysis. We are not focusing on ecology and creation or ecology and theology.[6] An ecological hermeneutic demands a radical change of posture in relation to Earth as a subject in the text. (Here the term "Earth" refers to the total ecosystem, that is, the web of life—the domain of nature with which we are familiar, of which we are an integral part, and in which we face the future.)

A radical ecological approach to the text involves a basic hermeneutic of suspicion, identification, and retrieval. This progression bears obvious similarities with several approaches of well-known feminist hermeneutics. The difference, of course, is that we are not reading from the worldview of women, but first and foremost from within the orientation of an ecosystem called Earth. We are reading as creatures of Earth, as members of Earth community in solidarity with Earth.

---

5. Ernst M. Conradie, "Toward an Ecological Biblical Hermeneutics: A Review Essay of the Earth Bible Project," *Scriptura* (2004): 135.

6. Habel, *Readings from the Perspective of Earth*, 35.

Suspicion

First, we begin reading with the suspicion that the text is likely to be inherently anthropocentric and/or has traditionally been read from an anthropocentric perspective.

At the outset, the term anthropocentric needs to be distinguished from anthropogenic (a text originating from humans) and from anthropotopic (a text in which humans are a central topos or theme). This facet of the approach was the focus of several papers at the 2004 SBL Consultation.

The anthropocentric bias that we are likely to find both in ourselves as readers and in the text we are reading has at least two faces. The first is the assumption or condition we have inherited as human beings—especially in the Western world—that we are beings of a totally different order than all other creatures in nature. In other words, the hierarchy of things is God, human beings, and the rest.

A second face of this anthropocentric bias relates to nature as "object." We have for so long viewed nature and all its parts—both animate and inanimate—as the object of many forms of human investigation of which scientific analysis is but one. This process has not only reinforced a sense of human superiority over nature, but has also contributed to a sense of distance, separation, and otherness. The rest of nature—especially the inanimate world—has been viewed as separate, other, and a force to be harnessed.

This phase of the hermeneutical process is related to the principle of intrinsic worth articulated in the Earth Bible project. When viewed with a traditional anthropocentric bias, other parts of nature are of less value. Often they are viewed merely as the stage or background for God's relationship with humanity, rather than as valued subjects in their own right.

Identification

The second element of a radical contemporary ecological hermeneutic is the task of empathy or identification.

In the light of my experience as an editor and writer in the Earth Bible project, it has become clear to me that the activity of identification now deserves to be highlighted as a distinct step in the hermeneutical process. As human beings we identify—often unconsciously—with the various human characters in the biblical story, whether it is an empathetic or antipathetic identification. We can identify with the experiences of these characters even if they are not necessarily individuals whom we could admire or emulate.

Even before reading the narrative or poetry of the text, a reader using this approach must, at least to some extent, come to terms with his or her deep ecological connections. Before we begin reading and seek to identify with Earth in the text, we need to face the prior ecological reality of our kinship with Earth:

that we are born of Earth, and that we are living expressions of the ecosystem that has emerged on this planet. This step relates to the fundamental principle of interconnectedness that we explored in The Earth Bible series.

Identification with Earth and members of Earth community raises our consciousness to the injustices against Earth as they are portrayed in the text, both at the hands of humans and God. The exegete who pursues a radical ecological approach ultimately takes up the cause of the natural world seeking to expose the wrongs that Earth has suffered—largely in silence—and to discern, where possible, the way Earth has resisted these wrongs.

RETRIEVAL

The third facet of this ecological hermeneutic is retrieval. The process of retrieval, it seems to me, has two basic characteristics, one related to the prior process of suspicion and the other to the process of identification.

As the interpreter exposes the various anthropocentric dimensions of the text—the ways in which the human agenda and bias are sustained either by the reader or the implied author—the text may reveal a number of surprises about the nonhuman characters in the story. Earth or members of Earth community may play a key role or be highly valued in the text, but because of the Western interpretative tradition we have inherited, this dimension of the text has been ignored or suppressed.

Where we meet nonhuman figures communicating in some way—mourning, praising, or singing—we have tended in the past to dismiss these as poetic license or symbolic language. Our anthropocentric bias leads to classifying these elements as mere anthropomorphisms.

Discerning Earth and members of Earth community as subjects with a voice is a key part of the retrieval process. In some contexts their voices are evident but have been traditionally ignored by exegetes. In other contexts the voice of Earth and Earth community is not explicit, but nevertheless present and powerful. These subjects play roles in the text that are more than mere scenery or secondary images. Their voice needs to be heard. It is a voice that need not correspond to the languages of words we commonly associate with human voices.

Discerning this voice may even take the form of reconstructing the narrative—as a dimension of the interpretation process—in such a way as to hear Earth as the narrator of the story. Such a reconstruction is, of course, not the original text, but it is a reading as valid as the numerous readings of scholars over the centuries. In such a narrative, Earth also becomes an interpreter.

EXEMPLAR

To illustrate the preceding steps of a radical ecological hermeneutics, I will outline briefly the key features of my presentation on Gen 1:26–28 at the 2005

Consultation. A more detailed analysis of this passage in found in *Word and World* Supplement Series 5.[7]

Suspicion

The suspicion that these verses are anthropocentric is immediately evident from the way that the status and role of humans are represented in the text. Human beings are given priority in relation to God, to other living creatures, and to Earth itself.

Regardless of how the *imago dei* is interpreted, the implied author portrays the creation of human beings as a unique event. Unlike other creatures, humans are the result of a consultation between God and certain beings designated as "us." Unlike other creatures, humans are made "in the image of God," thereby setting them apart from other beings and giving them a distinctive and superior relationship with the deity. They are "God-image creatures." Unlike other creatures, the blessing given to human beings involves "filling" creation with their presence and so giving them a privileged position. The relation of humans to God reflects an obvious anthropocentric bias.

A similar bias is evident when we consider how humans relate to other creatures and Earth itself. Humans are not one among many living creatures formed by God to share the planet, but that superior species who is given the mandate to "rule" (*rada*) over all other living creatures. And, as I have demonstrated elsewhere, the verb for "rule" in Hebrew involves the forceful exercise of power.[8] For humans to claim the right to "rule" like royalty further emphasizes the anthropocentric bias.

The third dimension of this bias is reflected by the commission to "subdue Earth." The verb "subdue" (*kabash*) is also a term that reflects the exercise of force. There is no suggestion of stewardship or care in this term. Joshua "subdues" the Canaanites by extreme force (Jos 18:1). And the presumption that humans are to subdue or conquer all of Earth is an arrogant anthropocentric attitude indeed.

Identification

If we now seek to identify with the characters in the narrative we gain a fresh appreciation this passage. In most traditional interpretations, human readers have quite naturally identified with the human subjects because in so doing they

---

7. Norman C. Habel, "Playing God or Playing Earth? An Ecological Reading of Genesis 1.26–28," in *"And God Saw That It Was Good." Essays on Creation and God in Honor of Terence Fretheim* (ed. Frederick Gaiser and Mark Throntveit; WWSup 5; St. Paul: Luther Seminary, 2006).

8. Habel, "Playing God or Playing Earth?," 39.

are closely linked with a dimension of God and that, in a sense, enables them to "play God."

If, however, we recognize that in ecological terms all living creatures are interrelated, and we dare to identify with our nonhuman kin in the narrative, we gain a very different perspective. We are then subjects, those "ruled" over by humans. These nonhuman creatures emanate, in the earlier stages of the Gen 1 narrative, from the land, the sea, and the air. Their bond with Earth and the natural world is explicit. Not so humans! They are not "natural" creatures connected with Earth who is a partner in the creation process. They are beings of a different order bearing the image of God.

When we identify with nonhuman creatures in the narrative, we become aware of the gulf between human and nonhuman creatures in this text, and that the assumption derived from this text is that the human domination of nonhuman species is legitimate. From the perspective of our nonhuman kin, the consequences that follow from such a position are unjust and inconsistent with the ecological reality of our planet.

As nonhuman kin we become aware that this text has been the basis for exploitation, oppression, and abuse of nature by arrogant humans. And in spite of claims to the contrary, as nonhuman readers we can readily see how this text has provided justification for a history of human domination of our kind.

Retrieval

Is it possible to retrieve the perspective or voice of Earth in this passage? The text quite explicitly states that humans are given the mandate to "subdue" Earth—an action that might quite naturally imply silencing or suppressing the voice of Earth and Earth community. On the basis of this text alone it might well be assumed that Earth is but a silent and insignificant object rather than a subject or central character in the narrative.

Even a cursory reading of the preceding narrative in Gen 1 reveals that Earth is a character who plays a lead role in the narrative.[9] Earth is first introduced as a figure waiting in the waters of the primal womb (verse 2). On the third day, the primal waters part and Earth "appears"—a spectacular event I have elsewhere designated a "geophany."[10] Earth then becomes a partner with God in the creation process. Vegetation emerges from Earth. Fish emerge from the sea. And all animals except humans emerge from Earth. Earth is their mother. Earth is a character with a positive perspective.

---

9. Habel, "Playing God or Playing Earth?," 38–39.

10. Norman C. Habel, "Geophany: The Earth Story in Genesis One," in *The Earth Story in Genesis* (ed. Norman C. Habel and Shirley Wurst; The Earth Bible 2; Sheffield: Sheffield Academic Press, 2000).

In Gen 1:26–28, however, that character seems to be suppressed and that Earth perspective is hidden from view. How might we retrieve the voice of Earth in the light of the wider Gen 1 context and our current ecological awareness? I suggest the following is indicative of Earth's perspective.

> *I am Earth. I was first revealed when God summoned the primal waters to part. I came forth from these waters as a living domain with potential to give birth. I count this a great honor and grounds for celebration. I am a valued part of the cosmos.*
>
> *At the request of God I brought forth, like a mother, all the flora that covers the land. I gave birth to vegetation that has the capacity to reproduce. All the flora that comes from within me is interconnected with me and is nurtured through me.*
>
> *At the request of God I also brought forth, like a mother, the fauna that live on Earth. They are my offspring and depend on me for subsistence. All fauna depend on the vegetation I produce for their survival and enjoyment of life. I am Earth, the source of daily life for the flora and fauna that I have generated from within me.*
>
> *Sad to say, there is another story that has invaded my world: the story of the so-called god-image creatures called humans. Instead of recognizing that these god-image creatures are beings interdependent with Earth and other Earth creatures, this story claims that the god-image creatures belong to superior ruling class or species, thereby demeaning their nonhuman kin and diminishing their value. Instead of respecting me as their home and life source, the god-image creatures claim a mandate to crush me like an enemy or a slave.*
>
> *My voice needs to be heard and the intrusive story about the humans in Gen 1:26–28 named for what it is from my perspective: the charter of a group of power hungry humans.*

3. Conclusion

Whether or not you hear the voice of Earth in precisely this way, the task of reading the text from an ecological perspective involves

(1) acknowledging the probable anthropocentric bias both within the text and within traditional interpretations;

(2) identifying with Earth and Earth community as kin who are subjects in the narrative;

(3) seeking to retrieve the perspective or voice of Earth and Earth community of whom we humans are but one species.

AIR, THE FIRST SACRED THING: THE CONCEPTION OF רוח IN THE HEBREW SCRIPTURES

Theodore Hiebert

In order to explore the radical reorientation to the biblical text that a new eco-logical hermeneutic requires, I have selected for study a particular natural phenomenon: the conception of the atmosphere in the Hebrew Scriptures. The atmosphere is one of the realms of nature in which the human relation to its environment is being tested most seriously in our own day. Fundamental changes in Earth's atmosphere, reflected in the phenomena of global warming and climate change, are now threatening the viability of the entire ecosystem and of human life itself in serious and unpredictable ways. It is now clear that international action, first placed before the world's attention at the Convention on Climate Change in Kyoto, Japan (1997), will be necessary to avert major disruptions for all species of life. Church bodies have responded, calling on their members to take this particular crisis with special seriousness. If we cannot find some way of valuing the atmosphere—and of identifying our future as a human race more closely with the future of the canopy of life that sustains us—we are indeed in danger.

Through an analysis of the biblical conception of the atmosphere, I want to show that biblical thought contains important resources for a more enlightened modern ecological ethic in which the environment and the human relationship to it are taken seriously. In this analysis, I want to show that nature played a foundational role in biblical thought rather than the peripheral role to which the Bible's interpreters have traditionally assigned it. I want to show also that humanity is regarded as an inseparable part of its larger natural environment, rather than a species of a different order as later theologians have claimed. I am not arguing that we try to recover wholesale the ideas about the world held by the pre-scientific, pre-industrial society of biblical Israel, but I do want to argue that biblical ideas can provide both inspiration and concrete resources for reconstructing new models for human existence that can move us beyond the anthropocentric thinking that has led to our current crisis.

In this analysis of the conception of the atmosphere in the Hebrew Scriptures, I will be employing at one time or another aspects of all three steps in the herme-neutical process developed in the SBL Consultation for Ecological Hermeneutics and spelled out by Norman Habel in the introduction to this volume: suspicion, identification, and retrieval. I want to show that we must be suspicious of the ways in which an anthropocentric bias and dualistic thinking have driven past interpreters—in sharp contrast to biblical authors—to regard the atmosphere as part of a totally different order of existence from that of humans and of God. Furthermore, I want to affirm the principle of human identification with creation by demonstrating how closely biblical writers connected humans and the atmosphere that sustained them. Finally, I want to retrieve the significance of creation in biblical thought by arguing that the atmosphere together with the natural world of which it is a part plays no peripheral role; rather, it occupies a foundational place in biblical theology.

1. רוח AS THE ATMOSPHERE

The closest we can get in the ancient language of the Hebrew Scriptures to a term approximating our English word "atmosphere," the envelope of air surrounding Earth, is the Hebrew word רוח (*rûaḥ*). The simplest translation for רוח is "air," and when it is used for the atmosphere, רוח refers to the great currents of air that produce surface winds and climatic changes. A few examples are sufficient to illustrate this. Qohelet uses רוח as part of a larger survey of the great rhythms of nature—the orbit of the sun, the flow of fresh water to the sea, the repetition of human generations—to describe annual atmospheric variations:

> Blowing toward the south,
> Then shifting toward the north,
> Shifting, shifting, the wind (רוח) blows,
> On its cycle, the wind (רוח) returns. (Qoh 1:6; translations are mine)

These winds, by which ancients referred to their atmosphere, may blow from the four points of the compass (Jer 49:36; Ezek 37:9), just as they are described by Qohelet as southerly and northerly. Yet the most common winds, or atmospheric conditions, mentioned by biblical writers are the drying east wind blowing off of the vast eastern deserts (Exod 14:21; Ezek 17:10), and the west wind—literally "the sea's wind," רוח הים—blowing in off of the Mediterranean laden with rain.

The use of רוח to describe the atmospheric conditions of thunderstorms that sweep in from the Mediterranean Sea and characterize the rainy season in ancient Israel is especially common in the Bible (e.g., 1 Kgs 18:45; 2 Kgs 3:17; Ps 148:8). Good illustrations are provided by the psalmist and by the author of Job, both of whom attribute wet season thunderstorms to divine activity:

> Who raises clouds on Earth's horizon,
> Making bolts of lightning for the rain,
> Leading out the wind (רוח) from his reservoirs. (Ps 135:7; cf. Jer 10:13)

Who made the wind (רוח) heavy,
And determined the amount of water,
When he made a rule for the rain,
And a law for lightning and thunder. (Job 28:25–26)

Such a preoccupation with the winds of the thunderstorm is not surprising from an agricultural society involved in dry farming. Israel's annual grain and fruit harvests—upon which its agricultural economy was based—were entirely dependent on precipitation produced when the middle-latitudes belt of cyclone winds or "westerlies" pulled moisture off of the Mediterranean Sea during the winter rainy season. The atmospheric conditions upon which Israel's survival was most directly dependent—the moisture bearing cyclone winds from the west—are those about which biblical authors write with most frequency and eloquence.

2. רוח AS BREATH

The salient feature of the Hebrew term רוח for our purposes is that, due to its basic meaning, "air," it is used for both "atmosphere" and "breath." While we recognize the connection between the atmosphere we inhabit and the air we breathe, especially during high pollution alerts in urban areas, we distinguish between these phenomena with different English words. In Hebrew, where a single term was used, the connection was always direct and indelible. Atmosphere and breath were the same thing, and this fact was recognized whenever the term רוח was employed. In the term רוח, therefore, the human being is inseparably linked to its non-human environment.

The integration within the term רוח of air as atmosphere and air as respiration is reflected perhaps most vividly in the image of a valley of dry bones described by the prophet Ezekiel. Though this image is metaphorical, signifying the restoration of the exilic community in Babylon rather than actual life after death, its details are drawn from Israel's understanding of ordinary realities. In order to capture more authentically the coalescence of the concepts of "wind/atmosphere" and "breath" in רוח, I have refrained from rendering רוח into English here:

He said to me, "Prophesy to these bones, and say to them, 'Dry bones: Hear the word of the Lord. This is what the Lord said to these bones: I am now putting רוח in you, and you will come to life.'" . . . When I prophesied, things immediately shook, and the bones came together, bone to bone. I saw first sinews on them, then flesh cover them, and then skin on top of it; but no רוח was in them. Then he said to me, "Prophesy to the רוח, prophesy mortal, and say to the רוח, 'This is what the Lord said: From the four רוחות,[1] come, O רוח, and breathe[2] into these

---

1. The plural form of רוח.
2. The same verb, נפח, used in the creation of the first human in Gen 2:7 below.

dead ones, and they will come to life.'" So I prophesied as he commanded me, and the רוח entered them and they came to life and stood on their feet. (Ezek 37: 4–5, 7–10)

In this narrative, רוח, "air," is summoned from the entire atmosphere (the four winds) to enter these human beings as breath and bring them to life. Every time the term is used, its double meaning as "atmosphere/breath" is prominent in the listener's mind. The language of the Hebrew Scriptures thus captures a fundamental self-understanding: human life is always and everywhere dependent upon רוח, "air," the canopy of air that it inhabits and which it breathes.

This connection between breath and atmosphere in the biblical term רוח is all the more significant because רוח, "breath," is the primary signifier of life in biblical thought: its presence indicates life; its absence death. Of course, we also link physical life with breath. Yet Western theology has relocated the notion of human life in its fullest sense to the soul or spirit, which is of a different order than physical life and which outlasts it. This shift in thinking has obscured an important aspect of the actual character of Israelite thought. For the ancient Israelites—who did not separate spirit from matter or soul from body—life in this world was life in its fullness, and this earthly fullness of life was defined by רוח, "breath."

According to Israelite thought, רוח, "breath," enters the fetus at birth (perhaps even before; Qoh 11:5), and it departs from the body, which returns to the soil, at death (Ps 146:4). When Israel's theologians wanted to claim that images of deities had no life or power, they said there was no רוח in them (Jer 10:14; Hab 2:9). Perhaps the most vivid account in the Hebrew Scriptures of breath as that which imparts life is the Yahwist's creation narrative, in which the customary synonym for רוח, נשמה, is employed:

> The Lord God formed the man (אדם) out of soil (עפר) from the arable land (אדמה), and he breathed into his nostrils the breath of life (נשמת חיים) and the man became a living being. (Gen 2:7)

Thus human life in its fullest sense, defined by biblical theologians as breath, is directly linked to and made dependent on the envelope of air which it inhabits and breathes.

By equating life with רוח, "breath," biblical writers link humans not just to the atmosphere they breathe but to all other animate life. The same term רוח that is used to define human life is also used to define animal life. Biblical authors make no distinction. This is illustrated in the phrase רוח חיים, "breath of life," a phrase used in Genesis by the priestly writer for all animate life, that which was destroyed by the great flood (Gen 6:17) and that which accompanied Noah onto the ark (Gen 7:15). The psalmist, who concludes a lengthy survey of creation and its forms of life with the claim that all living beings depend upon God, also reflects this conception:

When you hide your face they are disturbed,
When you take away their breath (רוח) they die
And return to their soil (עפר).
When you send out your breath (רוח) they are brought to life,
And you revive the face of arable land (אדמה). (Ps 104:29–30)

For both human and nonhuman life, רוח defines life, and its absence indicates death. In their understanding of life, biblical theologians do not place humans and animals in different categories. All living beings share the same breath and breathe the same air.

By using the same term both for the atmosphere and for breath, and by defining breath as life for humans and animals alike, biblical theologians placed the human and the nonhuman within a single conceptual world. In fact, it is now impossible to assign רוח to the human, on the one hand, or to the nonhuman, on the other. It dissolves the line we draw between the two. To take our atmosphere with ultimate seriousness, and to recover a sense that our survival depends upon it, we will have to develop some modern version of this biblical conception of the interrelatedness of humanity and its world.

3. רוח AS GOD'S ATMOSPHERE

רוח, the air of both atmospheric winds and animal respiration, is connected directly with God's being and God's activity in biblical thought, as is already clear in most of the texts quoted above. Air is not regarded as a material element of the natural world which, as a created substance, is empty of divinity. On the contrary, air as both atmospheric winds and breath is described in the Hebrew Scriptures as possessing a divine character. It originates from God, it is God's, it is a medium of the revelation of God, and it is an indication of God's presence. For the biblical theologian, רוח is sacred.

The sacral character of רוח for the ancient Israelite can be illustrated, in the first place, from those contexts where the term signifies atmospheric winds. The wind is called literally the wind of the Lord (רוח יהוה), or the Lord's wind (Hos 13:15), or it is described as coming from the Lord (Num 11:31). It is pictured as originating from God and controlled by God. God commands the wind (Ps 148:8), shifts the wind (Exod 10:19), guides it (Exod 10:13), and sends it across the earth (Gen 8:1). The psalmist depicts God raising the storm wind (רוח סערה) that whips up the sea's waves (Ps 107:25), a clear reference to the rainy season westerlies bringing thunderstorms from the Mediterranean.

This last example illustrates the most common context in which God is associated with atmospheric conditions: the Middle Eastern thunderstorm. The thunderstorm is in fact a characteristic setting for the theophany—the direct appearance of God—in the Hebrew Scriptures. The best-known example is the thunderstorm over Mount Sinai in which God speaks to the people in thunder and gives them the law (Exod 19–20). Many other instances of the storm theophany could be cited; e.g., Judg 5:4–5; Hab 3:8–15; Pss 29, 97. One of the most vivid storm theophanies is Ezekiel's vision of God's arrival to join the exiles in Babylon. Ezekiel sees a storm wind (רוח סערה; as in Ps 107:25 above), accompanied by all of the phenomena of the thunderstorm. He regards it as signifying God's presence with Israel in exile (Ezek 1:4, 28). It is the storm wind (סערה; as in Ps 107:25 and Ezek 1:4) after all, not a modest "whirlwind," from which God speaks to Job about the magnificence of creation (Job 38:1).

As noted above, biblical Israel's preoccupation with the winds of the thunderstorm is directly related to its agrarian economy of dry farming, which was dependent upon these seasonal rains. This fact lies behind Israel's association between these storm winds and God. Upon the regular return of the westerly blowing winds each winter and the moisture they bore, rested the success of Israel's annual harvests and the survival of its people. Thus, this particular atmospheric phenomenon was an especially obvious medium of the divine presence and activity, which ensured the lives of God's people in their land of "milk and honey."

This close connection between storm wind and deity, widespread in the Bible, is expressed in a particularly striking way in the vivid metaphors of Israel's oldest poetry. In the ancient hymn in Exod 15, God appears in the thunderstorm overwhelming Israel's enemies at the Sea of Reeds:

> At the wind/breath (רוח) of your nostrils
> The water swelled up,
> The currents rose up like a hill,
> The depths foamed in the heart of the sea . . .
> You blew with your wind/breath (רוח):
> The sea covered them,
> They sank like lead
> In the towering water. (Exod 15:8, 10)

4. רוח AS GOD'S BREATH

In this image from Exod 15, the storm wind is literally the breath of God. The combination of God's wind and God's breath in the term רוח is reflected also in an ancient poem preserved both in 2 Sam 22 and in Ps 18. A major section of this hymn is devoted to a detailed storm theophany (verses 8–16) in which the thunder is described as God's voice (verse 14) and the wind, as in Exod 15, as God's breath:

> The recesses of the sea appeared,
> The foundations of the earth were uncovered,
> At the roar of the Lord,

From the wind/breath (נשמת) of the wind/breath (רוח) of the Lord's nostrils.
(2 Sam 22:16)

I apologize for the unwieldy translation of the final line, but the poet has juxtaposed רוח and its nearest synonym, נשמה, used by the Yahwist for the creation of the first human in Gen 2:7. I do not want to gloss over all of these associations or the multivalence of the terms. Most translators, such as those of the New Revised Standard Version (NRSV) and of the Jewish Publication Society Version (JPSV), opt for something like "at the blast of the breath of the Lord's nostrils," an acceptable rendering but one that obscures some key nuances in the text.

5. רוח AS THE FIRST SACRED THING

With this background context, it is possible to turn to the very first and most familiar use of the term רוח in the Hebrew Scriptures—but it is now even less possible to translate it satisfactorily into English:

> When God began to create the skies and the earth—now the earth was formless, and darkness was over the surface of the deep, and God's רוח swept over the surface of the water—God said, Let there be light. (Gen 1:1–3)

Perhaps no other text so ably exploits the richness of the Hebrew term. Certainly, רוח evokes the atmospheric winds blowing over the primordial sea. This is a common ancient Near Eastern creation theme, reflected, for example, in the Babylonian creation epic *Enuma Elish* when Marduk uses winds as divine weapons to subdue the chaotic sea before he creates the world. As we have seen, Israel's poets have also depicted such winds as the very breath of God. And God's breath may also be associated with God's speeches that follow in Gen 1, an interpretation apparent in the psalmist's rendering of creation:

> By the word of the Lord the skies were made
> and by the breath (רוח) of his mouth all of their creatures (Ps 33:6).

God's breath may well anticipate the "breath of life" that will fill all living creatures brought into being at creation. All of these meanings—atmosphere, breath, speech—are imbedded in the first use of the term רוח in the Bible.

Furthermore, רוח is identified in Gen 1:2 not as a created substance but as an aspect of the divine being. The atmosphere is pictured here not just as created matter but as divine, and, as the first aspect of the world so described, the first sacred thing. This biblical way of thinking breaks down the sharp barrier Western theologians have erected between creator and creation. It makes the claim that God and the world are not separate but indissolubly connected, and that the atmosphere we inhabit is not just stuff but an aspect of God's own presence in creation.

6. רוח AS GOD'S BREATH AND ALL GOD'S CREATURES' BREATH

These biblical texts that identify wind as God's breath lead directly into a consideration of the connection between the breath of all living beings and God's own breath. In biblical thought, the air humans breathe is God's breath. In the first place, breath is given to humans by God (Zech 12:1; Job 33:4). This is especially well illustrated in the Yahwist's creation account quoted above in which God breathes into the nostrils of the first human being the breath of life (נשמת חיים; Gen 2:7). Another creation text reflects the same understanding:

> This is what God, the Lord, has said:
> Who created the skies and stretched them out,
> Who spread out the earth and what comes from it,
> Who gave breath (נשמה) to the people upon it,
> Breath (רוח) to those who walk in it. (Isa 42:5)

The breath of all creatures is not only given by God but is also sustained at every moment by God and God's own breath. Job speaks of staying alive

> as long as my breath (נשמה) is in me,
> as the breath (רוח) of God is in my nostrils. (Job 27:3)

He acknowledges the constant dependence of all life on God:

> In whose hand is the being of all living things,
> the breath (רוח) of all human beings." (Job 12:10)

This equation of the breath of God's creatures with God's own breath, and the dependence of all life on the divine, is perhaps most directly expressed in texts that describe God withdrawing God's breath, such as the selection from Ps 104:29 quoted above: "When you take away their breath (רוח) they die." A similar example is found in the speech of Job's counselor, Elihu, in which he surveys God's activity in the world:

> If he makes the decision,
> To gather to himself his air/breath (רוח), his breath (נשמה),
> All creatures die together,
> Human beings to the soil (עפר) return. (Job 34:14–15)

At death, says Qohelet, "breath (רוח) returns to God who gave it" (Qoh 12:7).

The use of רוח in the Hebrew Scriptures thus challenges the fundamental elements of an anthropocentric worldview. By identifying the atmosphere with the breath of life of all living creatures, רוח undermines the notion that humans are of a totally different order than the rest of nature and thereby superior to it. In Hebrew, רוח subverts the idea that nature is merely an object, without intrinsic worth, and separate from human existence. In fact, רוח not only signifies that humans and the rest of nature are inseparable; it also claims that the atmosphere and respiration are really aspects of God's own being and therefore sacred. It dissolves the sharp distinction between creator and creation that Western theologians have so staunchly defended. Such an integrated understanding of our ecosystem's atmosphere emphasizes its ultimate worth and its indispensability for human survival. To maintain the health of our world today and of ourselves, we will have to recapture in some modern form the holistic sense of the world reflected in the biblical conception of רוח.

7. רוח in Later Interpretation

In conclusion, one particular misinterpretation of the concept of רוח in the Bible must be addressed. Influenced by later dualistic philosophy and theology, which drew a sharp distinction between matter and spirit, body and soul, many interpreters have come to define רוח in certain contexts as an independent, incorporeal entity, which is customarily translated as the English word "spirit." By so doing they have introduced into the Bible a dramatic divide between spirit and matter, between body and soul, between human and nonhuman, which was not part of the biblical worldview and which has drawn an unbiblical divide between human beings and their environment.

The major Hebrew and English dictionaries in use today include this understanding of רוח as "spirit." Gesenius' lexicon, edited by Brown, Driver, and Briggs, for example, lists this as the fourth meaning of רוח: "*spirit* of the living, breathing being, dwelling in the בשר ["flesh"] of men and animals." While this lexicon here mentions "animals" as possessors of "spirit," the actual entry under "spirit" reserves this meaning for texts that connect רוח either with humans or with God. Examples include texts in which רוח should more simply and straightforwardly be translated "breath" (all cited above): Isa 42:5; Zech 12:1; Ps 104:29–30; Job 12:10, 27:3, 34:14–15; Qoh 11:5, 12:7. In their lexicon, Koehler and Baumgartner list this understanding as the sixth meaning of רוח: "(breath, element of life, natural) spirit of man." Anthropocentric limiting of "spirit" to humans is more obvious in this entry where references meaning "breath" cited include Ps 104:29; Job 12:10; 34:14; Qoh 12:7 (all translated above).

This attempt by translators to split off an immaterial reality reserved for God and for humans alone reflects an anthropocentric worldview not present among biblical authors or within their language. In our classic text, Gen 1:2, where God's רוח identifies God's breath with the atmospheric winds, the KJV and the RSV both use "spirit." While the NRSV and the JPSV have moved away from such unbiblical dualism with the translation "wind," other widely used recent translations—the NIV, NKJV, the New Living Translation, and The Message—have retained and even emphasized the older KJV/RSV tradition, granting רוח a special independent, spiritual status by capitalizing their translation: "Spirit." Another text whose translation illustrates this kind of post-biblical theological dualism is Ps 104:29–30, quoted below, where the NRSV translates רוח "breath" when it refers to God's creatures but "spirit" when it refers to God:

> When you take away their breath (רוח), they die
> And return to their dust.
> When you send forth your spirit (רוח), they are created
> And you renew the face of the ground.

Since the theologians of the Hebrew Scriptures nowhere else distinguish between material and immaterial parts of a human being, between matter and spirit, or between body and soul, it is improbable that the word "spirit" is ever a viable translation for the biblical Hebrew term רוח, and I have carefully avoided using it in this analysis. The word "spirit" can in fact be used in English with a more modest sense of mood ("high spirits") or character ("team spirit"). Yet its association with an independent immaterial entity is so strong in the English language and in the Western philosophical and theological tradition that its use, more often than not, can only seriously distort the biblical perspective.

I suspect that the impetus leading lexicographers and translators to distinguish the definition "spirit" from the definition "breath" derives largely from the strength of idealistic dualism in the Western philosophical and theological tradition rather than from the Hebrew Scriptures themselves. Idealism, originating with Plato and represented by Descartes, Kant, and Hegel, among others, has driven a sharp wedge between mind and matter, between spiritual and physical realities in Western thought. The result has been a trenchant dualism, by which God and humans, both possessors of spirit, have been set off from the material world and given a spiritual destiny unrelated to the material world's future. The world itself, by consequence, has been emptied of divinity and deprived of ultimate significance.

Indeed, this is a primary battleground in the modern struggle over values toward the environment in religious communities and in society at large. Will we perpetuate a dualistic style of thought that sets us off from other forms of life, and that carefully detaches divine and human realities from the natural world? Or will we cultivate new—or old—ways of thinking religiously that recognize and affirm the fundamental interconnectedness that the ecological sciences have brought to our attention anew?

The biblical concept of רוח, "air," indicates that the theologians of the Hebrew Scriptures entertained an understanding of the human in the world that is not dualistic but which, on the contrary, contained a deep appreciation for the interrelatedness of human life, other life, and the atmosphere upon which all life depends. In a single term, רוח, biblical theologians were able to affirm the correspondence between the respiration of all living beings and the atmosphere they inhabit. And with this same term, recognized as the רוח אלהים, the breath of God, they were able to affirm the sacredness of the atmosphere and the life it provides the creatures who inhabit it. רוח was regarded as foundational for rather than peripheral to life. Within the biblical conception of רוח, the air of atmosphere and the air that we breathe are at the same time united, sacralized, and granted ultimate significance.

ANIMAL SPEECH AS REVELATION IN GENESIS 3 AND NUMBERS 22

Cameron B. R. Howard

The retrieval of the voices of Earth in the Hebrew Bible is a hermeneutical project that requires listening for those voices, be they of animals or other parts of creation, to communicate in ways different from human speech. In two texts, however, nonhuman animals in the Hebrew Bible exhibit a human mode of conversation: the snake chats with Eve in Gen 3, and the donkey rebukes Balaam in Num 22. One might imagine that these Earth voices would require little or no "retrieval," since the animal characters speak in ways the story's human characters, as well as we human readers, can understand.

Biblical scholarship, however, has tended to obscure the subjectivity the snake and the donkey exhibit in these two texts, attributing their speech to literary conventions and nothing more.[1] Because the narrators of the two stories do not comment on animal speech as an extraordinary feature, many scholars follow the narrators' lead, never pausing to engage the talking animal characters as anomalies. In this view, the snake and the donkey have been elevated to the communicative status of human beings simply for narrative effect. A "dumb" donkey (both silent and stupid), who can see what the seer Balaam cannot, serves to ridicule the seer. And in the garden of Eden, only two humans have been created so far; who else will tempt Eve and Adam but another element of creation?

---

1. For paradigmatic examples, see Walter Brueggemann, *Genesis* (IBC; Atlanta: John Knox, 1982), 47, who emphasizes that the serpent "is a technique to move the plot of the story," and Ronald A. Veenker, "That Fabulous Talking Snake," in *The Challenge of Bible Translation: Communicating God's Word to the World* (ed. Glen G. Scorgie, Mark L. Strauss and Steven M. Voth; Grand Rapids: Zondervan, 2003), 265–72, who says, "Any story about a talking snake is, of course, a fable" (265). An exception is Terence Fretheim, "The Book of Genesis: Introduction, Commentary, and Reflections," in *General Articles on the Bible, General Articles on the Old Testament, Genesis, Exodus, Leviticus* (NIB 1; ed. Leander E. Keck; Nashville: Abingdon, 1994), 365–66.

I do not deny that inclusion of nonhuman animals speaking with humans via human speech reflects a literary artistry that uses the animals to develop the characterization of the story's humans—Eve and Balaam—and to help move the plot along. But the uniqueness of these talking animals within the biblical corpus prompts me to investigate these two texts together, to see if the snake of Gen 3 and the donkey of Num 22 share features or functions beyond conventions of genre. The text of each story is saturated with the vocabulary of divine revelation; the speech of the animals, who see and know what the humans cannot, mediates between God and the humans, giving humanity access to God.

That the animals serve to bring knowledge of the deity to humanity is part of the inherently anthropocentric nature of these texts. Yet these two texts also push beyond anthropocentrism, showcasing the snake and donkey as subjects who act on their own accord. I contend that rather than being simple "personifications"— depicted, literally, like "persons"—the snake and the donkey share with each other a distinct portrayal that sets them apart from—even above—their human counterparts. The characteristically human ability of the donkey and snake to converse in words with Balaam and Eve, respectively, is not a narrative elevation of the animals from subhuman to human capacities, but rather depicts their closer affinities with the deity. [2]

1. Beyond Fables

Within both the Hebrew Bible and the corpus of ancient Near Eastern literature, the snake's dialogue with Eve and the donkey's interrogation of Balaam stand out as anomalous instances of discourse *between animals and humans* using human speech. Talking animals and even plants do appear with some frequency in ancient Near Eastern texts. Sumerian and Babylonian literature, for example, feature an entire subgenre known as *Streitfabeln*, or contest literatures, in which pairs of animals or plants verbally spar with each other over which of the two

2. George Savran, in "Beastly Speech: Intertextuality, Balaam's Ass, and the Garden of Eden" *JSOT* 64 (1994): 33–55, has conducted an insightful intertextual examination of these two texts and the broader narratives of which they are a part. Savran recognizes that the snake and donkey both possess unique knowledge of the divine, that they transmit knowledge to humans via speech, and that the verbs of knowing and seeing are associated with the communication of knowledge in both stories. However, rather than regarding the episodes of animal speech as objects of study in themselves, Savran uses the similarities in the two animals' capacities for speech as part of a list of evidence for intertextual connections across the larger stories of the Garden of Eden (Gen 2–3) and Balaam the Seer (Num 22–24), focusing on the stories' thematic implications for the human community of Israel and its relationship with God. By contrast, deploying an ecological hermeneutic, as I am attempting to do here, amplifies the nonhuman voices of the story, making the animals and their speech independently worthy of analysis.

is superior.[3] It is rare, however, for the personifications in ancient Near Eastern literature to speak to human beings; most often they converse with each other or, in occasional instances, with deities. Only a few exceptions to this trend can be found, such as the Egyptian Tale of the Shipwrecked Sailor, in which the narrator, stranded on an island, is aided by a large snake who prophetically assures him that he will soon reach home again.[4]

The stories in Gen 3 and Num 22 can also be differentiated from other so-called fables in the Hebrew Bible featuring nonhuman talking protagonists.[5] In Judg 9:7–15, Jotham tells the story of trees who are searching among themselves for a king; in 2 Kgs 14:9–10, Jehoash responds to Amaziah's request for a meeting using an allegorical tale of a correspondence between a cedar and a thornbush. These two stories are not independent pieces of biblical narrative, but instead are placed in the mouths of other biblical characters. In Gen 3 and Num 22, the snake and the donkey are themselves indispensable elements of the primary narrative. No character recites a parable featuring the donkey or the snake, nor does a prophet use those figures as illustrations in an oracle. The snake and the donkey are biblical characters in their own right, further distinguishing them from any other ostensibly similar texts in the Hebrew Bible.

2. Genesis 3

The Yahwistic creation story in Gen 2 sets the scene for the snake's dialogue with the woman. At Gen 2:25, both the male and female have now been created, and both are "naked" and "unashamed." In an oft-noted pun, the two human beings are עֲרוּמִּים, naked, while the snake is עָרוּם, clever.[6] At the same time, the snake is distinguished from its fellow "creatures of the field" (חַיַּת הַשָּׂדֶה) by being more clever than them all. Within Gen 2:25 and 3:1a, the snake is both set apart from other animals and affiliated with the woman and man via the עָרוּם pun. Yet it will later become clear that, though the snake is aligned more closely with

---

3. Ronald J. Williams, "The Fable in the Ancient Near East," in *A Stubborn Faith: Papers on Old Testament and Related Subjects Presented to Honor William Andrew Irwin* (ed. Edward C. Hobbs; Dallas: Southern Methodist University Press, 1956), 5. Examples of contest literature include The Tamarisk and the Palm and The Ox and the Horse; they are included in W. G. Lambert, "Fables or Contest Literature," in *Babylonian Wisdom Literature* (Oxford: Oxford University Press, 1960), 150–212.

4. Miriam Lichtheim, "The Tale of the Shipwrecked Sailor," in *The Old and Middle Kingdomes* (vol. 1 of *Ancient Egyptian Literature*, Berkeley and Los Angeles: University of California Press, 1973), 211–15.

5. Cf. Ezek 17 and 19, in which plants and animals are protagonists but do not speak.

6. See, for example, the discussion of the pun's implications in Carol Newsom, "Common Ground: An Ecological Reading of Genesis 2–3," in Habel and Wurst, *The Earth Story in Genesis*, 60–72.

humanity than with other creatures, the snake's closest affiliation is actually with the divine being.

In the Yahwistic creation story, God creates the "creatures of the field" (הַשָּׂדֶת חַיַּת) only after creating the human being, placing the human in the garden, and articulating the rules governing the trees. The snake, as a creature of the field, is not present to hear God's admonition to the human regarding the tree of the knowledge of good and evil. The text is silent on how the snake comes to know that God has given such an injunction; nevertheless, the snake obviously knows something that God knows but the humans do not. In other words, the animal is somehow privy to a divine knowledge, while human beings know only what God tells them. The snake's first utterance is אַף כִּי־אָמַר אֱלֹהִים, "Did God say . . .?" or perhaps "Yea, God said . . . ." Whether we take the snake's speech as a question or not, the snake is nonetheless about to restate a speech that, as far as the text reveals, it did not hear.

The description of the snake as עָרוּם points to the "cleverness" of the snake's rhetorical move. It does not really need the woman to set its knowledge straight; instead, it wishes to engage the woman in dialogue. The woman answers the snake's query without hesitation; a talking snake prompts no astonished exclamation from her. Nor does the text note anything extraordinary. The direct discourse is undertaken in a matter-of-fact way: "it [the snake] said to the woman . . .," "the woman said to the snake . . .," and "the snake said to the woman . . . ." The dialogue passes back and forth between the two characters in simple, formulaic introductions, with the snake getting both the first and the last word.

The woman readily explains the discrepancy between what she understands God to have said and what the snake attributes to God. Notably, the woman also has not yet been created when God issues the directive about the tree, and her repetition of God's speech is by no means exact. She does not seem to know that the tree "in the middle of the garden" is the tree of the knowledge of good and evil, and she believes she will die merely by touching it—though God only mentioned eating its fruit as the cause of death. The snake corrects her, saying, "You will certainly not die! For God knows that on the day you eat from it your eyes will be opened, and you will be like God, knowing good and evil" (Gen 3:4–5). The snake's speech mediates between the words of God and the knowledge of the woman; it is a source of revelation for the human beings even before eating the fruit opens their eyes. The snake knows—or, at the very least, correctly predicts—what the consequences of eating the fruit will be. The humans do not die on that day, and instead their eyes are opened (3:7). Furthermore, while the text depicts the humans' own understanding of their new knowledge as an awareness of their nakedness (3:7), God realizes that "the human has become like one of us, knowing good and evil" (3:22), an assessment that lines up exactly with the snake's prediction.

The snake clearly can discern the immediate consequences of the humans' eating the fruit. Less clear is whether the snake knows the long-term effects of the action it initiates. The outcome of the snake's conversation incites God's anger against the snake, the woman, and the man. God now speaks curses, not conversation, to the three characters. Whereas the snake had been distinguished from the other creatures of the field by its cleverness, it now is distinguished from all such creatures by its state of being cursed. Rather than being partners in dialogue, the woman and the snake now will be enemies, engaging in physical assaults instead of verbal exchanges. If the snake intended to trick the woman into eating the fruit, then it must have known that its own downfall would be wrapped up in hers. If the snake sought some sort of positive consequence for the human couple, then it must have limits on its knowledge, since eating of the fruit brought curses rather than blessings. Or perhaps the snake was betrayed by the woman, who says to God, "The snake deceived me, and I ate" (Gen 3:13). The text suggests that the snake can predict God's behavior, but not the behavior of the humans. The human couple nevertheless expect imminent death at the hands of their creator because of their actions, despite the snake's declarations to the contrary.

Despite the text's ambiguity regarding the snake's motivations and the precise extent of its knowledge, an important point remains clear: the snake knows more about the ways of God than the humans do.

Moreover, the snake makes it possible for the human beings to acquire that knowledge. It is only after she converses with the snake that the woman is first able to *see*: "that the woman saw that the tree was good for eating, and that it was pleasing to the eyes, and that the tree was desirable to make one wise" (verse 6). Then, having eaten the fruit, "the eyes of the two were opened, and they knew . . ." (verse 7). God's hidden truths become accessible to the human beings only because of the snake, making the snake an agent of divine revelation.

3. NUMBERS 22:21–35

The story of Balaam and his donkey opens with a discrepancy between what God says and what God does—as in Gen 2–3. Balaam, a renowned seer, has been summoned by Balak, king of the Moabites, to curse the Israelites camped on the plains of Moab. In a curious move for a non-Israelite prophet, Balaam insists upon consulting Yahweh before consenting to travel to Moab to perform the curse. God says to Balaam, "Do not go with them; do not curse the people, for they are blessed" (Num 22:12). Repeatedly Balaam refuses to accompany the Moabite elders to Moab, because Yahweh has prohibited the journey. Pressed by the messengers from Balak, Balaam seeks a message from God one last time. This time God grants permission for Balaam to go with the elders, saying, "If the men have come to meet you, arise, go with them, but only the thing I tell you to do will you do" (22:20). Obedient to the words from God, Balaam goes. Given the great care Balaam has taken to follow the will of God, the reader is astonished when the text then says, "God became angry because he was going" (22:22a). God has told Balaam to go on the journey, and yet God has become angry precisely because

Balaam has gone. The narrative provides no explanation for this reversal in God's will—it gives no reason why God might tell Balaam to do one thing, and then seek to kill him for his obedience.

The donkey first appears in the story in Num 22:21. Balaam's saddling the donkey is the only action that does not directly echo God's commandment. Balaam is told to "arise, go with them" (קוּם לֵךְ אִתָּם); Balaam actually arises (וַיָּקָם), *saddles his donkey*, and then goes with the messengers (וַיֵּלֶךְ עִם־שָׂרֵי מוֹאָב). As the one aspect of his preparation for the journey not directly reflected in God's commandment, Balaam's donkey stands conspicuously ready to interfere in one way or another with Balaam's attempt to do the will of God.

When the angel of Yahweh appears in the road as an adversary (לְשָׂטָן) to Balaam, the narrative again draws attention to the presence of the donkey, but also to the presence of two of Balaam's servants (Num 22:22). Like the elders of Moab, who are not mentioned again until the end of the pericope in verse 35, Balaam's servants promptly disappear from the narrative. Of all this company of travelers, only the donkey sees (וַתֵּרֶא) the angel of Yahweh, sword in hand, standing in the road, and she[7] sees the angel all three times it appears. Balaam's blindness to God's messenger is particularly ironic, since he, a seer, has just engaged in direct conversation with God the night before he embarked on the journey. With each appearance of the angel, the donkey must take increasingly more drastic measures to avoid the angel's wrath, even injuring her rider and finally sitting down, refusing to go any farther. With each of the donkey's diversions, Balaam grows more angry, beating the donkey more severely each time, until finally the Lord opens the mouth of the donkey.[8] Unlike the snake's speech in Gen 3, here the donkey's ability to talk is attributed explicitly to God's intervention. Yet the donkey's speech is received by Balaam as no more extraordinary than the snake's conversation with Eve. The emphasis in both texts is not on the human characteristics that the animals display, but rather on the animals' abilities to see and know the ways of God when human beings cannot.

Like the snake, the donkey addresses her human companion interrogatively, but, as Savran notes, with "different rhetorical intent."[9] Whereas the narrator's description of the snake as עָרוּם may suggest intent to deceive, no adjectives are attached to the donkey. Her words stand alone to convey her meaning to the reader and to Balaam. She asks Balaam, "What have I done to you, that you have beaten me these three times?" Balaam's answer, in which he wishes for a

---

7. The Hebrew text uses אָתוֹן, indicating a female donkey, hence the feminine pronouns.

8. For Coats, a fable, of which the Balaam's ass story is the exemplar, "describes a static situation." To the contrary, in this story I have observed an increasing tension leading to a denouement, rather than a static situation. See George W. Coats, *Genesis, with an Introduction to Narrative Literature* (TFOTL 1; Grand Rapids: Eerdmans, 1983), 10.

9. Savran, "Beastly Speech," 38–39.

sword to kill the donkey for making a fool of him, is as ironic as his blindness; he might have asked to borrow the angel's sword—were he aware of its presence. The donkey then deploys two rhetorical questions that by their nature do not require answers, though Balaam still feels compelled to give one inadequate reply. She asks him, "Am I not your donkey, which you have ridden all your life to this day? Have I been in the habit of treating you this way?" Remarkably, rather than point to the fiery supernatural being blocking the road, the donkey appeals to the companionship—albeit a companionship forged through servitude—she and Balaam have shared. She puts her own subjectivity first, insisting that Balaam acknowledge the trust he owes her. Rather than serving as a folkloric convention that utters a few words to move the plot along, this talking animal is not only a character in its own right, but a self-aware, even "rounded" character. The fullness of the donkey's characterization at this point in the story contrasts with the deflation of Balaam's importance. Balaam's final, terse "no" (לא) in response to the donkey's questions is hardly worthy of a person who is expected to curse an entire people. Their conversation is, like the one between the woman and the snake, matter-of-fact in its presentation, yet extraordinary in its result.

Just as Yahweh has opened the mouth of the donkey, Yahweh also uncovers Balaam's eyes, but only after the donkey has spoken. Balaam's conversation with the donkey results in his ability to see the armed angel standing in the road; in the same way the conversation with the snake enables the woman to see the goodness of the tree.

But the interrogations are not yet over for Balaam. The angel of Yahweh asks nearly the same question that the donkey posed: "Why have you beaten your donkey these three times?" (Num 22:32). Before Balaam has a chance to revise his answer, the angel continues its address, explaining that the donkey's seeing and subsequent turning away have kept the angel from killing Balaam. The donkey, incidentally, seems never to have been in danger; the angel claims that it would have let the donkey live even had it slain Balaam (22:33). This talking animal emerges from her conversation with her human companion unscathed, and if she perceived danger before the angel spoke, she now learns that Balaam was the one who should have been wary.

4. KNOWING AND SEEING

Genesis 3 and Num 22 end with different fates for the human and nonhuman characters. The snake is cursed and Adam and Eve are expelled from the garden. Both Balaam and his donkey, on the other hand, survive their encounter with the messenger.

The presence of a talking animal by no means guarantees a happy ending for human or nonhuman animal; it does, however, guarantee some change in a human being's ability to know or to see. While this effect on the human reflects an inherent anthropocentrism in the texts, it also shows that the animals possess faculties that the humans do not—faculties that equip the animals to be messengers of God. For the animals to appear only as servants of *human* needs would be an unmitigated anthropocentrism. For them to be presented as agents of *divinity* is another matter.

Shemaryahu Talmon notes that revelations of God to humanity in biblical narratives often involve one or more of the verbs גלה, ראה, and ידע. Source critics attempt to categorize the nature of God's revelation according to different sources' uses of these verbs, proposing, for example, that where the Yahwist uses ראה for theophanies, the Priestly writer substitutes ידע at some instances, particularly those involving Moses.[10] Talmon resists this kind of strict categorization, pointing instead to numerous instances where two of the three verbs occur in parallel lines. Moreover, as Talmon points out, all three of the verbs are sometimes used together, such as in an introduction to an oracle delivered by one of our characters of note, Balaam: "An utterance of Balaam son of Beor, an utterance of the man of open eye, an utterance of one who hears the words of God, and knows (וְיֹדֵעַ) the knowledge of the Most High; the vision of *Shaddai* he sees (יֶחֱזֶה = ראה); one who falls down, yet his eyes are uncovered וּגְלוּי)" (Num 24:15–16).[11] Regardless of whether they can be separated by source—and they cannot be in this poem— these verbs of seeing, knowing, and uncovering all are clearly associated with God's revelations to humanity.

When Yahweh opens Balaam's eyes in Num 22:31, the verb is גלה. It connotes the removal of some covering, as though Balaam might normally have been able to discern angels in the road, but that ability has been temporarily obscured. As soon as Balaam's eyes are opened, he is able to *see* (ראה) the angel in the road, as his donkey has long been able to do. Balaam's response to the angel attributes his sin to not *knowing* (ידע), having just been indicted by the donkey and the angel for his failure to see. The presence of these three verbs emphasizes the revelatory nature of Balaam's rediscovered vision. Vision and knowledge are conflated: thanks to the donkey's vision, Balaam also acquires again both his prophetic vision and his knowledge of God's will.

Vision and knowledge are similarly synthesized in Gen 3:1–7. By communicating God's hidden knowledge to the human being, the snake already begins the process of eye-opening. Upon hearing the snake's clarification of God's statements regarding the tree, "the woman saw (וַתֵּרֶא) that the tree was good for eating, and that it was pleasing to the eyes . . ." (3:6). The fruit appeals to the woman's eyes, newly opened to the tree's pleasures. Moreover, before talking with the snake, the woman had not been able to "see" that the tree was good; the ability to know good is a promised consequence of eating the fruit, but even simple

---

10. Rolf Rendtorff, quoted in Shemaryahu Talmon, "Revelation in Biblical Times," *HS* 26 (1985): 53–70.

11. See Talmon, "Revelation in Biblical Times," 59.

knowledge of the true consequences introduces knowledge of good, described as an ability to see. Unlike Balaam, who has his eyes uncovered, the two first humans have their eyes opened, with the implication that they are acquiring for the first time the kind of sight enabling them to know (ידע) as God knows. They now become closer to God in a way that the snake, able to speak God's hidden truth to the humans, had already been.

5. Conclusion

By infusing the snake and donkey with the human characteristics of dialogue and speech, the narrative renders the realm of God's revelation accessible to the human characters. Beyond being merely a folkloric convention, personification in Gen 3:1–7 and Num 22:21–35 gives unique direction to the narrative. The talking animals allow Eve and Balaam to see that to which they previously were blinded, and with new sight comes new knowledge. Before the animals address their human companions, the first humans can neither see the goodness of the tree nor know the true consequences of eating its fruit. Balaam cannot know that God is angry with him for journeying to Moab (however capricious that anger may seem), nor can he see the angel blocking his path.

After conversing with the snake and the donkey, Eve and Balaam themselves acquire revelatory sight and knowledge of divine will. Thus the snake and donkey are revealed as mediators of divine revelation, possessing a closer relationship to God than their human counterparts. The texts' anthropocentrism, while still present, is mitigated by the privileging of the animals' revelatory agency over that of the humans'.

These two instances of animals talking with human speech cannot be said to comprise a unique genre, since there are no other biblical texts featuring animal personification with which to compare them. Nevertheless, this phenomenon operates in a very particular manner in Gen 3 and Num 22: the talking donkey and snake make God's revelation visible and comprehensible to humanity.

Yet the agency of these animals does not stop at the betterment of human beings. Instead, retrieving the voices of the snake and donkey from the obscurity of literary convention reveals that these two biblical animals exhibit far greater affinities with the deity than with their human counterparts who, by listening to the voices of the snake and the donkey, can hear the voice of God.

Earth Tells the Lessons of Cain

Kristin M. Swenson

1. An Ecological Hermeneutic

This essay is a creative reworking of the paper I gave in 2005 at the Ecological Hermeneutics section of the Society of Biblical Literature conference. In that paper, "Earth as Maternal Matrix of Relationships in Genesis 4:1–16,"[1] I talked about Earth as I demonstrated how the appearance, disappearance, and reappearance of one word in the stories of chapters 2–4 leads readers to conclusions with powerful ecological implications. Following that one word (Hebrew *shmr*) and its relationship to the greater literary context of these first stories in Genesis, readers discover that Earth is the hub of relationships. Human beings, God, and the land are in dynamic relation to each other by means of Earth. Human caretaking of the land is bound up with the caretaking of others, and such activity affords an experience of God.

This essay is different. In it I imagine how the same events might be perceived by Earth. I listen for the voice of Earth and seek to give Earth space for expression, an opportunity to be heard. That is, this essay is not about Earth so much as by Earth. Earth is the speaker. In an effort to incorporate all three working principles of the new ecological hermeneutic, I imagine Earth's perspective on the events and attempt to retrieve her voice. In an act of "radical re-orientation," as Norman Habel puts it, I portray Earth as subject, part of, and participant in the events related at the beginning of Genesis, with a voice of her own.

This requires suspicion that the texts focus primarily on human beings as unique within the world and the center of all purposeful activity. Giving Earth a voice challenges such anthropocentrism. Giving Earth a voice—indeed assuming the voice of Earth in this creative rendering—requires identification. It's a bit presumptuous to assume that any of us know the thoughts, feelings, questions, and dreams of another—much less Earth herself. Yet we are connected; we are members of Earth community; we are Earth-stuff.

---

1. I published another version of this paper in *Int* 60 (2006): 373–84.

Furthermore, these biblical texts include Earth as an important participant in the plot and character development, even occasionally making Earth an active subject (grammatically the subject of transitive verbs). Earth is a character in her own right in these stories, and goes by different names. Geographical place *erets*–Earth; arable land *adamah*–Earth; and paradise garden *gan*–Earth play a role in the stories' development of character and plot. So I took a chance and tried to imagine Earth's perspective. In the process of such retrieval, Earth is revealed as the matrix of relationships, central to the action, definitive of human purpose, and as a means of divine presence. In part because Earth functions in this astoundingly powerful way, attending to Earth's perspective allows us to see and understand these stories and events differently..

Indeed, the biblical text supports this creative rendering. That is, my exegetical work (represented in papers both presented and published) has led me to observe how reading the Cain and Abel story of Gen 4:1–16 in light of the Adam and Eve story of Gen 2:4b–3:24 portrays Earth as the means for humanity's experience of God. And this experience is inseparable from responsible caretaking of Earth and Earth community. While I depend for this essay on what I have learned from such careful reading and scholarship, I do not simply report the results but incorporate what I infer to be Earth's perspective on the narrated events. I have chosen to make the form a creative act of imagination partly to demonstrate that I recognize I am taking some liberties with the text. I have tried, however, to represent Earth with the kind of characterization that the text suggests, avoiding wild guesses about Earth's "thoughts" or "feelings" and concentrating on what the text suggests is Earth's point of view and role in the stories. Earth's narrative is represented in italics. My explanation and discussion along the way is represented in plain text.

2. By Way of Introduction

> *I am Earth, dynamic and vital, fragile and resilient, containing within me the life that you know. You are creatures of Earth, bound with blood and bone to the air, the waters, the very stones of my body. In the beginning, God moved on, in, and through me. The stories say so—and not only that, but that God continues to do so.*
>
> *I will tell you, from my perspective, how one man learned the dynamic connections of which we are all a part. His lesson is yours—to spare you his tragedy, perhaps. But you, like he, must discover these connections for yourself. (Neither God nor I stepped in to prevent the course of events told here.) Listen carefully, then, to the stories of the ancients. Be open to the questions. Wrestle with the answers.*

Earth in these biblical texts goes by several names specific to Earth's various aspects. *Erets*–Earth may be understood as the grand terrestrial globe on which we live; sometimes the term is used of particular territories. Earth in the Hebrew

Bible is also *adamah*-Earth, dirt from the ground. *Adamah* frequently functions as a term for soil, the arable earth out of which things grow—including human beings, according to Gen 2:7. Out of *adamah*, God fashioned and shaped *adam* the human being . . . and not without purpose.

The purpose of human beings, according to these texts, is grounded (pardon the pun) in Earth, as the following retelling notes. And through Earth, that purpose extends in relation to the whole Earth community (including but not limited to other people) and to God. Cain learned this the hard way. His story, when heard in light of his parents' experiences, leads readers to see for themselves that what seemed to be Cain's purpose—working in reverent service Earth—is inseparable from caring for others, no matter what the circumstances (even if they seem fair or not).

Finally, this integrally connected business of caring for Earth and caring for others affords an experience of the presence of God. The appearance, disappearance, and reappearance of one little word—like a firefly at night—takes readers down a path of questions and possible answers to a clearing lit with sudden realization. The story begins in Gen 2:4.

3. BEGINNINGS AND THE PURPOSE OF PEOPLE (GENESIS 2–3)

> *I am Earth. In the dawn of time, I was bare. I had no plants, no animals, and human beings had not yet come along. Two things contributed to my barrenness—the absence of human beings to work in reverent service to me, and the fact that Yahweh-God had not sent rain for me to drink to empower me to birth the living things that clothe me. I anticipated life then as now: the cycles of birth, death, and new birth, for flora and fauna alike. Then from my depths, a life-giving spring bubbled up with sweet water to animate my face and empower me. From* erets*-Earth a spring to water the face of* adamah*-Earth.*

What is God and what is Earth blurs in this commencement of creation. Genesis 2:5–6 tells us that Yahweh had not sent rain; but (and?) Earth produced the spring that provided the water necessary to cover the arable ground. Agency is ambiguous here. The narrator suggests that Yahweh is the determining factor—until God sends rain, there will be no water to vitalize the soil. Yet we read shortly after that that "a stream went up from *ha-erets*" (not "God caused a stream . . ."). Consequently, we can imagine Earth saying:

> *I was so eager for life in my presence that I brought up from the depths of my being clear fresh water so that plants and animals might grow and thrive. I accomplished this; but it was God who created the human being. Together, then, God and I made possible the conditions for life. And by my face, Cain later would exclaim, the face of God is known. But back to the beginnings:*
>
> *After the fresh waters came, Yahweh-God reached within me and fashioned a human from my humus, adam out of* adamah*-Earth. From my body, a human*

being, into whose nostrils God breathed life. So you can imagine how I might feel a special bond with this human being, fresh and new. Like a baby and its mother, adam *was shaped from my body and taken out of me. And the mysterious One who holds life gave life to this human, this creature of Earth. Again, the partnership between God and me made possible a new creation: a living, breathing human being.*

Whether or not Earth was an eager or even willing partner in this creation is less easy to determine than in Gen 2:6. Earth does not act outright but is acted upon in verse 7. Nevertheless, the partnership of Earth and God in growing life suggested in verse 7, and the manner of that action—taking the stuff of Earth and fashioning a creature named for its relation to Earth—suggests that Earth was not as unwilling as Earth proves able to be later in the story.

God immediately set to work growing a garden in which God set *adam*, the earth creature. The narrator then describes the garden as filled with nourishing beauty and food. "Garden" may be misleading, however, since the plants that filled it are described as trees. This forest serves as the human being's first home.

Like a nursemaid, then, I was gan*-Earth—the forest garden of God. I welcomed* adam *with sensual delights—things pleasing to look at and delicious to eat. I also held within me the means of life and moral reasoning, things of great value, and plenty of good, fresh water. So I would be for the human being . . . but the human would also be for me.*

When Yahweh-God settled adam *within me, it was in order to work in my reverent service and to guard my welfare. In the forest garden God announced the charter for human life, a two-part mandate that was life-giving and ultimately satisfying.*

These two things, *shmr* and *'bd*, the ancients tell, defined the purpose of the humans. One of them readers have heard before. The other is new to this part of the story. The verb *'bd* appeared earlier (verse 5) in the context of the necessary function of human beings to the vitality of Earth community. It means "to work, serve, worship," and is frequently translated "to till." But the word "till" does not do justice to the Hebrew word's range of meaning. Given the context in which it appears here, "work in reverent service to" is a better translation. Genesis 2:5 tells us that without human work in reverent service to *adamah*-Earth (and without water) Earth lay bare. The other verb, *shmr*, which appears in the context of *gan*-Earth, notes an occupation of guarding and can mean the work of protecting another's welfare. God's creative action built a dynamic and multifaceted relationship between Earth and *adam* that is described as mutually rewarding. Then the human was split and paired with another, which added to their mutual joy.

4. Growing Up in the Real World

Nevertheless, it couldn't last. I watched the human beings grow up, question-ing and challenging, experimenting, and rebelling. They needed to do this: to make decisions, to make mistakes. But the consequences of such maturation were painful for all of us, pulling relationships taut with tension, even to breaking.

Many scholars have noted how the Garden story in Gen 2–3 seems to tell the maturation of people. The human beings "grow up" in the course of the garden of Eden narrative, going from innocence to intention to separation and distinc-tion.[2]

Self-conscious, the humans came to know shame, unhappy with bodies that are an extension of me and shaped by God. Furthermore, man turned against woman and woman against snake with finger-pointing and blame. The humans' relationship to God, to me, and within the Earth community became marked by distance and pain. I watched the breakdown of interanimal relationships (woman and the snake, for example) and between the humans (a parity relationship became unequal, with new burdens for both parties). Like an empathetic mother, I took on the curse of God, making the human's work with me difficult and frustrating.[3]

I would no longer be the nursemaid gan–Earth to the human beings. God sent them away, and Eden became as unavailable as childhood is to an adult. Neverthe-less, even in a(n adult) world of choices, dilemmas and pain, the human beings are still linked to me. Earth–creatures and I are intimately related, and I will take them back to me when they die. In the meantime, human purpose outside of Eden is still to work in reverent service ('bd) to me.

That is how the Garden story ends. And this raises a question: What happened to the other word *shmr*, the verb describing the second part of God's two-part mandate to human beings? After the humans were driven from the garden, they were still defined by *'bd* working in reverent service to *adamah*–Earth, just as they were before God planted the garden. But there is no mention of *shmr*. The

---

2. S. R. Driver, *The Book of Genesis: With Introduction and Notes* (London: Methuen, 1904); Hermann Gunkel, *Genesis übersetzt und erklärt* (Göttingen: Vandenhoeck & Ruprecht, 1902); Umberto Cassuto, *From Adam to Noah* (Jerusalem: Magnes Press, 1961); L. M. Bechtel, "Rethinking the Interpretation of Genesis 2.4b–3.24," in *A Feminist Companion to Genesis* (ed. A. Brenner; Sheffield: Sheffield Academic Press, 1993), 77–117; Ellen van Wolde, "Facing the Earth: Primaeval History in a New Perspective," in *The World of Genesis: Persons, Places, Per-spectives* (JSOTSup 257; Sheffield: Sheffield Academic Press, 1998), 22–47. See also Harold Kusher, *How Good Do We Have To Be?* (Boston: Little, Brown & Co., 1996).

3. Here I follow Shirley (Joh) Wurst's insightful reading of Earth's curse as a choice Earth made—to take the curse rather than see Earth's child, the human being, cursed. Shirley Wurst, "'Beloved, Come Back to Me': Ground's Theme Song in Genesis 3?," in Habel and Wurst, *The Earth Story in Genesis*, 87–104.

context of its absence suggests that the business of "guarding, keeping the welfare of" may be irrelevant outside of Eden.

5. The Purpose of People in the Real World

Yet the next episode seems to give an answer. Cain was born, and then Abel, and immediately readers learn that while Cain worked in reverent service to *adamah*–Earth, Abel kept sheep. It sounds like a division of the labor that defined the human being's purpose in the Garden—"guarding" or "keeping"; but it wasn't . . . quite. That is, Abel's work was not the *shmr* of Gen 2:15, a general "guarding" or "keeping." It was *ro'eh*, a term used specifically of shepherding.

> *At the time, I wondered if this was enough. After all, where was the second part of the two-part charter for human beings? Shmr is absent from the description of human work outside of Eden at the end of Gen 3. I wondered if shmr is specific to Edenic conditions, not the real-world, adult-life of humans outside of the garden. Perhaps in the difficult and dangerous conditions outside of paradise, it is enough that human beings 'bd (work in reverent service to) me as adamah–Earth.*
>
> *I was there when Cain was born into this adult world and noted that Eve announced Cain an adult. She declared that she had "gotten (qnh)" Cain (Qayin) as "a man" "with Yahweh-God." "How odd!" I thought. Cain was born not a baby, not a child, not a son, but a man . . . and associated with God. Furthermore, I noted how Abel is identified—auspiciously—only in relation to Cain (as Cain's brother) and by his name which means "emptiness, transience," like mist that evaporates. With a sense of foreboding, I thought about how the implications of these statements would bear on the events to come.*

In a concise opening phrase, the narrator suggests that Abel would not be around very long and that Cain was responsible for him. Furthermore, the oddity of identifying Cain at birth as "a man" suggests that Cain's responsibility is an adult one, complicated by the ambiguities and difficulties that mature persons must deal with in life.

After learning of their work vis-à-vis the Earth and Earth community (Cain works in reverent service to *adamah*–Earth and Abel ensures the health and vitality of sheep), readers learn that they make offerings to God from the produce of their particular labor.

> *I was the conduit of human relationship to God. I was the stuff of the gifts that linked Cain and Abel to God. But God's response to the sacrifice was unpredictable—accepting Abel's offering while ignoring Cain's. I don't know why God reacted in this way, ignoring my contribution—both offerings were worthy expressions of different types of work. But God is God, therefore not subject to anyone else's expectations or demands.*
>
> *Cain, as you'll remember, was described at his birth as an adult. Cain was born into the real world of ambiguity, unfairness, and only partial understanding.*

He got a bitter taste of reality when God ignored his gift. It made Cain angry and discouraged.

I feared for Cain—how he'd handle himself, what he'd do. God got involved immediately, asking Cain why he was so upset. At the time, I wondered: "Now why would God ask such a thing, isn't it obvious?"

Yet with this question, God suggested that Cain's response to the vicissitudes of life was not the only possible one. And God continued by reminding Cain (asking "is it not so,") that if he would do well, Cain would be encouraged, "lifted up" (*ns'*) in contrast to his "fallen" face. The alternative: if he did not choose the good, sin like a beast was lying in wait for him. Finally, God told Cain that he must master the impulse to wrongdoing.

I was a silent party to this exchange. I was not involved; yet I was there, hoping that Cain would do the right thing. I observed how God managed to shift attention away from the business of the offering and onto the matter of what Cain would do with his feelings. I noted how God's silence about the justification of favoring one offering over the other contrasted with God's warning to Cain—a contrast that emphasized that Cain couldn't control God's behavior; but Cain could, and was expected to, control his own—and that that was the important point.

Cain did not handle the situation well. The very next thing he did was get Abel into the field (sadeh–Earth, another of my particular forms).[4] And Cain killed his brother, Abel. "Ah, Abel, so this is how it goes!" I thought. This is your fragility, your transience, vis-à-vis the man described as your brother. Just as neither I nor God tried to stop the couple in the garden from making choices with painful consequences, so we did not try to stop Cain . . . even from murdering his brother.

Maybe Cain thought that out in the sadeh–Earth, no one would know, no one would see. Or maybe Cain thought that I would cover for him because his vocation was to care for me. But I am Earth and my face mediates the presence of God. I witnessed the murder and absorbed the red river of Abel's life running from Cain's hand. And I knew already what Cain had not yet learned—that our relationship was inseparable from others and from God. Connections, responsibilities, and purposefulness are multifaceted.

In no time at all, Yahweh-God approached Cain with another question: "Where is your brother Abel?" Cain's infamous response "I do not know; am I my brother's keeper?" is a much more shocking hook than readers typically appreciate. For

---

4. Readers might not suspect that things would go badly when "Cain rose up." After all, God had said that if Cain did well, then he would "be lifted up." However, there is a subtle shift in vocabulary. Although in translation *qwn*, rise up," appears to be a synonym for *ns'* ("lift up"), it is a different verb in Hebrew, and has a slightly different meaning. Furthermore, Cain is the agent of the action. God had said that if Cain did what is good, he would "be lifted up," the passive form suggesting that someone or something other than Cain would make it happen. Instead, Cain took it upon himself to "rise up" (Gen 4:8).

here at last is the long-lost word *shmr*, the word that appeared in Gen 2 as the second part of the two-part purpose of people in the Garden—to *'bd* and *shmr* it. It is the word that Abel's vocation came so close to meeting . . . yet didn't.

When readers answer the question, "Yes! Yes, you are supposed to guard the welfare of your brother!," they acknowledge that the work of *shmr* is not relevant only in the paradisiacal conditions of Eden. It is required also in the difficult world of disappointment and unfairness outside of Eden. Not only that, but it is connected with care not simply for the garden of Eden, not simply for Earth in any shape or form, but also with caring for the other. Cain's care for Earth, Cain's work in reverent service (*'bd*) to Earth was not isolated from guarding the welfare of others . . . and that this was expected even in the problematic world east of Eden.

> With Cain's question, I wanted to weep at his ignorance of this integral connection that proves so costly. I am a matrix of connection. It isn't possible to care for members of the Earth community without caring for me; and it isn't possible to care for me without caring for others. Furthermore, such caretaking is not limited to the easy conditions of the garden of Eden—but it is expected also in a world where people experience anger, betrayal, and injustice. That is what people listening to this story are led to conclude, when they answer Cain's question with "Yes, yes of course!" Yet Cain's lesson continues to be lost to people who simply think he was a murderous idiot. They fail to appreciate how answering "yes" to Cain's question involves them in a timeless web of connections and responsibilities that run through me. Taking care of Earth cannot be done without taking care of others and vice versa.
>
> But even that is not all. Cain's failure to appreciate that the responsibility he had to his brother was inseparable from his work for me cost him our relationship, too. With the bitter taste of violence in my mouth and God's presence animating my face, Cain was cursed—by me, through me, on account of me. That's a tough thing for me to say. And it all happened so fast.
>
> Then he had to leave. Forced to flee from my presence, Cain cried out that this was more than he could bear. Through me, he said, he experienced the very presence of God. Cain's speech equates my face with the face of God.[5] Cain understood his alienation from me as alienation from God. And he was bereft.
>
> I am a matrix of life and connection, corrective, and rewarding. Serving me, serving others, and serving God are all part of the same piece. And Cain knew that work in reverent service to me, adamah–Earth, was not merely tilling the soil but basking in the presence of God—a privilege and a delight. But he failed to appreciate that enjoying this relationship meant taking seriously his responsibility to others . . . even when things seemed unfair.

---

5. The text makes this point using chiastic parallelism.

Cain learned, and careful readers learn with him, a startling lesson of responsibility and divine presence: even in the difficult and sometimes unfair conditions east of Eden, working in reverent service to Earth is inseparable from guarding the welfare of others. And the process of such caretaking, as they suggest in this story, may allow a person to experience the very presence of God.

I would like to end there, but there is another implication of the story worth mentioning. It is a harsh corrective to those who profess that God will step in and correct the effects of our destructive actions, or that Earth will find a way to heal Earth and Earth community despite our assault on both. Notice how neither God nor Earth prevented Cain from murder.

Of course, none of us can say what God will or will not do; and none of us knows Earth so well as to predict the planet's adaptability and potential for healing. But this story should give pause to anyone who assumes that God and/or Earth will arrest the violence of our (in)action and simply fix everything. We are responsible.

How Lonely Sits the City:
Reading Lamentations as City and Land

Peter Trudinger

In the summer of 586 B.C.E., according to the biblical history, the officers and army of the king of Babylon conquered Jerusalem after a long siege. They burned the temple, destroyed the palace and mansions, tore down the fortifications of the city, and relocated the population (2 Kgs 25; cf. Jer 39, 52). The fall of Jerusalem and the exile are usually considered to be pivotal events that shaped the religion, identity, and literature of Israel.

The biblical accounts emphasize one perspective on the exile: widespread destruction, massive deportations, and the depopulation of Judah with only the poorest remaining in the land. Yet they also contain indications contrary to this— the figure for the number of deportees given in the book of Jeremiah is relatively small (Jer 52:28–30), and major cities, such as Mizpah the new capital, remained functional (2 Kgs 25:22–24). The archaeological evidence is correspondingly complex.[1] The territory around Jerusalem shows evidence of destruction, but cities further away do not. These observations underscore the point that the biblical texts were produced from a particular viewpoint by writers with certain interests.

The dominant biblical perspective on the exile appears to be that of the elite upper classes who lost the most when Jerusalem was destroyed, who were deported to refugee camps, and who eventually regained control of Judah—now a Persian province—a few generations later. As an alternative to this view, one might write a history of the exilic period from the perspective of those who continued to reside in Judah—perhaps the peasants who fled to the hill country

---

1. A discussion of Judah after 586 B.C.E. is found in Jill Middlemas, *The Troubles of Temple-less Judah* (OTM; Oxford: Oxford University Press, 2005), esp. 37–42; see also Hans M. Barstad, "After the 'Myth of the Empty Land': Major Challenges in the Study of Neo-Babylonian Judah," in *Judah and the Judeans in the Neo-Babylonian Period* (ed. Oded Lipschitz and Joseph Blenkinsopp; Winona Lake, Ind.: Eisenbrauns, 2005), 3–20.

during the fighting, but returned after the siege to farm their traditional lands in a territory free from unrest and the depredations of the old elite.

Both these perspectives are anthropocentric. They tell the history of the destruction and "exile" from the point of view of humans. How would Earth or a nonhuman member of Earth community tell the story of the exile? Would they speak of the devastation of the surrounding countryside by the construction of siege works, or of a scorched-earth policy, or perhaps even remember wistfully a period of rest from farming following the deportation (compare 2 Chr 36:21)?

In this paper, we adopt a geocentric perspective. We take a biblical text from the period of the exile (in this case, Lam 1–2) and decenter the interpretation of this text away from an anthropocentric subject, rereading it with a member of Earth community as subject. There is a sense in which this process is an experiment in hermeneutics: what sort of interpretation results if we consciously reject key anthropocentric interpretative assumptions and go against the flow of traditional interpretation for this exilic text? Embedded in this process is another question: to what extent does the text itself give voice to nonhuman subjects? All biblical texts, of course, were shaped by humans and in the first instance we suspect them to express human interests. To what extent can a geocentric perspective be retrieved from any text, particularly one that deals with a decidedly human experience like the exile? Our rereading visits the three aspects of an ecological hermeneutic—suspicion of the biblical texts and their prior interpretation as anthropocentric, identification with a nonhuman subject, and retrieval of the voice of that subject if possible.

1. Texts and Center

The exile appears as subject, motif, or background in many texts in the Hebrew Bible. The present study will focus on the first two chapters of the book of Lamentations. The five laments in this book, usually thought to be written in Judah at the start of the exilic period, deal directly with the destruction of Jerusalem and the start of the exile. The book does not present an historical account of these events, but an emotional response to them, interlaced with circumstantial details. The language is skillfully chosen and emotionally charged in order to convey the grief and horror felt by the people. The primary perspective in Lamentations is anthropocentric. Can this work express the voice of the nonhuman?

Surprisingly, the first two chapters of the work do contain what appears to be a nonhuman voice: the voice of "the city" (1:1), that is, Jerusalem.[2] Lamentations 1 and 2 are almost entirely given over to describing Jerusalem during and after

---

2. In Lam 1 and 2, several terms are used to denote the city, the most common being "Zion" and "Jerusalem."

the destruction. What is more, the city is a character in the poems; Jerusalem is personified and speaks.

In the tradition of interpretation of Lam 1 and 2, this remarkable voice is handled in an entirely anthropocentric fashion: the city, Jerusalem, is assumed to stand for the people.[3] The metaphor is usually explained as a psychological ploy on the part of the author to enable the grieving people to distance themselves from the horror of the destruction. It facilitates the grief process. "Through [the city's] personification the Jerusalem community can deal with its own pain and anxiety on a more profound level."[4] "When the poet intends to convey the full force of community anguish, he adopts a female persona."[5]

Subsequent interpretation appropriates the fall of Jerusalem as a symbol for other human catastrophes.[6] The narrator's description of the excess of suffering and the cries of the city are seen as paralleling human responses to situations of intense, excessive suffering that challenge the notion of the kindness of God. Under this trajectory of interpretation, the city as such has no independent value. It is a persona created purely for the psychological palliation of humans.

At this point, a hermeneutic of suspicion comes into play. Should we accept this anthropocentric tradition of interpretation, or is there another way? Certainly cities are linked with people. They are constructed by humans for the use of humans. Nevertheless, must the city be seen as a cipher for human interests? Or might it be in some way a nonhuman member of Earth community? Might a city have an independent voice? Or would its interests be so aligned with that of its human creators that the voice of a city can only be anthropocentric?

In Lamentations we are dealing not with any city, but with a specific city, Jerusalem. This city is special. An extensive network of biblical traditions—the so-called "Zion" traditions—surrounds this city.[7] In the first instance, the Zion

---

3. Often the equation is made without comment, e.g., for F. W. Dobbs-Allsopp, verses like 1:5b and 8a are "explicit" examples of the "acknowledgment of human sin and guilt;" see *Lamentations* (IBC; Louisville, Ky.: Westminster John Knox, 2002), 29; similarly Middlemas, whose chapter on Lamentations is entitled "Lamentations: The Voice of the Land," sees the land as representing the people and interprets verses 1:5a and 18 as laying the blame on the exiles; see *The Troubles of Templeless Judah*, 213–14.

4. Knut M. Heim, "The Personification of Jerusalem and the Drama of Her Bereavement in Lamentations," in *Zion, City of Our God* (ed. R. S. Hess and Gordan J. Wenham; Grand Rapids: Eerdmans, 1999), 129–30. This essay is an illuminating analysis of the process of personification: the community is transformed into the city, which in turn is portrayed as a grieving person.

5. Barbara Bakke Kaiser, "Poet as 'Female Impersonator': The Image of Daughter Zion as Speaker in Biblical Poems of Suffering," *JR* 67 (1987): 175.

6. See, e.g., Tod Linafelt, *Surviving Lamentations: Catastrophe, Lament, and Protest in the Afterlife of a Biblical Book* (Chicago: University of Chicago Press, 2000).

7. The Zion traditions are discussed in many places, see, e.g., Philip S. Alexander, "Jerusalem as the Omphalos of the World: On the History of a Geographical Concept," pages 104–19 in *Jerusalem: Its Sanctity and Centrality to Judaism, Christianity, and Islam* (ed. Lee I. Levine; New

traditions stress the association of the city with God. The temple in Jerusalem is the principal place on Earth where God is manifested or may be encountered. It is God's dwelling place on Earth—the metaphor does not limit God, but exalts the status of the city.

In addition—and this is significant for the present discussion—the traditions also assert the centrality of Zion in the cosmos. Zion is the place where three worlds—heaven, Earth, and the underworld—touch. Zion was the starting point of creation, and it is envisioned to be the source of continuing life for Earth, for example, as the wellspring of fructifying rivers (Ezek 47:1–12). The city is the center of the world, preeminent among all lands (Ezek 5:5; 38:12; Pss 48:1; 87:1–2). As such, in biblical texts it often becomes the representative *par excellence* of the surrounding land of Judah or the rest of Earth. For example, the settlement of the land is the settlement of Zion (Exod 15:17; Ps 78:54–55); the people of Judah are the people who come to the city (Jer 7:2); Jerusalem is placed in synonymous parallelism with other towns (Pss 48:11; 97:8; compare Isaiah 40:9); and in Ps 74, the destruction of the sanctuary parallels the fate of all the places of God in the land. The city is associated with a larger territory or Earth in such a way as to suggest that a thought progression from one to another was considered natural—or even that the two were identified. The city is the hub of Earth community and the sacred center of the cosmos. The biblical traditions suggest that Jerusalem may be considered more than an anthropocentric cipher; rather it may be regarded as a nonhuman member of Earth community with an independent voice and, what is more, may represent the interests of a larger entity, the land.

There are, then, two ways of approaching a text that features Jerusalem. One way is guided by the view that any city is so closely tied to its inhabitants that it can only represent human interests. In this case, Jerusalem is a *metaphor* for its people. The other notes the special role of *physical* city Jerusalem as center of the web of the cosmos and regards it as a member, and representative (through metonymy), of Earth community.

This paper explores Lamentations 1 and 2 along the latter path, identifying with the physical city, Jerusalem, as nonhuman subject, asking the extent to which the texts express or suppress the voice of the city, and seeking to recover this voice

York: Continuum, 1999); and Jon D. Levenson, *Sinai and Zion: An Entry into the Jewish Bible* (San Francisco: HarperSanFrancisco, 1987), esp. 111–36. Sometimes a distinction may be made between the terms "Jerusalem" and "Zion," with the former being used to refer to the mundane city and the latter to the city imbued with religious significance. However, such a distinction in usage does not apply in Lamentations where, for example, both terms appear in tight parallel constructions (1:17; 2:10, 13). The two names are used to signify the same entity and any separate connotations they carry join together. In this text, there is only one city, "the city" (1:1).

in the story of the events of 586 B.C.E., the story of the destruction of the city and the subsequent exile of its people.[8]

2. Lamentations 1 and 2

Lamentations 1 and 2 are expressions of extreme grief at the calamity that has befallen Judah, specifically, the destruction of Jerusalem and the fate of its inhabitants. The two chapters are cast as a series of speeches that contain vignettes about the city and its inhabitants. In this section we will review the speeches and what they say about the catastrophe. Later we shall consider how they say it and raise questions of consistency. Our readings will center on the city Jerusalem.

It is generally agreed that there are two speaking voices in these chapters, the voice of the narrator and the voice of the city, Jerusalem personified.[9] In Lam 1, the narrator speaks in the third person in verses 1–11b and the city in the first person in verses 11c–22, although the two interrupt each other in verses 9c and 17. In Lam 2, the narrator speaks in the third person in verses 1–10, cries in grief in verses 11–12, and addresses the city in the second person in verses 13–19. The city speaks in verses 20–22.

Lamentations 1:1–11B

In this speech, the narrator addresses an audience external to the poem (except for the interruption in verse 9c). All attention is on Jerusalem. The city, or something associated with it, is the grammatical subject of almost every verse in the speech. The wretched state of the city is described in two ways. The first and more prosaic of these concerns the fate of its inhabitants. Jerusalem has suffered depopulation through exile (verse 3), captivity (verse 8) or flight (verse 6), and in the process, the people have suffered (verses 4, 7, 11). The description suggests total depopulation. No one is coming to religious events and the city's thoroughfares are empty (verse 4). Despite references to the grief of the people (verse 4),

---

8. Other texts that link the city with the effects of the exile are Isa 40–55 and Haggai. The writings of Isaiah of Babylon are often associated with Lamentations; see Linafelt, *Surviving Lamentations*, 55; Carol A. Newsom, "Response to Norman K. Gottwald, 'Social Class and Ideology in Isaiah 40–55,'" *Semeia* 59 (1992): 73–78; Patricia Willey, "Sing to God a New Song: Using the Past to Construct a Future," *Reformed World* 46 (1996): 37–46.

9. The identification of the voice of the city is made on the basis of the context of the speeches and the narrator's identification in Lam 2:13–20. The narrator does not identify himself. Two other characters in Lam 1 and 2 do not speak: Yahweh and the passersby. For a summary of theories on the speaking voices in the whole book, see Iain Provan, *Lamentations* (NCBC; Grand Rapids: Eerdmans, 1991), 6–7. Personification is a literary device. The personified city in the text may refer to either the city as metaphor for its people or the physical city.

the passages do not indicate that any survivors live in the city. Because of this depopulation, the city has suffered a loss of status (verses 1, 5, 6).

The lament opens with a powerful metaphor for depopulation—the death of a spouse. This image implies a strong link between a place and its residents. The city is associated with its people (עָם), just as other inhabited districts (מְדִינוֹת) have their own population groups (גּוֹיִם). Now the city is widowed. The personification of Jerusalem as widow is not continued by the narrator in the rest of the chapter, but is replaced by the image of a mother who has lost her children. To these personifications is added the repeated identification of Jerusalem as daughter (בַּת) and sometimes virgin (בְּתוּלָה).[10] The use of a female figure in all these personifications opens the way for the second description of the fate of Jerusalem.

The second metaphor for the catastrophe is rape. Jerusalem has been violated. Rape is not asserted explicitly but built out of double entendres borne by the description of the sack of the city. Jerusalem has been exposed naked in public (verse 8); enemies have touched its "precious things" (verse 10) and nations (גּוֹיִם, recalling the human consorts of other inhabited areas in verse 1) have entered the "sanctuary" (verse 10).[11]

The reason for this tragedy is stated in verses 5a and 8b: Jerusalem has sinned. In other words, Jerusalem bears responsibility for the catastrophe. However, the sins that caused its downfall are never made explicit. There are hints of sexual impropriety on the part of Jerusalem: the reference to lovers recalls the common prophetic metaphor of sin as adultery carried out by the unfaithful wife (verse 2, echoed by Jerusalem in verse 19); the public "uncleanness" (טֻמְאָה; verse 9) displayed by the city could refer to traces of adulterous intercourse; and a schema of adultery punished by rape is consistent with the biblical fondness for a motif of reversal (however unpalatable the idea of rape as punishment seems to us today). The evidence, however, is not incontestable: the term "lovers" is paralleled by "friends," "priests," and "elders," and so need not mean anything more than "supporters;" in Lamentations, the sexual metaphor has different nuances

---

10. For a discussion of the female terms, see Adele Berlin, *Lamentations: A Commentary* (OTL; Louisville, Ky.: Westminster John Knox, 2002), 7–11. Elaine R. Follis argues that the term "daughter" implies unity between people and place; see "The Holy City as Daughter," *Directions in Biblical Hebrew Poetry* (ed. Elaine R. Follis; JSOTSup 40; Sheffield: JSOT Press, 1987), 178.

11. On the rape imagery, see F. W. Dobbs-Allsopp and Todd Linafelt, "The Rape of Zion in Thr (Lamentations) 1,10," *ZAW* 113 (2001): 77–81; and Deryn Guest, "Hiding Behind the Naked Women in Lamentations: A Recriminative Response" *BibInt* 7 (1999): 415–20. Xuan Huong Thi Pham has argued that much of the imagery is drawn from mourning rites, but this does not preclude a sexual innuendo; see *Mourning in the Ancient Near East and the Hebrew Bible* (JSOTSup 302; Sheffield: Sheffield Academic Press, 1999), 48–49, 75–76.

than in the prophetic literature;[12] and the uncleanness might be the result of rape, or of a menstrual flow.

The agents who have brought about Jerusalem's suffering are human foes and the Lord. Human agency is emphasized; the role of God is mentioned only in verse 5, although Jerusalem appeals to God in verse 9c.

LAMENTATIONS 1:11C–22

This section contains a lament by the personified city (except for verse 17). Whereas the narrator's speech contained two descriptions of events, namely, depopulation and sexual violence, the city's speech concentrates only on the loss of population (verses 15, 16, 18, 19, 20), and does not allude to rape or sexual violence. Depopulation is attributed to deportation and slaughter. The city acknowledges guilt at least twice in this speech (verses 18a, 22b, possibly also 14a and 20c).[13] The tone is one of grief (verses 16, 20), tinged with anger (verses 21–22). The role of the Lord in the catastrophe is highlighted. God is the grammatical subject of verses about as often as Jerusalem. The narrator echoes this in his interjection (verse 17).

Both the narrator's speech and the words of the city associate the miserable state of the city to the suffering and loss of its people. Indeed, the only occurrence not tied to this is the transgression of the sanctuary by the invaders described in verse 10, but even in this verse, the "precious things" may be humans (compare Hos 9:6; Lam 1:7, 11; 2:4). Hence an anthropocentric core underlies this first lament. War, siege, and destruction, however, affect more than just humans. The fields, vineyards, and land in the path of the invading city and around the city would have been devastated. Their trauma could aptly be portrayed as rape, as would the physical damage to the city which is not described until Lam 2. The narrow anthropocentric focus fosters a suspicion that the voice of the physical city is not truly represented in the Lam 1 and that what is heard is the voice of the city as metaphor for its inhabitants.

LAMENTATIONS 2:1–19

Although lament over the fate of the people is still in evidence, in verses 1–10 the narrator's description of the fall of the city widens beyond this motif to take in the physical destruction of the sanctuary, fine houses, and fortifications. As if taking courage from Jerusalem's lament in the first chapter, the narrator now shows no reservations about attributing the destruction to God. Verses 1–9 are

---

12. Dobbs-Allsopp, *Lamentations*, 63–65.

13. Verses 14a and 20c have textual uncertainties; see Provan, *Lamentations*, 50–51, 54–55.

a litany of God's actions in the destruction of Jerusalem. Lamentations 2:11–12 returns to an anthropocentric focus with the narrator expressing personal grief over the lost population. God is not mentioned, nor is the physical destruction of the city. In verses 13–19, the narrator addresses Jerusalem. He acknowledges the city's grief (verse 13) and adds a list of anguish contributed by human agents (verses 14–16). Nevertheless, God is confirmed as the ultimate cause of destruction acting without mercy (verse 17). The narrator encourages the city to complain to God. The narrator's closing verse returns to the fate of humans (verse 19).

LAMENTATIONS 2:20–22

The city again utters a short lament to God, bewailing only the death of its inhabitants. Chapter 2 is dominated by a sense of excessive suffering. The final verse implies that God, as the one who controlled Jerusalem's enemies, is ultimately responsible for the unwarranted suffering.

Again in this chapter, an anthropocentric interest in the fate of the city's human inhabitants is very much in evidence, particularly in the speech of the personified city.

3. THE NARRATOR AS A FRIEND OF THE CITY?

The preceding overview has brought to the fore the extent to which the laments concentrate on human suffering associated with the fall of Jerusalem rather than on the broader suffering of creation. On its own, this tendency is not enough to convict the text of silencing the nonhuman voice in irredeemable anthropocentrism. An ecological hermeneutic sees all elements of creation as being interrelated: the injury to one member reverberates through all. Jerusalem is portrayed as traumatized by the slaughter of its inhabitants.

Conversely, as the second lament develops, the human speaker aligns himself more closely with Jerusalem. The narrator stands alongside Jerusalem, and uses his voice to publish the excessive extent of the city's sufferings, pointing the finger at God and encouraging the city to cry out. His concern goes beyond the death of people—something that is clearly of interest to a human—to include the damage done to Jerusalem. Do we see in this narrator the human face of the interconnectedness of creation? The narrator cannot take away the pain, but can stand alongside the mourning city and grieve with it. Does the narrator become the comforter Jerusalem lacked in Lam 1 (1:17, 21)?

On the other hand, the narrator in Lamentations has not escaped criticism in recent scholarship. Feminist scholars have noted the negative implications of his personification of Jerusalem as female in a text that portrays violence and rape. A strong and thorough critique in this vein has been made by Deryn Guest, who sees the choice of gender as shifting the blame away from the leaders of Jerusalem (who would have been male) onto a female figure.[14] Ultimately Guest's critique remains anthropocentric—albeit gynocentric rather than androcentric. On the other hand, Guest provides many useful insights for furthering an ecological hermeneutic of suspicion. With this in mind, let us place the narrator under investigation.

Can we trust the narrator? If all Jerusalem's friends have betrayed the city (1:2), can the narrator be a friend of the city? The blanket accusation of 2:14, that the prophets saw false visions, cannot stand. Some prophets, such as Jeremiah, warned of disaster. These may appear to be small points, but they serve to raise our suspicion of the narrator.

There is an imbalance of power between the narrator and the city. The narrator speaks first, and so sets the scene. The narrator defines the metaphor of the city as female, and in doing so assigns the city to a lower status in society (contrary to the elevated position it occupies in the Zion traditions). In addition, by assuming the authority to name the city as female, the narrator subordinates the city to himself.[15] Later, the narrator commands the city (2:18–19). The narrator is thereby positioning himself as superior to the city. If the city is regarded as the center of the web of the cosmos in the Zion traditions, then, as a consequence of this naming and commanding, the narrator is also distancing himself from nature and its suffering.

The city bears the blame for what has happened. The narrator asserts this and the city confesses this. How can this be? Elsewhere in the Hebrew Bible, responsibility for the exile is placed on the actions of the people; for instance, for incorrect worship (such as under Manasseh, 2 Kgs 21:3–15; or by the elders, Ezek 8:7–18). How can the *physical* city err, while the leaders and those living in it remain blameless?

Furthermore, the city is personified as female. To what extent would a woman in ancient Israel be considered a responsible agent in politics or society independently of her husband or (adult male) children?[16] Can a mother/daughter/wife alone be considered to be responsible for a catastrophe? Yet beyond the relatively minor charges in 2:14, neither Lam 1 nor Lam 2 ascribe guilt to humans.

What is more, by virtue of being in a position to command the city the narrator must be aligned with the leaders of the city. Does this implicate him in the sin attributed to the city?

And what were the sins that the city committed? The text does not explain. The narrator may be alluding to a prophetic metaphor linking sin and adultery,

---

14. "Hiding Behind the Naked Women in Lamentations," 429.

15. Charles W. Miller, "Reading Voices, Personification, Dialogism, and the Reader of Lamentations 1," *BibInt* 9 (2001): 394.

16. Guest, "Hiding Behind the Naked Women in Lamentations," 425.

but this is not certain—and, in any case, the narrator admits that the prophets cannot be trusted (2:14)!

An analysis of the rhetorical strategies in Lam 1–2 reinforces our suspicion of the narrator. At the start of Lam 1, the narrator adopts a perspective that is removed from the city and describes the situation in Jerusalem. His speech lacks the anguish of Jerusalem's response or the compassion in Lam 2. He describes the situation of the city in a way that is tempting to call "objective," although, of course, the literary technique of personification is anything but objective. Nevertheless, the reader, who is accustomed to an omniscient and trustworthy narrator elsewhere in the Hebrew Bible, is inclined to accept the essential veracity of the narrator's description. It may be colorful but it is built on history, and the color conveys the extreme nature of the city's distress.[17] While the narrator may use imaginative language, the situation described is congruent with reality. Or so the trusting reader thinks.

Embedded in the narrator's opening speech are two short statements about the guilt of the city (1:5b, 8a). If the narrator is credible on the description of disaster, surely the reader should accept the allocation of blame to the city? Yet there is no explanation given for the nature of this guilt and no evidence cited to support the claim. As indicated above, guilt must extend beyond the city as such.

The personification of the city also contributes to the reader's acceptance of the accusation against the city. The opening personification of the city as widow is very strong, and captures the elements of death, loss, and powerlessness. Then personification slides from widow to mother (1:5), both of which include the category "wife." And a wife, of course, is open to a charge of adultery. The ground is laid for the innuendo of sexual sin on the part of Jerusalem. Overall, in the opening speech, the focus on Jerusalem distracts attention from other potentially guilty parties.

Sexual impropriety or assault is not mentioned in the subsequent speeches made by Jerusalem in Lam 1 or 2, although the city admits guilt for (unspecified) sin. Jerusalem's speech concentrates on the depopulation of the city, primarily an issue for humans. What about the damage to nature and the environs of the city as a consequence of the rebellion and siege? Do we have here a depiction of a bereaved parent who laments the loss of only some of her children—the human ones—but not others? Or is this a co-opted voice?

Jerusalem's speech does, however, emphasize the agency of God in the intensity of the suffering and the fate of the city. The narrator picks this up in the second chapter. He magnifies the suffering, and encourages the city to protest to

---

17. Iain Provan swims against the scholarly tide here, arguing that the author's use of devices such as hyperbole and stereotyping renders problematic the recovery of the historical background of the poems; see Provan, "Reading Texts against an Historical Background: The Case of Lamentations 1," *SJOT* 4 (1990): 130–43; idem, *Lamentations*, 12–15.

God. It is as if the narrator, having found another to take the blame (God) and another charge (that the pain is not matched to the sin) no longer needs the innuendo of sexual misconduct against the city.

By the end of Lam 2, responsibility for the tragedy has been spread around widely—Jerusalem, a past generation of prophets, and God have all been blamed. The only character untouched by guilt is . . . the narrator. In fact, the narrator, as we noted above, appears to be quite a noble character as he becomes the only friend and comforter of Jerusalem.

It is common for commentators to observe that Lam 1–2 is not so much about (human) sin, but about extreme pain and suffering that goes beyond anything that might reasonably be expected in the circumstances. In doing this, they are following the trajectory set by the narrator's speeches. The interpreter has become caught up in the rhetorical strategy of the narrator—moving from condemnation of the city to sympathy, and to apprehension towards God. At the same time, the readers do not see what the narrator has not said, namely, that responsibility must extend to human agents and in particular to the narrator himself.

From a literary point of view, the voices speaking in the text—the narrator and Zion—are no more than personas created by the author(s) of Lam 1–2.[18] The voice of Jerusalem is not the voice of the physical city, but the author's construction of such a voice.

Is this construction eco-friendly? Our analysis suggests not. In the speeches, the concern of the personified city focuses on the loss of people; Jerusalem is explicitly blamed for the tragedy; and the flow of the poems serves to deflect assignment of blame away from human agents onto Jerusalem and then God.[19] What is omitted is telling: human culpability.

4. Conclusion

Our exploration started with two questions: What happens if the first two chapters of Lamentations are read without the central traditional anthropocentric assumption that the city is a human voice? Does the text then allow a nonhuman subject to speak? Alas, our attempt to read with the city as a nonhuman subject has come to naught. The city does indeed speak with an anthropocentric voice.

---

18. On the speaking voices in Lamentations, see William F. Lanahan, "The Speaking Voice in the Book of Lamentations," *JBL* 93 (1974): 46–56. Miller, in "Reading Voices," traces the interactions of the voices in Lam 1. The speeches of the different personas interact to add another layer of complexity to the text: in Lam 1 and 2, these voices gradually raise the issue of excessive divine response to sin.

19. Alan Cooper suggests that the poet avoids acknowledging personal accountability in the whole of Lamentations—in Lam 1–2 by using the persona of Jerusalem to take the blame; in 3:41 and 5:15 watering down confession by using the first person plural; see "The Message of Lamentations," *JANES* 28 (2001): 13–14.

What might have been the voice of the physical city is co-opted and manipulated to serve human ends. Little wonder God does not choose to speak!

This text hides something: a nonhuman subject, the city, that suffers on account of human behavior, that is cursed for human sin, and whose voice is co-opted for human ends. The list has a familiar ring to it. At the start of the biblical story, from Gen 3 on, Earth, like the city, is cursed and suffers on account of human disobedience rather than its own sin. Yet, even if Lamentations mutes the city's voice, we can imagine what Jerusalem might say:

> I am Jerusalem,
> > the center of the Land of God,
> > apple of God's eye.
> I mourn
> > my broken form,
> > and my broken people
> but also
> > the ravaged the lands about me,
> > the scorched earth,
> > ground ripped up for siegeworks,
> > the animals and soil
> > all suffering under a fall,
> > cruel collateral damage
> > imposed by God
> > and provoked by humans.
> I mourn
> > because biased humans
> > only see a city fallen
> > and not the pain
> > of trees, mountains, land
> > whose souls reside in me.[20]

20. Thanks to Norman Habel for his helpful comments on this paper.

"Therefore the Earth Mourns": The Grievance of Earth in Hosea 4:1–3

Melissa Tubbs Loya

In Hos 4:1–3 the prophet warns,

שִׁמְעוּ דְבַר־יְהוָה בְּנֵי יִשְׂרָאֵל	Hear the word of the Lord, O people of Israel:
כִּי רִיב לַיהוָה עִם־יוֹשְׁבֵי הָאָרֶץ	for the Lord has an indictment against the inhabitants of the land.
כִּי אֵין־אֱמֶת וְאֵין־חֶסֶד	There is no faithfulness or loyalty,
וְאֵין־דַּעַת אֱלֹהִים בָּאָרֶץ:	and no knowledge of God in the land.
אָלֹה וְכַחֵשׁ וְרָצֹחַ	Swearing, lying, murder,
וְגָנֹב וְנָאֹף פָּרָצוּ	stealing, and adultery break out;
וְדָמִים בְּדָמִים נָגָעוּ:	bloodshed follows bloodshed.
עַל־כֵּן תֶּאֱבַל הָאָרֶץ	Therefore Earth mourns,
וְאֻמְלַל כָּל־יוֹשֵׁב בָּהּ	and all who live in it languish;
בְּחַיַּת הַשָּׂדֶה	with the animals of the field,
וּבְעוֹף הַשָּׁמָיִם	and the birds of the air,
וְגַם־דְּגֵי הַיָּם יֵאָסֵפוּ:	even the fish of the sea are perishing.

Various aspects of this pericope have been the focus of past interpretation. These verses have been understood as an introduction to a new section of the book of Hosea, in which the prophet adopts corporate, rather than personal language to outline Israel's crimes and punishments.[1] The pericope has been read as an example of the רִיב genre, in which Yahweh brings a "covenant lawsuit" against

---

1. For differing opinions on the function of Hos 4:1–3 as an introduction to various parts of the book, see Hans Walter Wolff, *Hosea: A Commentary on the Book of the Prophet Hosea* (ed. Paul D. Hansen; trans. Gary Stansell; Hermeneia; Philadelphia: Fortress, 1974), 65, 68, 73–74; Jörg Jeremias, *Der Prophet Hosea* (ATD 24/1; Göttingen: Vandenhoeck & Ruprecht, 1983), 59; Edmond Jacob, *Osée* (3d ed.; CAT 11a; Geneva: Labor et Fides, 1992), 39; Francis I. Andersen and David Noel Freedman, *Hosea: A New Translation with Introduction and Commentary* (AB 24; Garden City: Doubleday, 1980), 332.

the people of Israel.[2] The passage has also been seen as discourse on the Decalogue (Exod 20:13–15; Deut 5:17–19), as Yahweh appears to use parts of the law code (or some version of it) to argue the case.[3] Each of these foci addresses an important aspect of the text. Yet each also concentrates rather exclusively on the crimes of humanity and their prosecution.

Such anthropocentric readings obscure the role played by Earth in Hos 4:1–3. When the passage is read in a new way, from the perspective of Earth, new questions emerge. Some of these questions have yet to be fully explored, and in this study I will focus on three such questions. First, what role does Earth play in Yahweh's רִיב? Second, what effects do Earth and its inhabitants suffer as a result of Earth's actions? And third, why does Earth respond to Yahweh's indictment of Israel's crimes in the way that it does?

In answer to these questions I will argue that Earth is the active agent through which Yahweh's judgment is rendered in Hos 4:1–3. Yahweh acts in bringing the lawsuit; however, Earth acts in bringing about its consequences. It is Earth, then, and not Yahweh, that acts in verse 3, where nothing less than a systematic undoing of creation is described. Yet, Earth does not act outside of Yahweh's purposes. Rather, Earth—indeed, the entire cosmos—is governed not only by physical laws, but also by the moral order Yahweh builds into creation at its inception. The mourning, languishing, and perishing of Earth and its inhabitants described by Hosea are consequences of Israel's breach of this moral order through the crimes they commit against one another.

---

2. Cf. Hermann Gunkel, introduction to *Die Grossen Propheten*, by Hans Schmidt (SAT 2/2; Göttingen: Vandenhoeck & Ruprecht, 1923), lxiii; Ernst Würthwein, "Der Ursprung der prophetischen Gerichtsrede," *ZTK* 49 (1952): 1–16; Herbert B. Huffmon, "The Covenant Lawsuits in the Prophets," *JBL* 78 (1959): 285–95; Dwight Daniels, "Is there a 'Prophetic Lawsuit' Genre?" *ZAW* 99 (1987): 339–60.

3. רָצַ֖ח, "murder," אָלֹ֔ב, "stealing," and נָאֹ֑ף, "adultery," are expressly forbidden in the Decalogue. The terms אָלֹ֔ה, "swearing," and כַּחֵ֖שׁ, "lying," do not appear in the Decalogue, but the actions they describe are prohibited in the third and ninth commandments, respectively. On the continued debate regarding whether the verse cites a fixed form (or any form) of the Decalogue see Katherine M. Hayes, *"The Earth Mourns": Prophetic Metaphor and Oral Aesthetic* (AcBib 8; Atlanta: Society of Biblical Literature, 2002), 48, n. 41; Andersen and Freedman, *Hosea*, 336–67; James Luther Mays, *Hosea: A Commentary* (OTL; Philadelphia: Westminster, 1969), 64–65.

1. The Role of Earth in Yahweh's רִיב

The Primary Role of the Land in Hos 4:1–3

אֶרֶץ, "land", or "Earth,"[4] plays an essential role in Hos 4:1–3. Earth's importance is underscored by its appearance at each stage of Yahweh's lawsuit: in the summons (יוֹשְׁבֵי הָאָרֶץ, "the inhabitants of the land," Hos 4:1b), the indictment (אֵל הַיָּם בָּאָרֶץ וְאֵין־דַּעַת, "for there is no knowledge of God in the land," verse 1d), and the sentence (עַל־כֵּן תֶּאֱבַל הָאָרֶץ, "so Earth mourns," verse 3a).[5] Moreover, in the lawsuit the land is mentioned as often as the deity (verses 1b, 1d, and 3a, and verses 1a, 1b, and 1d respectively), and more often than human beings.[6] In one of the two instances in which human beings are mentioned, they are spoken of as יוֹשְׁבֵי הָאָרֶץ, "inhabitants of the land" (verse 1b; compare בְּנֵי יִשְׂרָאֵל, "the people of Israel," in verse 1a). Not only, then, is the land a primary focus in Hos 4:1–3, the role that human beings play in the pericope is defined by their relationship to the land.

The land holds primary place, too, when the prophet spells out Israel's crimes. It is not merely that Israel shows no faithfulness, no loyalty, no knowledge of God (Hos 4:1c, 1d). It is that Israel does not show these qualities בָּאָרֶץ, "*in the land*" (verse 1d; emphasis added). The specific crimes outlined in Hos 4:2—those also prohibited by the Decalogue regulations that define Israel's covenant relationship with Yahweh (Exod 20:13–15; Deut 5:17–19)—suggest that in the summons and indictment of Yahweh's רִיב "the land" refers to the political entity of Israel. In other words, the "inhabitants of the land" *of Israel* are brought up on charges because there is "swearing, lying, murder, stealing, and adultery" *in the land of Israel* (verses 1–2).

אֶרֶץ has a wide range of meanings, however. Not only can it mean land as political entity or people, but also land as Earth.[7] In the sentencing of verse 3, אֶרֶץ takes on this more general meaning, described as home not just to the political entity Israel, but also to the animals of the field, the birds of the air, and the fish of

---

4. The context determines which English translation is most appropriate; however, a Hebrew reader would be aware of the range and nuances of the term.

5. Cf. Walter Brueggemann, "The Uninflected Therefore of Hosea 4:1–3," in *Social Location and Biblical Interpretation in the United States* (vol. 1 of *Reading from this Place*; ed. Fernando F. Segovia and Mary Ann Tolbert; Minneapolis: Fortress, 1995), 241.

6. So the Masoretic Text (MT). The Septuagint (LXX), following the MT, speaks of γῆς twice in verse 1 and once in verse 3, but the term also appears (unlike the MT) in verse 2: ἀρὰ καὶ ψεῦδος καὶ φόνος καὶ κλοπὴ καὶ μοιχεία κέχυται ἐπὶ τῆς γῆς, "cursing, and lying, and murder, and theft, and adultery abound in the land" (emphasis added). Cf. Mays, *Hosea*, 60, 62, who argues that בָּאָרֶץ ("in the land") could have been lost from the end of verse 2b in the MT through *homoioteleuton* (with verse 1d).

7. Brueggemann, "Uninflected Therefore of Hosea 4:1–3," 241; Hayes, *Earth Mourns*, 42.

the sea. In other words, the אֶרֶץ of verse 3 is that which sustains all creation. It is Earth in its broadest sense, then, that acts in Hos 4:3, mourning the crimes Israel has committed in and against its own land.

The important role played by the land in this pericope should not be surprising. As Laurie Braaten suggests in his study of thematic threads in Hosea, the prophet gives prominence of place to the land throughout his work.[8] The land plays a key role in the call of the prophet, who in Hos 1:2 is told to take a wife and children of whoredom because "*the land* commits whoredom by forsaking the Lord" (emphasis added). While most understand "the land" in this verse as a reference to the land's inhabitants,[9] Braaten explores the notion that it is the "land *per se*" that commits whoredom when its sanctity is violated by the bloodshed and whoredom of its inhabitants.[10] In his reading of Hos 4:1–3, Braaten concludes that "the land is clearly presented as a victim, suffering for the sins of her human inhabitants. The land responds to this suffering as sufferers often react in the Hebrew Bible—she 'mourns.'"[11] This assessment is no doubt true. Earth, however, is more than a mourning victim in Hos 4:1–3. Earth is, in fact, also an active agent.

Earth as the Active Agent in Hos 4:3

In the Earth Bible project, various scholars question whether, in certain biblical passages, Earth stands as a subject, "capable of self-expression in some form."[12] Specifically, they ask whether passages that speak of Earth rejoicing or mourning are "more than metaphor,"[13] revealing "unknown," "latent," or "hidden" qualities[14] of Earth as a nonhuman and nondivine actor in the biblical drama. While Hos 4:1–3 is not a main focus of any of the scholars writing in this series, it is a text that begs the same question. Is Earth's mourning described in Hos 4:3

---

8. Laurie Braaten, "God Sows: Hosea's Land Theme in the Book of the Twelve," in *Thematic Threads in the Book of the Twelve* (ed. Paul L. Redditt and Aaron Schart; BZAW 325; Berlin: de Gruyter, 2003), 104-32. Cf. his "Earth Community in Hosea 2," in *The Earth Story in the Psalms and the Prophets* (ed. Norman C. Habel; The Earth Bible 4; Sheffield: Sheffield Academic Press, 2001), 185–203. Similarly, creation is recognized as a main theme in Hosea by Stefan Paas in his *Creation and Judgment: Creation Texts in Some Eighth Century Prophets* (OTS 47; Leiden: Brill, 2003), 325–59.

9. For example, see Andersen and Freedman, *Hosea*, 169, who conclude that "land" is a "comprehensive word, with sacred associations, [and it] covers everybody—kings, priests, people."

10. Braaten, "God Sows," 105, 108–9.

11. Braaten, "God Sows," 112.

12. The Earth Bible team, "The Voice of Earth: More than Metaphor?," in Habel, *The Earth Story in the Psalms and the Prophets*, 23–28.

13. Earth Bible team, "The Voice of Earth," 28.

14. Earth Bible team, "The Voice of Earth," 27.

more than metaphor? What motivates Earth to act? And, if Earth's mourning has real effects, what are they?

To understand Earth's actions in Hos 4:3, we must first identify Yahweh's role in the ריב. It is clear that the deity brings the suit against the people of Israel, indicting them for their breech of covenant. As Brueggemann rightly notes in his study of the pericope, however, there is "no intervention or instigation by Yahweh" in the judgment outlined in verse 3.[15] Not only does the verse refrain from identifying Yahweh as an active agent in the punishment described, it does not refer to the deity in any way. In a conclusion that does not necessarily follow, however, Brueggemann contends that because "the first two verbs [in the verse] have 'eres and "inhabitants" as subject, and the third is a passive verb (niph'al) . . . there is no active agent of punishment, not even Yahweh."[16] Other scholars conclude that even if Yahweh is not explicitly mentioned, the deity is the implicit subject who metes out Israel's punishment in Hos 4:3.[17]

Yet as Brueggemann notes, the first verb in the verse does have an explicit subject: אֶרֶץ. Katherine M. Hayes goes a step further in noting that in Hos 4:1–3 "Earth becomes an actor in the ongoing relationship between YHWH and Israel."[18] What remains to be said is that Earth is *the* actor in Hos 4:3. When this verse is read from a perspective that understands Earth as an actor—Earth as subject—and Earth's mourning as more than metaphor, Earth emerges as the active agent of the punishment meted out against Israel. In a sequential parallelism,[19] "Earth mourns, and all who live in it languish." It is the action of Earth that sets in motion all other actions described in the verse. Earth's mourning, then, ultimately leads to the languishing of its inhabitants and the perishing of all creation.

EFFECTS OF EARTH'S MOURNING

The Verbs of Hos 4:3

The series of events begun by Earth's mourning is drastic. The roots used in Hos 4:3, when taken separately, indicate destruction and despair. When taken together, however, and when accompanied by the very particular descriptions of Earth and its inhabitants that appear in verse 3, these roots portray utter annihilation. The root used to describe Earth's action in verse 3, אבל, generally means

15. Brueggemann, "Uninflected Therefore of Hosea 4:1–3," 241.

16. Brueggemann, "Uninflected Therefore of Hosea 4:1–3," 242.

17. Cf., for example, Andersen and Freedman, *Hosea*, 341.

18. Hayes, *Earth Mourns*, 64.

19. Or a parallelism that represents a sequence of actions. Cf. James L. Kugel, *The Idea of Biblical Poetry: Parallelism and Its History* (Baltimore: John Hopkins University Press, 1981), 4.

"to perform mourning rituals."[20] It is not uncommon, however, to find the root in parallelism with verbs that connote dryness, not only in Hos 4:3, where אבל is paired with אמל, "to be weak, languish" (compare Isa 24:4, 7; 33:9; Joel 1:10),[21] but also in various passages that pair אבל with יבש, "to be dry" (Amos 1:2; Jer 12:4; 23:10; Joel 1:10). Moreover, the Akkadian cognate *abālu* means "to dry out" when used to speak of plants and fields.[22] Such parallels led G. R. Driver and many commentators after him to propose a secondary meaning for אבל: "to dry up." It has become common, then, to translate Hos 4:3 as "therefore the land dries up."[23]

This desiccation of Earth leads to the languishing of all who live on it. Like the root used to describe Earth's mourning, the root most commonly translated "to languish" also connote a dryness of sorts. אמל can mean "a loss of fertility," as for example in Jer 15:9: אֻמְלְלָה יֹלֶדֶת הַשִּׁבְעָה, "she who has born seven has languished."[24] When used collectively, as in Hos 4:3, this root may also indicate the diminishing—the drying up—of an entire people.[25] The picture painted is one of deadly drought, annihilation of the fertile lands that sustain life and of the fertile wombs that birth it.

Moreover, as the animal list at the conclusion of Hos 4:3 demonstrates, the drought depicted by the prophet is no ordinary one. This drought is global, affecting all Earth's inhabitants. As such, it echoes the theme of "dry chaos" found throughout the Hebrew Bible, most notably in the Yahwist's creation account (Gen 2:4b–6) which describes Earth as dry and altogether barren prior to Yahweh's creative act.[26] Hosea 4:3 describes a return to this pre-creation state. As

---

20. This is often true in the hithpael form; cf. Joseph mourning Jacob, whom he believes to be dead in Gen 37:34; Samuel's grief over Saul's death in 1 Sam 15:35; 16:1.

21. The waw + suffix form of וַאֲמְלַל in Hos 4:3 suggests that it stands in relation to the verb that precedes it. This coupled with the fact that the root from which it is derived, אמל, is not attested in active form (BDB, 51a), makes וַאֲמְלַל difficult to translate. A wide range of meanings is indicated by the various translations proffered: "languish" (NRSV; Mays, *Hosea*, 60; Hayes, *Earth Mourns*, 37); "enfeebled" (Andersen and Freedman, *Hosea*, 331, 340); "shall fade away" (Wolff, *Hosea*, 65, 67).

22. Cf. G. R. Driver, "Confused Hebrew Roots," in *Occident and Orient, being Studies in Semitic Philology and Literature, Jewish History and Philosophy and Folklore in the Widest Sense, in Honor of Haham Dr. M. Gaster's 80th Birthday. Gaster Anniversary Volume* (ed. B. Schindler and A. Marmorstein; London: Taylor's Foreign Press, 1936), 73–82.

23. NJPS, "withered;" Andersen and Freedman, *Hosea*, 339; Mays, *Hosea*, 60, 65.

24. Cf. 1 Sam 2:5; BDB, 51ab; Hayes, *Earth Mourns*, 42.

25. L. Koehler, W. Baumgartner, and J. J. Stamm, *Hebräisches und aramäisches Lexikon zum Alten Testament* (5 vols; Leiden: Brill, 1967–95), 61a. Cf. Wolff, *Hosea*, 68; Hayes, *Earth Mourns*, 42.

26. Cf. Nicholas J. Tromp, *Primitive Conceptions of Death and the Nether World in the Old Testament* (Rome: Pontifical Biblical Institute, 1969), 132; Arent J. Wensinck, *The Ocean in the Literature of the Western Semites* (Verhandelingen der Koinklijk Akademie van Wetenschappen

Michael DeRoche has suggested and as I shall discuss in more detail below, in this verse the prophet envisions nothing less than a reversal of creation.[27]

The last verb in Hos 4:3, אסף, stresses the scope of the destruction suffered by creation as a result of Earth's mourning. The semantic range of אסף is broad. In its meaning "to destroy, remove, perish," it is perhaps best translated as "sweep away," a translation that recalls the sounds of the Hebrew consonants אסף.[28] Such a reading of אסף in Hos 4:3 would indicate that, as a result of Earth's mourning, "the animals of the field, and the birds of the air, even the fish of the sea" are swept away. אסף also, however, means "to gather," as, for example, in a fishing net, or in a harvest.[29] The latter connotation is reflected in the use of אסף to speak of the autumnal harvest festival of Booths, or the Ingathering (e.g., חַג הָאָסִף in Exod 23:16). While harvests in general, and the harvest festival in particular, have positive associations—through harvests life is sustained—to harvest is also to destroy. It is possible that Hosea here plays with this meaning of אסף: there will be a harvest, but God will be the reaper, and all creation his crop.[30] Moreover, by pairing אסף with verbs that connote Earth's drying up, the prophet paints the destruction in verse 3 as Earth's *final* harvest.

This image of a final harvest is particularly well suited to Hosea's larger arguments. A main concern of the prophet is what he sees as rampant apostasy in Israel. In particular, he accuses Yahweh's people of worshipping Baal, the Canaanite storm god, controller of rain and, as a result, fertility (cf. Hos 2:6, 18; 13:1). In Hos 4:1–3 the prophet warns that it is Yahweh, and not Baal, who will try Israel, and that the punishment for the nation's crimes will be a cosmic drought over which the Canaanite fertility deity has no control (cf. Hos 2:18–25).

The Scope of Earth's Mourning: Creation Uncreated

Not only do the Hebrew verbal roots used in Hos 4:3 indicate utter annihilation, so too does the prophet's description of the affected parties. Early in verse 3, the prophet states that Earth's mourning will affect "all those who live in it" (Hos 4:3b). In the last lines of verse 3, the prophet further identifies the victims of Earth's mourning by specifying the parts of which "all" consists, namely the animals of the field, the birds of the air, and the fish of the sea. As DeRoche and

---

27. Michael DeRoche, "The Reversal of Creation in Hosea," *VT* 31 (1981): 400–409.

28. See Adele Berlin, *Zephaniah: A New Translation with Introduction and Commentary* (AB 25A; New York: Doubleday, 1994), 72.

29. BDB, 62ab–63a.

30. Cf. T. H. Gaster, *Myth, Legend, and Custom in the Old Testament* (New York: Harper & Row, 1969), 679.

others argue, the creatures listed in verse 3 serve as a merism for all creation throughout the Hebrew Bible[31] and other ancient Near Eastern literature.[32]

One notable biblical example of such a list appears in the Priestly writer's account of God's creation of the heavens and Earth in Gen 1:1–2:4a. On the fifth and sixth days of his work, the deity creates first fish (Gen 1:20a) and then birds (verse 20b), cattle and then wild animals (verse 24), and lastly human beings (verse 26).[33] An analogous ordering of creatures is found in God's command to the newly created human beings to "have dominion over the fish of the sea and over the birds of the air and over every living thing that moves upon the earth" (Gen 1:28b). DeRoche argues that Hosea reverses the order of the established merism: whereas first fish, then birds, and finally wild animals are listed in these Genesis texts, in Hos 4:3 first wild animals, then birds, and finally fish are said to perish. This reversal of the order of creation, when read in the context of the cosmic devastation described in verse 3, depicts an unmaking of creation.[34]

WHY IS IT THAT EARTH MOURNS?

In answering the first two questions with which I began this study, I have established that it is Earth that acts in bringing about the consequences associated with Yahweh's רִיב, and that these consequences are cosmic in scope. One question remains: why does Earth respond to Yahweh's indictment of Israel's crimes in the way that it does? Or, put another way, what is it about the relationship between

---

31. E.g., Pss 8:7–8; 104:11–12. Some animal lists contain a fourth member of the merism: things that creep along the ground; so Gen 9:2; Ezek 38:20 (which also speaks of uncreation). Deuteronomy 4:16–18 lists animals, birds, creeping things, and fish in its warning against making idols (in the Decalogue, however, a more general three-part list is given in the commandment against casting idols, whether they be of creatures "in heaven above, on the earth beneath, or that is in the water beneath the earth" [Exod 20:4; Deut 5:8]). For more on such merisms, including arguments contra DeRoche, see W. M. Clark, "The Animal Series in the Primeval History," VT 18 (1968): 433–49; Marvin Sweeney, Zephaniah (Hermeneia; Minneapolis: Fortress, 2003), 63.

32. E.g., in the Egyptian texts "Hymn to Aton" and "Gratitude for a God's Mercy" (ANET, 370, 380). A similar list appears in the Ugaritic account of the creation of dawn and dusk in CTA 23 (UT 52).62–63; cf. DeRoche, "The Reversal of Creation," 403–4.

33. On the possible dependence of Hosea on the creation narrative of the Priestly source see DeRoche, "The Reversal of Creation," 404; and Hayes, Earth Mourns, 60, n. 87.

34. An important question in the interpretation of Hos 4:1–3, but one that is outside the scope of this study, pertains to the tense of the verbs in the pericope. Specifically, do the imperfect verbs in Hos 4:3 refer to the present or the future? Does the verse describe events that are already unfolding, and which verses 4–14 (and perhaps all of Hos 4–11) depict in more detail? Or, does 4:3 refer to a threat of future punishment, and thus stand to some degree in contrast with the description of the present situation in verses 4–14? Both possibilities are supported by the prophet's use of language.

the three parties present at the רִיב—Yahweh, Israel, and Earth—that causes Earth, by its mourning, to render Yahweh's punishment against Israel? The language Hosea uses to speak of the רִיב suggests that Earth mourns because Israel's crimes disorder Yahweh's creation to such a degree that it can no longer operate as intended at its inception.

There is a causal link between the human crimes explicated in Hos 4:2 and the action and fate of Earth in verse 3. That the link is causal is signaled by the connecting phrase עַל־כֵּן, meaning "therefore; so; as a result." As Jörg Jeremias has suggested, it is significant that this phrase, rather than the similar לָכֵן is used to connect the crimes described in verse 2 to the consequences discussed in verse 3. While both עַל־כֵּן and לָכֵן can be translated (among other things) as "therefore," there is an important, if subtle, distinction between the two: לָכֵן, especially in prophetic texts, tends to come before a divine declaration or command;[35] כֵּן־עַל, on the other hand, most often introduces a "statement of *fact*, rather than a *declaration*."[36] In Jeremias's words, עַל־כֵּן indicates, "die (notwendige) Folge einer Tat," the (necessary) result of an action.[37] In the context of Hos 4:1–3, עַל־כֵּן indicates the necessary result of crimes committed by humanity. Earth's mourning, then, is a response, and the necessary result of Israel's swearing, lying, murder, stealing, and adultery.

As the necessary result of Israel's crimes, Earth *must* mourn. That it does so in the context of Yahweh's רִיב, however, suggests that Earth is operating within a system governed by the deity. This impression is strengthened by the use of עַל־כֵּן to connect verses 2 and 3. Earth's mourning is necessary because Earth and its inhabitants are governed by a particular order. As Klaus Koch demonstrates in his seminal essay (not on creation, but on the doctrine of retribution), for some biblical writers there exists an "organic structure of order" in creation made up of "spheres of influence."[38] Actions, therefore, have consequences, and it is possible for these consequences to be produced without the direct intention of the deity.[39] Terence Fretheim puts it another way: "The most common agent of divine judgment is the created moral order. That is, God has created the world in such a way that deeds (whether good or evil) will have consequences."[40]

---

35. BDB, 486b.

36. BDB, 487a.

37. Jeremias, *Der Prophet Hosea*, 33. Cf. Hayes' analysis in *Earth Mourns*, 45.

38. Klaus Koch, "Is There a Doctrine of Retribution in the Old Testament?" in *Theodicy in the Old Testament* (ed. James L. Crenshaw; Philadelphia: Fortress, 1983), 57–87. For an illustrative critique and sharpening of Koch's argument, see John Barton, "Natural Law and Poetic Justice in the Old Testament," *JTS* 30 (1979): 1–14.

39. Brueggemann, "Uninflected Therefore of Hosea 4:1–3," 235.

40. Terence Fretheim, *God and World in the Old Testament: A Relational Theology of Creation* (Nashville: Abingdon, 2005), 163.

Yet, this system is not deistic. Yahweh continues to be intimately involved in its operations. Yahweh's dynamic participation is demonstrated, for example, in the vastly different messages of Hos 4:1–3 and Hos 11. In Hos 4:1–3 Yahweh acts in bringing the רִיב against Israel. Earth acts, however, in bringing about Israel's punishment. Earth's independent action in response to human crimes suggests that the moral requirements Yahweh places upon Israel reflect the governing principles of Yahweh's entire creation. Earth's mourning, therefore, is the verdict and the punishment given in response to Israel's injustices. It is not unprecedented, as Hermann Gunkel and Joachim Begrich point out, for "natural elements," such as land, vegetation, and animals, to serve as witness, or even judges, in a רִיב.[41] Earth stands as both judge and victim in Hos 4:3, mourning in response to Israel's crimes and suffering the cosmic devastation that is the result of its own grief. In this way Earth plays an essential role in the pericope. Earth is *the* actor in Yahweh's lawsuit.

Conclusion

As I have demonstrated, it is not only the deity and human beings who act within the governing system of creation. When Hos 4:1–3 is read from the perspective of the land, Earth itself emerges as the active agent, simultaneously imposing and suffering the sentence of Yahweh's רִיב against Israel. In this prophetic oracle, creation is not simply the scenery in which the story of Israel's relationship with Yahweh plays out. Rather, creation actively mourns the subversion of the created order, and this results in the languishing and perishing of all who live on it: the animals of the field, the birds of the air, and the fish of the sea. Hosea's oracle, then, serves as an instruction to readers of biblical texts to refrain from strictly anthropocentric approaches that obscure the active role that Earth—and other elements of created order—play in the relationship between Yahweh and creation.

---

41. Hermann Gunkel and Joachim Begrich, *Einleitung in die Psalmen: Die Gattungen der religiösen Lyrik Israels* (HKAT, Abt. 2 Supp.; Göttingen: Vandenhoeck & Ruprecht, 1933), 364–65. Cf. Huffmon, "Covenant Lawsuits in the Prophets," 286, 292.

Earth Community in Joel: A Call to Identify with the Rest of Creation[1]

Laurie J. Braaten

1. Introduction: The Approach of this Study

The Book of Joel offers an excellent example of a text with a major focus on Earth community. Earth is a major subject in Joel 1–2, and even set forth as an example to humans of the proper response to a crisis. Before we commence our study, however, we need to make some brief observations concerning the terminology and methodology employed in this paper.[2]

Definition of Terms

First, the term "Earth," without the article (and capitalized), will connote what is commonly called "nature," the land and nonhuman realm of the ecosystem. "The earth," with the article (and lower case), connotes the planet, or a comprehensive portion of land. "Land" or "the land" connotes a narrower subject than Earth, often connoting territory inhabited by humans or animals. "Ground" is often a synonym for "land," although it usually connotes the arable land, or soil.

"Earth community" is a comprehensive term for the entire ecosystem, or web of life. Since humans are part of the created order, and cannot survive apart from Earth, humans, as well as Earth, are members of this community.

---

1. A longer version of this paper was originally published as "Earth Community in Joel 1–2: A Call to Identify with the Rest of Creation," in *HBT* 28 (2006): 113–29. I am grateful to the editors for allowing me to reprint this paper here.

2. The terminology employed in this study generally follows that adopted by The Earth Bible series; see Norman C. Habel, "Introducing the Earth Bible," in Habel, *Readings from the Perspective of Earth*, 25–37. Bible translations in this paper are my own unless otherwise noted.

I would like to argue for a third member of Earth community: although the biblical tradition often fixes the deity's dwelling place in heaven, God has *chosen* to dwell among a people, the nations, and Earth.[3] This makes God a member of Earth community by choice. God, however, unlike other members of Earth community, can be self-sustaining and has a power in and over Earth community that no other member has. Earth community comprises a symbiotic whole: when one member acts in a non-life-affirming manner, the whole community is affected.[4]

Toward an Ecological Reading of Joel

An ecological reading of Joel starts with the premise that Earth is an intrinsically worthy subject in the text. Earth is not just a setting for the drama of human salvation, or an object of human desire. Recent studies have begun to take more seriously the idea that Earth is presented as a viable subject in Joel 1–2, but these readings are still predominantly anthropocentric interpretations.[5] As long as Joel is approached from this anthropocentric perspective, Earth's role in the text will be in danger of being treated in piecemeal fashion as an interesting, but quaint, relic of an ancient worldview.

The current study will attempt to approach Joel 1–2 from a geocentric perspective. To some this may appear to be an exercise in creative imagination. Since, however, nearly every verse in Joel 1–2 mentions Earth, I would argue that such a reading is appropriate to the subject matter. Indeed, since we know very little about Joel, can we state with certainty that this "son of Petuel" did not consider himself called to be a spokesperson for Earth?[6] Admittedly, as a human author, Joel (or a later scribe) could not help but leave some anthropocentric biases in the text. But would this necessitate viewing Joel 1–2 as primarily a tool of an anthropocentric ideology? What is to prevent the reader from identifying primarily with Earth in the text, rather than with the human community? What if, rather than assuming that the text is thoroughly anthropocentric unless proven otherwise, instead we start from the opposite perspective and assume that it is

---

3. For God's identifying with the world as the divine dwelling place see Terence E. Fretheim, *The Suffering of God: An Old Testament Perspective* (OBT; Philadelphia: Fortress, 1984), 37–39. See also my discussion concerning God as a member of Earth community in Laurie J. Braaten, "Earth Community in Hosea 2," in Habel, *The Earth Story in Psalms and Prophets*, 185–203.

4. For one treatment of this topic, see H. H. Schmidt, "Creation, Righteousness, and Salvation: 'Creation Theology' as the Broad Horizon of Biblical Theology," in *Creation in the Old Testament* (ed. and trans. Bernard W. Anderson; IRT 6; Philadelphia: Fortress, 1984), 102–17, esp. 103–11.

5. E.g., G. W. Ahlström, *Joel and the Temple Cult of Jerusalem* (VTSup. 21; Leiden: Brill, 1971), 46 n. 2, recognizes that the animals seem to have more knowledge of God's gifts than do the people.

6. For the sake of convenience, the author will be identified with the prophetic speaker.

Earth-centered—unless clearly stated to the contrary? This study will attempt such a consistent Earth-centered reading. While I have no doubt that much has been missed in Joel by typical anthropocentric readings, I also recognize the provisional nature of many of my own proposals. More research, discussion and reflection are needed.

THE NATURE OF THE BOOK OF JOEL

Our final preliminary task is to provide an overview of the book of Joel. Recent studies have affirmed the unity of the book. Ogden has helped us see that the entire book is in the form of a community lament and God's answer. Joel's presentation is literary, however, and not a historical report.[7] Joel describes typical problems, and proposes typical responses.

The introduction to the Book of Joel identifies it as the word of YHWH to Joel. This word is present as the prophet, speaking for God, summons Earth community to mourn. This same divine word identifies with and articulates the suffering of Earth community. Joel's descriptions of the suffering, voice, and restoration of Earth are found primarily in Joel 1–2 [1:1–2:27 Eng.], the focus of this study.

2. JOEL 1—EARTH COMMUNITY CALLED TO LAMENT

APPEALS FOR EARTH COMMUNITY TO MOURN AND EARTH'S RESPONSE

Joel 1 begins with a comprehensive summons for the elders and "all inhabitants of the land" to listen to and hand down God's word to later generations. "All the inhabitants of the land" may well include nonhuman inhabitants, as it does in Hos 4:1–3 and other passages that report Earth mourning. Immediately after this all-inclusive summons to hear, the crisis at hand is described: locusts have consumed everything.

Next, two sets of appeals to lament are made to specific groups. The first set (verses 5–9) addresses drunkards (verse 5), an unnamed female subject (verse 8, f. sg. impv.), and priests (verse 9).[8] Included are motivations to lament because of the locust damage: drunkards will lack their wine, priests will lack offerings.

Joel 1:6–7 is of special interest; it states that a nation has invaded God's land and destroyed God's plants. I suggest that this attests God's lament. "My land! . . .

---

7. Graham S. Ogden, "Joel 4 and Prophetic Responses to National Laments," *JSOT* 26 (1983): 103–5.

8. With the LXX we read אבלו in verse 9 as an imperative (see *BHK*) rather than an indicative, since verse 13 (again) commands the priest to lament, indicating that they have not yet mourned.

My vines! . . . My fig trees!"—are similar to the human laments, "Alas, my daughter!" or "Alas, my brother!"[9] Furthermore, this divine lament probably begins in verse 4 with the announcement of the damage of the locusts. While verses 6–7 might be viewed as background for the lack of offerings reported in verse 9, I propose that they also function as an initial motivation for the female subject of verse 8 to mourn, but who is this subject? This individual is probably Earth,[10] the subject of God's lament. This is supported by the following verses. Between the first and second appeal for human subjects to lament, we find this statement in verse 10: "Field is destroyed! Ground mourns! Surely grain is destroyed, wine is put to shame, olive oil languishes!" Katherine Hayes has convincingly argued that the verbs connoting damage to Earth in this section of Joel are appropriate to mourning subjects.[11] It is instructive to observe here that Earth, represented by fields, ground, grain, wine, and oil, is the first *subject* to respond to God's call to lament. This lends credibility to the proposal that the initial address to "all inhabitants of the land" is a call to the *entire* Earth community—not just its human members.

The second set of appeals to lament addresses farmers and vine tenders, and ends again with the priests (verses 11–14). Once more the motivation for the priests is the lack of grain and drink offerings. This time, however, the priests are commanded to convene a comprehensive mourning ritual: they are to call a public fast by gathering the elders and "all inhabitants of the land" to God's house to cry out to God (verse 14). In this case the lack of offerings seems to be a motivation for YHWH to act: the God-honoring sacrificial cult will cease unless God does something. But this motivation also contains a subversive word on behalf of Earth. While it is common understanding that the proper functioning of the cult maintains the order of creation, or Earth,[12] here the opposite is stated: it is the proper functioning of *Earth* that maintains the order of the *cult!* The divine–human interaction in the cult is incomplete without a third partner, Earth.

The prophet continues by giving the priests the words to cry, indicating that the events portend a destructive Day of YHWH (verse 15). The dawning of this Day is announced by the rhetorical question of verse 16: "is not food cut off from before our eyes, and from the house of our God rejoicing and joy?" One reading of this text is that humans lack food for their daily needs and for cultic celebra-

---

9. For YHWH's mourning over God's people or land see Jer 12, a passage with similarities to this one. See the treatments by Fretheim, "Jeremiah 12," esp. 98–108; cf. Suffering of God, 107–26, 130–36, 159–62. See also Laurie J. Braaten, "All Creation Groans: Romans 8:22 in Light of the Biblical Sources," *HBT* 28 (2006): 162 n. 29, and 164.

10. Ibn Ezra (*ad loc.*) suggested that the female subject might either be the ground, or the prophet's self נפש.

11. Hayes, *Earth Mourns*, esp. 189–96.

12. E.g., Marvin A. Sweeney, *The Twelve Prophets* (Berit Olam; 2 vols.; Collegeville: Liturgical Press, 2000), 1:160; Ahlström, *Joel and the Temple Cult*, 6–7.

tions. Since up to now Earth community has been included in the lamenting, however, we would include the full Earth community. Further, while the temple is in view in the reference to "God's house" in verse 14, in verse 16 God's house has a more comprehensive meaning: it is God's land, at the cosmic center of which stands God's temple.[13]

This proposal is supported by the way the speech continues. After reference to the failure of seed and grain (verse 17), the lamenting of the animals is reported (see Hayes for a discussion of the language[14]): animals sigh (אנח), cattle are confused (בוך) and sheep suffer punishment (נאשם[15] verse 18)! Up to this point, these are the only "inhabitants of the land" who *actually* articulate their "lack of food." More mourning behavior is reported in verse 20 due to a drought, "Even the animals (בהמה) of the field long for (ערג)" God because they lack pasturage. This withered pasturage is part of the "house of our God" from which food is cut off. Rejoicing is lacking in this house because such joy is always deemed inconsistent with mourning.[16]

The last issue we will take up in this section is the voice in verses 19–20, which begins: "Upon you, Oh YHWH, I call!" It is obviously the prophet intoning the community's lament; but who *is* the community here? Since this lament focuses exclusively on the nonhuman world, the most appropriate speaker would be Earth. This is entirely consistent with what we have read so far. Up to this point we know that Ground mourns, and we have heard the groaning and seen the dismay of the domestic and wild animals. Earth has spoken, but until now we have not heard Earth's speech articulated. Here, finally we hear Earth calling out to God. We hear Earth complaining about the destructive Day of YHWH announced earlier. This day has come like a raging fire consuming Earth's meadows, burning Earth's trees, drying up its watercourses, and causing Earth's animals to long for God's salvation. Implied in the lament is Earth appealing to God for deliverance, which is now explicitly articulated.

THE HUMAN COMMUNITY CALLED TO IDENTIFY WITH EARTH

So far we have read Joel 1 almost exclusively from the perspective of Earth. Earth and God (through the prophet) clearly mourn the crisis at hand, yet the people

---

13. For a discussion of the land as God's dwelling place and cosmic center with reference to the West Asian context see, e.g., R. E. Clements, *God and Temple* (Oxford: Blackwell, 1965), 51–54; Jon D. Levenson, "The Temple and the World," *JR* 64 (1984), esp. 282–87; Jon D. Levenson, *Sinai & Zion: An Entry into The Jewish Bible* (San Francisco: HarperCollins, 1985), 111–37.

14. The lament vocabulary used of the animals is discussed in Hayes, *Earth Mourns*, 177–204.

15. BDB s.v., but cf. *BHS*, and *HALOT*.

16. See Saul M. Olyan, *Biblical Mourning: Ritual and Social Dimensions* (Oxford: Oxford University Press, 2004), 13–19.

have not yet responded. By presenting the languishing and mourning Earth as the first to respond to a crisis, Joel is employing a widely known concept: eight other passages in the Hebrew Bible depict Earth mourning in response to human sin, God's judgment, or a combination of both.[17] In most cases it is understood that humans should be engaged in similar behavior, but they are not. Earth's mourning is a sign that something is wrong, and it behooves humans to find out what, and take measures to correct it. For example, Jeremiah depicts God as complaining that the land is mourning and desolate, "but no one takes it to heart" (Jer 12:11). We see the same idea expressed in the Ugaritic Aqhat narrative, where Aqhat's family mourns in response to languishing vegetation.[18] Once they discover that a murder is the cause of the crisis, they take action to remove the pollution from the land.[19]

In Joel, the call to lament, due to the languishing of members of Earth community by the locusts, is reason enough for humans to mourn. The crisis intensifies, however, when Earth's mourning rises in ever increasing crescendos, and the human community remains silent. As Saul Olyan has argued recently, the solidarity of the mourning community is necessary for the reincorporation of the primary mourners into their proper social relationships. In Joel, the humans hold out, so Earth remains in a liminal state.[20] It seems that the hazy condition of the drunkard in Joel 1:5 is symptomatic of the entire community; perhaps they care about nothing except their self-gratifying consumption which insulates them from feeling the pain of others.

2. Joel 2—Repentance and Restoration in Earth Community

The Problem Revealed: A Call for Repentance

The summons of God and the mourning Earth fail to get humans to identify with Earth in the petitionary mourning rites in Joel 1.[21] Joel 2, however, indicates

---

17. The passages are discussed in what Hayes determines to be their chronological order: Amos 1:2; Hos 4:1–3; Jer 4:23–28; 12:1–4; 12:7–13; 23:9–12; Isa 24:1–20; 33:7–9; Joel 1:5–20.

18. See CTU 1.19 I 1–49 (UNP 66–68; *ANET* 129–55). These mourning rituals involved tearing of garments and weeping in the heart.

19. Parker calls attention to the similarity between this response and David's response to a famine in 2 Sam 21:1–2. Concerns for the expiation for the land due to the pollution of bloodguilt are found in Num 35:33. See Simon B. Parker, *The Pre-Biblical Narrative Tradition* (SBLRBS 24; Atlanta: Scholars Press, 1989), 122–23, 131.

20. Olyan, *Biblical Mourning*, 6–19, 46–61. Making special reference to van Gennep's classical study on rites of passage, Olyan argues that mourners are cut off from the larger community and have entered a liminal state.

21. "Petitionary mourning rites in response to a crisis" is one of the four categories of mourning rites identified by Olyan, *Biblical Mourning*, 25–27, and throughout the work.

that the failure of humans to mourn is a double tragedy since human sin is the source of the problem. Joel never indicates the nature of the people's sin, [22] but it is implicit in the announcements that the locust invasion and drought are harbingers of the Day of YHWH (Joel 1:15; 2:1–2), and in the call for God's people to repent (Joel 2:12–14). Locusts and drought are signs of God's judgment elsewhere in the Hebrew Bible.[23] In summary, Earth is suffering and mourns. In the process, Earth serves as a model for proper human mourning, and calls for humans to identify with Earth's suffering. Earth also condemns human sin; Earth's suffering stands as a sign to humans that they have not repented of the damage they have done to Earth.

Once again there is a call to convene an assembly (Joel 2:15–16). This time the priests are commanded to weep and pray on behalf of Earth community. "Have compassion, YHWH, upon your people, and do not give over your allotment to taunting, for the nations to rule over them. Why should it be said among the peoples 'where is their God?'" (Joel 2:17b). The term נחלה "allotment" is usually understood as being in synonymous parallelism with God's people. The oracle that answers this prayer in verse 18, however, responds to God's land and God's people separately, implying the same distinction in verse 17.[24] Therefore, I suggest that its primary meaning here is God's allotment or entitlement, that is, the land. In the narrower context of this prayer, the reference to the disgrace of God's allotment and the lack of compassion toward God's people serves as a motivation clause—YHWH's reputation is tied up with the way the deity's beloved are being treated.

Despite this bargaining aspect, these words are still presented as *God's word*—the prophet, in the name of God, instructs the priests to speak in this manner. These prophetic words introduce a subversive element—they essentially undermine any human claim to the land as a commodity at their disposal. In

---

22. The only possible hint concerning this human sin might be given in the odd beginning, where "drunkards" and "wine drinkers" are the first groups called to lament. The prophets sometimes connect excessive wine drinking with conspicuous consumption that accompanies apathy for the poor, and oppression of the weak; see Amos 6:4–7. See also Isa 5:11–13, 20–23, where the context (verses 8–10) condemns land theft.

23. Locust invasions and drought are among the curses that come upon the land when humans sin (Deut 28:23–24, 38; Lev 26:19–20). In Solomon's temple-dedication prayer, locusts are among the disasters that God sends to judge and motivate the people to repent and ask for God's forgiveness (1 Kgs 8:35, 37; cf. 2 Chr 6:26, 28). This is reiterated in the Chronicler's version of God's appearance to Solomon after the dedicatory prayer (2 Chr 7:13–14). God will "forgive their sin and heal their land" if the people humbly repent and call on God's name.

24. The answer to this prayer in Joel 2:18 addresses the subjects of verse 17—"people" and "allotment"—in the opposite order ("land" and "people") forming an AB–B'A' chiastic pattern. The same usage can be found in Joel 4[3]:2b: "I will enter into judgment with them there concerning my people and my allotment—Israel whom they have scattered among the nations, and my land which they apportioned" (AB // A'B' pattern).

their attempt to negotiate with God for the loss of crops by making it an issue that affects God's reputation, the people unwittingly surrender their exclusive entitlement to the land. Only God can claim an entitlement to the land, so the human community must surrender to God their claim to land as commodity, and look to God to ascertain how to live with Earth as community partner.

In the end, this prayer functions to erode the consumer claims of the human community, and offers hope to Earth and Earth community as a whole. We must still ask, however, how Earth will fare when considered to be God's land?

The Resolution: Divine Mercy

An initial answer to the question above has been anticipated earlier: God laments for the sake of "my land" (Joel 1:6). This lament indicates that though God has led the locusts to the land as the harbinger to the Day of YHWH, God has taken no joy in it. Earth has suffered collateral damage in God's judgment against human sin.[25]

The way the priest depicts God responding in the people's prayer gives us a more direct answer: "YHWH will be zealous for [YHWH's] land, and YHWH will have compassion for [YHWH's] people" (Joel 2:18).[26] The promises of God's salvation that follow are primarily articulated in terms of the restoration of Earth, and are directed both toward the people and Earth. Verse 19 is explicitly directed to the people: God will send to them grain, wine, and oil, and remove their reproach. Verse 20 may be a continuation of this human address—but it also could be directed to Earth community, namely to both humans and Earth. God promises to remove the locusts (referred to as "the northerner"[27]), driving them into a parched land. Verses 21 and 22 address Earth directly. "Fear not, O Ground, be joyous and rejoice, for YHWH has done great things. Fear not, O animals of the fields, for the pastures of the wilderness will sprout, for the tree will bear its fruit, and the fig tree and vine will yield their strength."

---

25. See the discussions concerning God's mourning in the works of Fretheim—see n. 8 above, esp. "Jeremiah 12," 108, where he refers to the "collateral damages" that ensues when God uses imperfect means to render divine judgment.

26. Deist argues that the imperfect verbs are logical imperfects, indicating what will happen after the supposed action, rather than as historical sequences reporting actual events (he cites *GKC* § 111i-l). See Ferdinand E. Deist, "Parallels and Reinterpretation in the Book of Joel: A Theology of the Yom Yhwh?," in *Text and Context: Old Testament and Semitic Studies for F. C. Fensham* (ed. W. Claassen; JSOTSup 48; Sheffield: Sheffield Academic Press, 1988), 75–76 n. 1.

27. "Northerner" reflects a traditional name for Israel's enemies, who usually attack from the north. See Brevard S. Childs, "The Enemy from the North and the Chaos Tradition," *JBL* 78 (1959): 197. Here it is used as a designation for the locusts, which usually enter the land from the south or east.

At this point I would like to pause to offer some observations. First, the grain, wine, and oil, considered from the perspective of Ground in Joel 1:10—are viewed from the side of human need in Joel 2:19. Similarly, the fig trees and vines, identified as God's in Joel 1:7, are portrayed as Ground's in Joel 2:22. This interchangeability of "ownership" in Joel 1 and 2 suggests the interconnectedness of the three members of Earth community—Earth, Humans, and God. No one member of the community can claim exclusive rights to Earth's bounty. Second, the command to Ground to be joyous and rejoice in 2:21 confirms our proposal that the "house of God" that lacked food, joy, and rejoicing in Joel 1:16 includes Land as God's habitation.

Returning to God's answer to the priest's prayer, Joel 2:23–24 addresses the "Sons of Zion," promising rain and the filling of threshing floors and wine vats. Joel 2:25–27 alternates between a direct addressee, "you" (2d per. m. pl.), and references to "my people." I suggest that the "you" addressee is Earth community, properly understood as comprising both Earth and people. When this passage is read in terms of Earth community, verse 26 completes the reversal of Earth community's mourning. We have already seen in verse 21 that God has replaced Ground's mourning with joy, a common theme in the Psalms. In verse 26, Earth community is now fully restored to one of its primary functions: praising YHWH for God's great deeds. Humans praise God in cultic celebration, which includes lauding God's works and articulating Earth's praise of God (Pss 145:1–21; 147:1–20; 149:1–3). Earth praises the name of God by acting according to Earth's nature: displaying God-given fertility in abundant vegetative yields and flourishing animal populations.[28]

EARTH COMMUNITY'S FATE IN THE HANDS OF GOD AND HUMANS

The survey above may suggest that all is well for Earth and Earth community. Yet we have left untouched some troublesome issues raised by the text.

The first issue emerges in Joel 2:25. God promises to remove the locusts, describing them with the same terms employed in God's lament in Joel 1:4. As in Joel 2:11, they are portrayed as a great army with God as their leader. The terminological linking of God's lament in Joel 1 with this acknowledgment of participation in the problem articulates the polarity of God's activity in Joel. God laments the problem, God announces sending the problem, then God promises to remove the problem!

A reader coming to the defense of Earth might suggest a simpler solution to the locust problem: perhaps God should not have sent the locusts in the first place! While this effort to identify with suffering Earth is noble, unfortunately it

---

28. Ps 148:7–13; see Terence E. Fretheim, *God and World in the Old Testament: A Relational Theology of Creation* (Nashville: Abingdon, 2005), 249–68.

oversimplifies the issue. Foremost, it fails to reckon with the fact that the locusts are not just a "problem" to be eliminated; rather, they are themselves full members of Earth community! It is often stated that God does not violate human freedom to stop destructive behavior, but that God can use that destructive behavior for divine purposes. For example, God can use the militaristic and self-aggrandizing policies of Assyria and Babylon as a means of judging God's people. Likewise, God can use so-called forces of nature for similar purposes. Unfortunately, that makes God responsible for the collateral damage that ensues.

In the case of the locusts, they don't have a military agenda of conquering and taking territory; rather, they are simply doing what locusts do, namely, consuming what they need. It is instructive to observe how the text avoids demonizing the locusts. While they are the harbingers of the destructive and fearful Day of the Lord (Joel 1:15; 2:11), they are also a "nation" (Joel 1:6), a "great and vast people" (Joel 2:2 and 5). They are YHWH's חיל, ("army," Joel 2:11, 25; NRSV), the same term used to describe the yield of the fig tree (Joel 2:22). As a matter of fact, in Joel 2:25 God persists in referring to them as "my great army" even after promising to remove them and make restitution for their damage! The reader cannot help but notice that in the detailed description of the locust invasion in 2:4–9, there is a hint of admiration for their highly efficient and well-organized foray; they are elite troops, obedient to YHWH, their commander-in-chief![29] Nevertheless, the locusts have become the enemy of other members of Earth community, and God has identified with the enemy.

In this bad news, there is also good news: God has not abandoned Earth community. Rather, God has continued to be a part of it. For a little while God was present with the locusts in judgment. Ultimately, however, God will drive them to a parched land for the sake of the rest of Earth community (Joel 2:20). Yet the possibility is always open that, in response to human sin, this polarity of divine action may once again manifest itself and divide sibling against sibling. This division in Earth community will be a recurring problem unless humans sincerely repent of the sin that brings this judgment.

Humans do repent in Joel, don't they? The answer is not clear. First, we have to remember that Joel is not a historic report, it is a literary presentation of a community lament and God's typical answer. The most we can say is that the book of Joel advises the human community how to respond in a typical crisis brought on by God's judgment, and indicates how God typically answers this human response.

---

29. While their behavior is destructive, is it any less so than the drunkards of Joel 1, who consume in excess of their needs? Perhaps the anti-creation behavior of the human community has elicited God's judgment as an uncreation of the land, as in the exodus narrative; see Terence E. Fretheim, "The Plagues as Ecological Signs of Historical Disaster," *JBL* 110 (1991): 385–96.

Second, while the text clearly presents YHWH as calling humans to repent both in liturgical actions and by rending their hearts, it nowhere depicts them as actually doing this (Joel 2:12–14). Rather, the text portrays God's response as conditional on the priest's prayer. As we have seen above, the bargaining chip in this prayer contains a subversive element—it calls the people's bluff as they essentially confess that the land isn't really theirs. While this confession has an element of repentance, it lacks the full-scale turning from evil that the occasion demands. Someone needs to teach the people the way to repentance as part of their proper response to the crisis in Earth community. Perhaps this is the function of the "teacher of the right way"—one of the gifts granted to the people in connection with the rain (Joel 2:23).[30]

What then, has brought about God's response? The answer is tucked away in Joel 2:13–14: while humans may not have fully repented of their actions, God has repented of God's actions. In this passage the prophet calls humans to repent on the prospect that God "may repent and be sorry, and leave behind a blessing." God's response in 2:18–27 is just that—God goes even so far as to promise restitution to Earth community for the locust damage in 2:25! The reader has the uneasy feeling, however, that perhaps this is not a real solution. While God alone has the power to set Earth community right, it is usually not achieved without the cooperation of its human members. Earth has been saved for now, but will the human community learn to live by God's mercy, or will they presume upon it? Will they repent of their evil, or will they soon cause more suffering in Earth community?

The open-endedness of Joel 1–2 invites readers to become the prophet's audience. The unresolved issues are issues that readers are called upon to address. The text seems to point the way. Earth mourns—should not readers identify with Earth's mourning? Earth suffers violence—should not readers repent of the evil that made this happen? Readers pray for a transformed Earth—should they not depend upon the mercy of God, and trust in the power of God's great deeds to effect this change? Readers desire God's salvation for Earth community—should they not confess that they have no valid title to Earth, that Earth is not theirs to do with as they please? In the meantime, Earth laments:

> How long, Oh God, will you allow my enemy to destroy me,
> > how long will your fire burn against me?
> My animals cry to you, my vegetation withers, my land is parched.
> We long for your salvation, Oh God;
> > abandon not the life of your Earth to destruction.

---

30. Ahlström presents a convincing case for this translation of מורה לזדקה in *Joel and the Temple*, 98–110.

My companions who have shared my table since my youth
     have betrayed me.
"Come" they say, "no one is watching, has not God given 'this' to us?
Come, let us eat, let us drink,
     let us fashion for ourselves goods without limit.
Come, take what is hers, she will not miss it,
     she is but dirt, what does she care?
Let us do as we please, let us not fear.
     What does God care about such matters?
Is this not a small thing?
     Is not our God patient? Surely God will forgive us."

How long, Oh Lord, must I suffer these insults?
     How long will my children languish?
My children have gone without food, they wander without a home.
They open their mouths in hunger, they can no longer utter your praise.
They are considered objects, uprooted and refashioned into images.
Will these images offer you praise? Will they save their human masters?

God, you have been my companion since my youth,
     you called me forth from the waters.
How long, Oh Lord, will your patient tolerance of human sin last?
     Will you be with my enemy forever?
Will your loving kindness and slowness to anger toward humans endure,
     while my suffering is without end?

Instruct them, Oh God, send them a teacher of the right way.
Yet I will hope in God, who alone can deliver me
     from the hands of my enemies.

The Other Prophet! The Voice of Earth in the Book of Amos

Hilary Marlow

Using a threefold hermeneutic of suspicion, identification, and retrieval to explore biblical texts from an ecological perspective has resulted in a wide variety of readings that challenge traditional interpretations. In this study of the book of Amos I have focussed mainly on the interconnected tasks of identification and retrieval. In the process, I have, however, undertaken a different form of suspicion, directed not at the biblical text but at myself as reader. How can I have read the book of Amos so many times and not noticed the part that the natural world plays within it? Why have I allowed my anthropocentric bias to muffle the voices of the rest of creation? This reflection on the book of Amos will hopefully redress the balance and encourage others to read the prophetic texts through new lenses. One initial discovery has been that the hermeneutical categories of the SBL symposium do not always exactly "fit" with the biblical material, leading to difficulty in separating the task of identification with the nonhuman figures, voices, and forces in the text from retrieval of the unnoticed voices and roles of Earth community. So I make no apology if in this paper the distinction between these two interrelated and mutually dependant concepts is somewhat blurred.

The Hebrew Bible, in particular the prophetic books, is full of language describing the natural world or using it as metaphor or analogy, much of which still goes unnoticed in the secondary literature. But there is more to identification and retrieval that just noting images of nature in the text. The questions raised by the Earth Bible project include asking whether the Earth is an active voice in the text or a passive lifeless entity, and whether the Earth is treated unjustly, and if so, to what extent this is acknowledged in the text. These concerns have prompted my reexamination of the text of Amos, and a discovery that the natural world is an active participant in the Earth's story in this book—although in ways that are not necessarily beneficial to its human population.

1. Speech in Amos

The book of Amos is characterized by speech. Not only is YHWH portrayed as the one who speaks, and Amos the prophet as his spokesperson but the author also uses the literary device of direct speech to set up the tension between the prophet Amos and the priest Amaziah (Amos 7:10–15), and puts words into the peoples' mouths that highlight their failings (see, for example, 4:1, 8:5). Various commentators have drawn attention to the rhetorical and didactic skills exhibited by the book, whether of the eighth century prophet or his redactor/redactors.[1]

More specifically a number of modern studies have applied classical rhetorical theory to biblical prophetic texts. A recent example is Möller's analysis of rhetorical structure and strategy in Amos.[2] Such studies focus on aspects of human and divine speech in the text. But what about the Earth? In what ways does the natural world "speak" in the book of Amos, and with what effect?

Attributing a human quality such as speech to inanimate objects is not without its difficulties, and begs the question whether the "voice" of the Earth is not itself a human creation, "a thoroughly anthropocentric device."[3] Yet it is no less problematic to speak of the voice of Earth than of the voice of God. Both are metaphors that enable humankind "to appreciate the reality of communication with a 'thou' other than ourselves."[4] Metaphor is more than a rhetorical device; it becomes a hermeneutical tool that enables those of us operating from a Western dualistic perspective "to begin relating to Earth as kin rather than commodity, as partner and co-creator rather than property."[5] However, in the book of Amos, as we shall see, metaphor becomes a means through which humanity and the Earth either connect or are contrasted.[6]

---

1. See, e.g., Shalom M. Paul, *Amos: A Commentary on the Book of Amos* (Minneapolis: Fortress, 1991); Hans Walter Wolff, *Joel and Amos: A Commentary on the Books of the Prophets Joel and Amos* (Philadelphia: Fortress Press, 1977).

2. Karl Möller, *A Prophet in Debate: The Rhetoric of Persuasion in the Book of Amos* (Sheffield: Sheffield Academic Press, 2003). See also Mary E.Shields, *Circumscribing the Prostitute: The Rhetorics of Intertextuality, Metaphor and Gender in Jeremiah 3:1–4:4* (ed. D. J. A. Clines and P. R. Davies, JSOTSup 387; London: T&T Clark, 2004); Ernst R.Wendland, "The 'Word of the Lord' and the Organisation of Amos: A Dramatic Message of Conflict and Crisis in the Confrontation Between the Prophet and People of Yahweh," *Occasional Papers in Translation and Textlinguistics* 2 (1988): 1–51; Joyce Rilett Wood, *Amos in Song and Book Culture* (Sheffield: Sheffield Academic Press, 2002).

3. Tim Meadowcroft, "Some Questions for the Earth Bible" (paper presented at the ANZATS Conference, Christchurch, New Zealand, July 2000).

4. Norman Habel, ed., *The Earth Story in Psalms and Prophets* (The Earth Bible 4; Sheffield: Sheffield Academic Press, 2001), 24.

5. Habel, *The Earth Story in Psalms and Prophets*, 28.

6. See Gören Eidevall, *Grapes in the Desert: Metaphors, Models and Themes in Hosea 4–14* (Stockholm: Almqvist & Wiksell International, 1996); Kirsten Nielsen, *There is Hope for a Tree:*

Before looking in detail at ways in which the voice of the Earth may be heard in Amos, I will make two general observations on the interaction between God and the natural world in the book.

2. THE EARTH RESPONDS

In a number of instances in Amos the natural world is portrayed as responding to the call of YHWH. For example, when God summons the waters of the sea in Amos 5:8 and 9:6, they are apparently obedient to his "call," in contrast to the people who have not heeded YHWH's voice. A more drastic response is presented in 1:2: "YHWH roars from Zion and from Jerusalem (he) utters voice, and the grazing pastures mourn and the top of Carmel dries up." The landscape undergoes a significant and visible change in response to of God's voice. The language used of YHWH is that of the divine warrior (roaring), and of the storm God (thundering); both suggest divine anger.[7]

But is God's anger directed at the natural world, and if so, why should it be the focus of God's rage? Doesn't this verse imply wanton destruction of Earth's landscape by YHWH? A careful examination of the text suggests that a subtle process is at work: the Earth acts as a channel for YHWH's message rather than being the recipient of divine displeasure.

Three observations highlight this process:

1. The author's choice of the root אבל, with its ambiguous meaning (primarily "to mourn" with a secondary nuance meaning "to dry up") to describe the response of the pastures to YHWH's voice (1:2).[8] This attribution to the natural world of the capacity for emotion is by no means unique to Amos. It suggests that the Earth is somehow involved in YHWH's coming—not as a passive victim, but actively responding to God's call for action.[9]

2. The mourning of the pastures parallels the forthcoming judgment by fire on the foreign nations, and the defeat of Israel in the succeeding oracles (Amos 1:3–2:16). The juxtaposition of 1:2 with the following sections establishes a connection between the devastation of Earth and that of

---

The Tree as Metaphor in Isaiah (Sheffield: Sheffield Academic Press, 1989); Shields, *Circumscribing the Prostitute.*

7. Elsewhere in the Hebrew Bible קולו נתן is associated with thunder: e.g., Ps 18:14[13]; Ps 68:34[33]. See Frank M. Cross Jr., *Canaanite Myth and Hebrew Epic* (Cambridge, Mass.: Harvard University Press, 1973), 174; Hayes, *Earth Mourns,* 22.

8. See discussion in Hayes, *Earth Mourns,* 12–18; also David J. A. Clines, "Was There an *'bl* II 'Be Dry' in Classical Hebrew?" *VT* 42 (1992): 1–10.

9. The image of the Earth mourning occurs in nine prophetic texts in the Hebrew Bible; see Hayes, *Earth Mourns,* 2 and *passim.*

human political landscapes. More specifically, suggests Hayes, "the Earth responds to the punishment YHWH will inflict because of the sins of the community."[10]

3. On a more local level, it is notably the shepherds' pastures that are affected by the drought, with the inherent possibility that their flocks will lack food. In other words, Earth's response to YHWH affects the economic well-being of the people, and as we shall see, this is part of YHWH's judgment on them.

From the outset, the book of Amos is setting up a three-way connection between the voice of YHWH, the response of Earth, and the fate of human beings.

The opening "hymn" setting out the effect that YHWH's judgment has on the natural world (1:2) is reversed in the closing verses of the book: "The mountains will drip sweet wine and the hills will melt" (Amos 9:13b). Although YHWH does not speak or call in this section, he is clearly the cause and initiator of the restoration—of human social and political institutions (9:11–12, 14) as well as of the Earth's fertility (9:13). The book of Joel ends in a similar way (Joel 4[3]:18); the promise is preceded by announcement of YHWH's theophany couched in the same language as in Amos 1:2 (Joel 4[3]:16). In Joel as in Amos, the Earth acts as a mediating voice between YHWH and the people; in both texts, the Earth is a conduit for the blessings of fertility or the sorrow of famine.

3. THE EARTH COOPERATES

Having discussed ways in which Earth responds to YHWH's call, our second general observation relates to Amos 9:2–3, which describes the futility of trying to escape God's hand. In these verses, the whole cosmos, physical and mythical, appears to be in cooperation with YHWH. Although the remnant of the people make great effort to plumb the depths of Sheol or ascend to the heavens, they will not find refuge (verse 2). Although the highest mountain and the bottom of the sea might provide good hiding places, they make no attempt to shelter the escapees. The cosmos works along with YHWH to expose those who are attempting to flee his judgement.[11]

Following these two general observations, let us now examine three specific ways in which the voice of the Earth can be heard in the book of Amos: the use of natural world imagery, nature's role in revealing YHWH, and nature as a means of judgement. Together these form part of a rhetorical structure that highlights the importance of the Earth and its relationship with God and humanity.

---

10. Hayes, *Earth Mourns*, 30.
11. Compare Ps 139:7–12 and Job 28:12–22.

METAPHOR AND VISION

First, examples drawn from nature provide the vehicle of metaphors and the substance of visions. In Amos 2, the size and strength of the Amorites is likened to that of cedar and oak trees (verse 9), but this physical advantage does not prevent their destruction at the hands of YHWH, just as even the mightiest trees can be felled or burned down. Is this imagery merely a metaphor for the downfall of a great nation? Or does it also imply a negative or instrumental view of trees themselves?

Kirsten Nielsen's study of tree imagery in First Isaiah notes that the tree bears both a "material status" and an "ideological status."[12] The former term denotes what is observable and known by everybody, that is, the "evident accuracy" of the image.[13] In addition, suggests Nielsen, the view of the tree as sacred by virtue of its association with fertility myths in the ancient world also informs the metaphorical use.[14] If these two factors are brought to bear on Amos 2:9, the tree metaphor can implicitly be seen to indict the Amorites for their pride and their pagan religious practices, as well as their military power.[15] However, the trees are not themselves intrinsically proud or hostile to YHWH, and indeed the tree metaphor is used in both a positive and negative sense in the Hebrew Bible.

In other texts the imagery is drawn from animal rather than agricultural life. In Amos 3:12 the deliverance of Israel is likened to snatching part of a domestic animal from the jaws of a lion, while in 5:19 the dangers of nature (lions, bears, and snakes) are used as metaphors for the danger about to come upon the Israelites. As Jobling and Loewen point out, it is not that these animals are dangerous because God uses them as a means of punishment, rather that the peoples' "experience" of nature precedes their experience of God.[16] These wisdom similes and metaphors invoke the audience's understanding of the natural order of the world as it applies to them by alluding to what happens in the rest of nature; such an understanding is an important prerequisite for understanding the prophet's message of condemnation or hope. Moreover, part of the powerful impact of Amos' message lies in the potential reversal of apparently known and secure elements of life.[17]

---

12. Nielsen, *Hope for a Tree*, 71–85.

13. Nielson, *Hope for a Tree*, 140.

14. Nielson, *Hope for a Tree*, 79–84.

15. The Hebrew root רום, normally referring to a spatial characteristic, "to be high," is also used in a figurative sense signifying "to be proud"; e.g., Isa 2:13–17, 10:33–34 (Nielson, *Hope for a Tree*, 129–30).

16. David Jobling and Nathan Loewen, "Sketches for Earth Readings of the Book of Amos," in Habel, *Readings from the Perspective of Earth*, 83.

17. See Susan Gillingham, "'Who Makes the Morning Darkness': God and Creation in the Book of Amos," *SJT* 45 (1992): 165–84.

In Amos 3:4–5 and 6:12 we find use of several metaphors that suggest "unnatural behavior." In each case the rhetorical question draws on observable animal behavior and begs the answer "No, of course not!" So, for example, in 6:12 the reader is asked "Do horses run on the crags or does one plough the sea with an ox?" The force of the image lies in what Wolff calls "the antithetical relationship between the similes and that to which they are compared."[18] It contrasts the natural wisdom of a horse whose hooves are unsuited to mountaineering with the foolishness (and danger) of setting justice aside, and compares the absurdity of an ox ploughing the sea with the stupidity of neglecting righteousness.[19]

Some have asked whether it is problematic to use nature imagery to describe human situations, arguing that "the world, rather than sharing in human reality, becomes merely an instrument for thinking about human reality"?[20] However, this implies that the vehicle in a metaphor is necessarily of secondary importance to the tenor, which undermines the whole thrust of figurative language. Indeed, one could argue that the mental image conjured up by the vehicle is what gives the metaphor focus and substance. In any case, is using images of nature to describe human life substantially different to using anthropomorphic language to describe nature—or even God? And what would human conversation and literature be like if all imagery of the natural world were removed (assuming that were possible)?

In Amos the metaphors enrich and enliven the language, and give color and immediacy to the pronouncements of the prophet. Furthermore, the natural world is a reference point, a yardstick, at times even an ideal, against which human experience is measured. Metaphor becomes a means through which humanity and Earth either connect or are contrasted.

In addition to the use of metaphors and similes drawn from nature, we find that three of the five visions of Amos involve images of the natural world. Two describe the devastation of the land by YHWH's judgement in terms of a locust plague (Amos 7:1–2) and a raging fire (7:4). The third in 8:2 uses a word play between קיץ (summer fruit), and הקץ (the end, or reaping time). In each of these visions, as well as in most of the metaphors we have considered, the outcome is a negative one for the Israelites, although, in many cases, the "voices" of nature are not themselves intrinsically negative. Rather, the natural environment itself has provided the material that the prophet shapes into his oracles and that inspires his visionary experiences. In this respect, then, Earth has a voice that can be heard clearly.

---

18. Wolff, *Joel and Amos*, 284.

19. See also Isa 1:2; see John Barton, "Natural Law and Poetic Justice in the Old Testament," *JTS* 30 (1979): 1–14; repr. in *Understanding Old Testament Ethics: Approaches and Explorations* (Louisville, Ky.: Westminster John Knox, 2002), 32–44.

20. Jobling and Loewen, "Earth Readings of Amos," 84.

REVEALING YHWH

If the first way in which nature is heard is by use of figurative language, the second voice of the Earth, implicit rather than explicit in the text, is that which proclaims something about YHWH himself. In the three "hymnic fragments" (Amos 4:13; 5:8; 9:5, 6), the author does not specifically describe a speech act; the language is that of God communicating, both with humanity and with nature: YHWH "reveals his thoughts" to humans in 4:13 and "calls" to the waters in 5:8 and 9:6. In each of these three texts, natural phenomena reveal something of the name (and therefore the character) of YHWH. There is an interesting parallel in Ps 19, where the capacity for speech is specifically attributed to cosmic phenomena: "The heavens recount the glory of God . . . day to day pours forth speech" (Ps 19:1). The Psalmist goes on to address the very problem we have already discussed, that of using anthropomorphic language to describe nature ("there is no speech; there are no words"; verse 3), but he still maintains that by their very existence these cosmic events speak ("through all the Earth their voice has gone out, and their utterances to the end of the world"; verse 4).

Unlike Ps 19, which uses the splendor of the natural world as a call to worship and cultic obedience, in Amos these descriptions are designed to provoke a response of awe and dread at the name of YHWH. If mountains, wind, and sea are powerful, unpredictable, and dangerous, how much more so their creator. If changing days and seasons, and the movement of the night sky, are mysterious and unfathomable, how much more so the one who causes them. In Amos 4:13, the only reference to humanity—"he declares to a mortal his thoughts"—is sandwiched between descriptions of God as the creator of geological features (mountains), of unseen meteorological forces (the wind), and of the natural diurnal rhythms (dawn and darkness). This deliberate positioning conveys the smallness and insignificance of humanity (or possibly of the author himself) in comparison with these natural phenomena.

The other two hymnic fragments both invoke wider cosmic evidence of YHWH's power—the constellations of Pleiades and Orion in Amos 5:8 and the "upper chambers in the heavens" of 9:5. As we have already mentioned, they suggest a partnership of cooperation between the cosmos and YHWH that will have devastating effects on the people.

MEANS OF JUDGMENT

This leads us to the third aspect of the voice of the Earth in Amos, namely, the natural world as the means of YHWH's judgment and punishment. A wide variety of natural elements seems to be available to YHWH to direct at those who have warranted judgment. In the oracles against the nations (Amos 1:3–2:5) we read that YHWH will "send fire" on the individual nations indicted.[21] This phrase both evokes the concept of the Divine Warrior, and also describes the physical devastation of war. Similarly, in 7:4 YHWH is portrayed as summoning fire to consume the land (using the same verb קְרָא "to call" as is also used of the sea in 5:8 and 9:6).

In a number of other places, natural disasters first speak a warning to the people of God, and subsequently become the means by which God executes judgment on them. In Amos 4 the basic requirements for life (bread and water in verses 6–7) have already been withheld, and pests and diseases have struck the crops (verses 9, 10). Each of these calamities was intended to provoke a change of heart but to no avail: "Yet you did not return to me" (4:8, 9). Other catastrophes are yet to come: floods (5:8, 9:6), earthquake (8:8, 9:5, see also 1:1), and disruption of the cosmic rhythms. As we have seen, this demonstrates the all-powerful name and character of YHWH: "I will make the sun go down at noon . . . and the Earth dark in broad daylight" (8:9).[22] These judgments are a consequence—nature voicing YHWH's verdict on Israel's sin: "On account of this [Jacob's deeds], will not the land quake and all who dwell in her mourn?" (8:8). Rather than declaring God's glory as in Ps 19, the natural world pronounces God's anger, and so is part of the dialogue between YHWH and the people. Since the people have not listened to warnings mediated through God's human agent the prophet, God chooses to speak through a cosmic one.

So far, Earth, acting as YHWH's agent, has spoken entirely with a negative voice. But the other side of this picture of devastation and natural disaster is the hope of restoration of land and fertility. This is a theme that occurs frequently in other prophetic texts; in Amos, it is only found in the final verses of the book (Amos 9:13–15).[23]

Here, in a reversal of the book's opening verses, as already noted, the author describes the agricultural endeavors of the people (Amos 9:14) alongside the natural productivity of the Earth (verse 13). The predominant metaphor is that of grapes and wine, frequently found in prophetic texts to depict the ideal of abundance and fertility. The statement that "the mountains will drip sweet [or fresh] wine" (verse 13) invites a supernatural interpretation, implying that this is achieved without human agency, and this abundance of natural fertility speaks of the restoration of harmony between land and humanity as well as between YHWH and his people (verse 15).

---

21. See Amos 1:4, 7, 10, 14; 2:2, 5.

22. Gerard Pfeifer, "Jahwe als Schopfer der Welt und Herr ihrer Machte in der Verkundigung des Propheten Amos," *VT* 41 (1991): 475–81.

23. Particularly in Isaiah; see, e.g., 30:23–26, 35:1–9, 41:18–21; but see also Ezek 34:27; Hos 2:18–23.

4. Conclusion: A Prophetic Voice

The book of Amos puts a strong emphasis on communication. YHWH, Amos, Amaziah, and the people all have a voice. Apart from Amos who speaks in obedience to YHWH's will, all the human voices are set in opposition to the voice of YHWH. However, the natural world is not excluded from this conversation; the Earth is part of a cosmic dialogue between Creator and creation. Although the Earth has a message to communicate, like Amos it too only ever works at YHWH's bidding, whether for destruction or restoration. Indeed, in the book of Amos the relationship between the Earth and YHWH is no different to the dynamic between the prophet himself and God, since the prophet has also been called to be God's voice to the people.

Furthermore, there are several direct similarities between the voice of Amos and that of Earth. Both depend on hearing YHWH—Amos speaks in response to YHWH's revelation; Earth speaks following YHWH's call. Both bear witness to God before the people of Israel—Amos repeats the words YHWH gives him in the peoples' hearing; the natural world reflects the very nature of YHWH. Both are concerned to execute YHWH's judgement: Amos pronounces it and the Earth fulfills it. In a very real sense, then, the voice of Earth in the book of Amos may be said to be a "prophetic voice."

The Role of Nonhuman Characters in Jonah

Raymond F. Person Jr.

Discussions of character in the book of Jonah generally overlook the role played by nonhuman characters. That is, characterization is generally understood as being limited to human and divine beings, and the nonhuman characters are understood simply as an extension of the human and divine characters.[1] The winds, the fish, the plant, the worm, and the wind are simply tools of the Lord. The Ninevite animals wearing sackcloth and ashes are simply property of the people of Nineveh.

However, if we take a closer look at the narrative, we see that these non-human characters should be understood as characters with their own individual integrity who respond obediently to the Lord and are valued as such by the Lord. In order to make this point clear, I will first examine closely how these nonhuman characters are referred to in the narrative. I will then examine more closely two anthropocentric interpretations of these characters, before proposing interpretations that move beyond the anthropocentric interpretations, thereby retrieving the nonhuman perspective in the narrative.

1. Nonhuman Characters in the Jonah Narrative

The non-human characters in the Jonah narrative include the "mighty wind"/ "mighty storm"/the sea (Jonah 1:4–15), the ship (1:4), the lots (1:7), the "large fish" (2:1–2, 11), the animals of Nineveh (3:7–8; 4:11), the "*qiqayon* plant" (4:6–10),[2] the worm (4:7), a "fierce east wind" (4:8), and the sun (4:8).

---

1. See R. F. Person, Jr., *In Conversation with Jonah: Conversation Analysis, Literary Criticism, and the Book of Jonah* (JSOTSup 220; Sheffield: Sheffield Academic Press, 1996). In this monograph, I discussed nature as characters and noted that this perspective was generally overlooked (58–59). However, I did not fully explore the implications of this observation at that time. I strive to do this more effectively in this essay. All translations are my own as given in *In Conversation with Jonah* (see esp. 32–36).

2. My translation of the Hebrew noun *qiqayon* follows that of J. M. Sasson, *Jonah* (AB 24B; Garden City: Doubleday, 1990), 291–92.

When Jonah tries to flee from the Lord, the Lord responds by casting "mighty winds towards the sea so that a mighty storm raged upon it" (Jonah 1:4). This description makes it clear that the winds, sea, and storm are controlled by the Lord. Furthermore, Jonah's speech to the sailors confirms this when he says, "the Lord, the God of Heaven, I worship—he who made the sea and the dry land" (1:9). However, once the storm has been initiated by the Lord, it appears to take on a life of its own, at least as an active participant in the narrative. This active role is evident in the way the sea is referred to thereafter. Jonah 1:11 reads: "And they [the sailors] said to him, 'What must we do to you for the sea to calm down for us?' for the sea was becoming increasingly violent." Here the sailors and the narrator refer to the sea as if it has a will of its own. It is as if the Lord gave the sea a job to do and it is obediently following through with this task. Jonah's answer to the sailors' question has the same perspective: "Pick me up and cast me into the sea. Then the sea will calm down for you" (1:12). The narrator's report of the consequences of Jonah being thrown overboard also has this perspective: "and the sea ceased its raging" (1:15). Note that the narrative could read "the Lord calmed the sea," but it does not. Rather, the sea becomes an active agent in the story, doing the Lord's will.

With the storm fully under way, "the ship threatened to break up" (Jonah 1:4). The most literal translation of the Hebrew שבה, meaning "think, devise, plan,"[3] would be "the ship thought to break up." It is as if the ship carefully assessed its situation and, in an act of desperation, decided that giving up might be the best option if the sailors did not take its warning seriously enough and respond appropriately in order to save the ship.

In response to the ship's threat, the sailors pray and then lighten the load. They then use the pagan practice of casting lots as a way of seeking an answer to the question "Who on board the ship is the cause of the gods' anger?" and "the lot fell on Jonah" (1:7). The pagan sailors' understanding of this practice would be that the gods use the lots to answer their question. Ironically, the lot speaks the truth—even though the writers of the narrative would probably condemn this pagan practice. That is, despite the pagan assumptions underlying the practice of casting lots, the lot seems to do the Lord's will by revealing the truth to the sailors.

The role of other nonhuman characters as active agents responding to the Lord's command is even more explicit in the narrative in that, as we will see, the fish, the Ninevite animals, the plant, the worm, and the wind respond to verbal commands of the Lord, even if these commands are not explicitly reported in the narrative. This is most evident in Jonah 2:11: "Then the Lord spoke to the fish and

---

3. In *In Conversation with Jonah* I overlooked the ship as an active agent. This insight comes from K. M. Craig, Jr., *A Poetics of Jonah: Art in the Service of Ideology* (Macon, Ga.: Mercer University Press, 1999), 49.

it vomited Jonah upon dry land." The Lord speaks a command to the fish and it obeys. The use of a form of אמר here is unusual in that it is not followed by direct speech. In his study of direct discourse, Samuel Meier concludes that אמר rarely occurs without introducing direct discourse (only 2.7 percent of the time).[4] In the book of Jonah, this is the only occurrence. In Jonah 2:1 the narrative reads "The Lord appointed a large fish to swallow Jonah." Again, the verb used here (that is, ימן) suggests that the Lord addresses the fish with speech (see Ezra 7:25; Dan 1:10, 11; 2:24, 49) and the narrative suggests that the fish obeys the Lord's command—it states that "Jonah was in the belly of the fish for three days and three nights" (Jonah 2:1).

The Lord also "appoints" the plant to shade Jonah (4:6), the worm to kill the plant (4:7), and the wind presumably to destroy Jonah's booth (4:8); each of these characters responds obediently. With the plant and booth no longer providing shade, "the sun attacked Jonah's head" (4:8). That is, even without any reference to God appointing the sun to some task, the sun seems to understand its role in the Lord's plan after the worm and wind have done their job and, therefore, the sun obediently responds.

The above discussion certainly suggests that from the narrative's perspective, these nonhuman characters are understood as active, independent agents who obediently respond to the Lord. As the Creator of "the sea and dry land" (Jonah 1:9), the Lord is portrayed as controlling all of creation, but this does not require an understanding of these nonhuman characters as mere puppets of the Lord. As active agents, it is possible that they, like Jonah, may disobey the Lord. However, from the perspective of the Jonah narrative, such attempts at disobedience are futile—that is, everything that the Lord commands in the book of Jonah is done, even if the Lord had to work hard to force Jonah into reluctant obedience. In fact, Jonah's initial disobedience is contrasted with the obedience of the nonhuman characters, the pagan sailors, and the pagan Ninevites.

That nonhuman entities are considered active agents with value is confirmed in the final words of the narrative: "Then the Lord said, '. . . Yet I should not have compassion on Nineveh, that large city, which has in it more than one hundred and twenty thousand people, who do not know their right hand from their left hand, and many cattle as well?'" (Jonah 4:10–11). The Lord's rhetorical question certainly can be understood as a divine statement of the worth of the animals of Nineveh; the Lord has compassion for them as created beings. This statement also suggests that the Lord values the nonhuman characters as active agents in the divine plan for creation.

---

4. S. A. Meier, *Speaking of Speaking: Marking Direct Discourse in the Hebrew Bible* (VTSup 46; Leiden: Brill, 1992), 60–61.

2. Anthropocentric Interpretations

Most interpretations of the nonhuman characters in the book of Jonah do not represent these characters as active agents.[5] This does not mean that most interpreters dismiss or reject this interpretation; I suspect that this interpretation does not even occur to most interpreters. This is not to say that most interpreters completely overlook the role these characters play; however, the role these characters play is generally limited to two specific observations, namely, the Lord's use of these characters to advance the plot, and their characterization as an element of the satirical tone of the narrative. Below I will discuss each of these observations further, showing how they certainly reflect an important element of the Jonah narrative. However, I will then discuss how these observations nevertheless fall short of understanding the important role of the nonhuman characters as active agents who respond obediently to the Lord's implicit and explicit wishes.

The nonhuman characters, much like the sailors and the people of Nineveh, are important to the plot development of the narrative.[6] For example, when Jonah disobeys the Lord's command and the sailors unknowingly participate in this disobedience, the Lord's uses the "mighty wind," the "mighty storm," and the sea to stop Jonah's flight. The Lord then uses the fish to deliver Jonah where he was required. These nonhuman characters are certainly essential to the plot of the narrative; however, it would be a misinterpretation to limit one's understanding of the role of these characters to this one function in the narrative.

The Jonah narrative is often understood as having a satirical tone and the role of some of the nonhuman characters certainly adds to the satirical tone.[7] For example, it seems ridiculous for Jonah to be offering a prayer of thanksgiving to the Lord—proclaiming "Deliverance belongs to the Lord" (Jonah 2:11)—when he is still in the belly of the fish. Furthermore, while in the fish, Jonah still thinks himself better than the pagan sailors, despite the fact that the sailors are now safe in their boat on a calm sea. Jonah says, "Those who hold to empty faiths, their hope for mercy they give up. But, I, with a grateful voice, sacrifice to you; that which I vow, I shall fulfill" (2:9–10). Certainly a thankful Jonah in the belly of the fish adds to the satirical tone. Another example includes the Ninevite animals, who repent with their human counterparts by wearing sackcloth and ashes. Such a scene of all the animals in "that large city" dressed in sackcloth and ashes begs credulity and certainly adds to the satirical tone of the narrative. Despite the

---

5. However, see M. Mulzer, "Die Buße der Tiere in Jona 3,7f. und Jdt 4,10," *BN* 111 (2002): 76–88. Mulzer discusses the motif of the repentence of animals in Jonah and Judith in the context of parallels in Greek and Roman literature, specifically Herodotus, Plutarch, Euripides, and Virgil.

6. See further, Person, *In Conversation with Jonah*, 52–54.

7. See further, Person, *In Conversation with Jonah*, 69–88.

observation that the role of some of the nonhuman characters in the narrative adds to the satirical tone, it would be a misinterpretation to limit the importance of these characters to this role in the text.[8]

3. Beyond Anthropocentric Interpretations

Nonhuman characters play important roles in plot development and the satirical tone of the Jonah narrative. I have also asserted above that limiting the importance of these characters to these roles would be a misinterpretation of the narrative. I will defend this assertion as I strive to retrieve the understanding of the nonhuman characters as active agents in the narrative.

All the characters in the Jonah narrative play important roles in advancing the plot and in establishing the satirical tone. In the narrative, there is no distinction between, for example, Jonah, the fish, and the Ninevite animals. In fact, the most significant distinction between the characters concerns obedience to the Lord, with disobedient Jonah contrasted with all of the other human and nonhuman characters. In other words, the pagan humans (that is, the sailors and the people of Nineveh) are in the same category as the nonhuman characters (for example, the fish, the plant, and the wind), that is, the category of those who obey Jonah's God without reluctance or delay. For example, the people and animals of Nineveh immediately repented with sackcloth and ashes once they understood God's judgment. If this is the case in the Jonah narrative, then why would one conclude that some characters (that is, the nonhuman characters) are only important to some limited narrative functions, when other characters who have similar roles in the same narrative functions (that is, the human characters) play important roles in other aspects of the narrative? That is, why would one conclude, for example, that the Jonah narrative contrasts disobedient Jonah and his ethnocentrism with the repentant, obedient people of Nineveh as a way of critiquing an understanding of the Hebrew prophets' ethnocentrism, but exclude the animals of Nineveh from having any role in this critique? The only reason I can see is based on an anthropocentric assumption that such nonhuman characters must not be as important as the human characters in the narrative. If the interpretation of the Jonah narrative given above is accurate, the target of the satirical tone is not simply prophetic ethnocentrism but also anthropocentrism in general. In the

---

8. Similarly R. W. L. Moberly, "Preaching for a Response? Jonah's Message to the Ninevites Reconsidered," *VT* 53 (2003): 156–57, n. 4: "It is difficult for the modern reader not to see animals in sackcloth as purely humorous, despite the general high valuation of animals in relation to humans elsewhere in the OT which could suggest a more positive and serious construal."

words of Phyllis Trible, the theology of the Jonah narrative "embraces plant and animal, perhaps even a worm."[9]

If the satirical targets of the Jonah narrative are the ethnocentrism and anthropocentrism of its ancient readers, then it certainly seems likely that the readers are being asked seriously to consider identifying with those other beings that the Lord created, including even Israel's enemies, the people of Nineveh, and their "many cattle as well" (Jonah 4:11). In a similar way, we contemporary humans must overcome our anthropocentrism in order to construct our own theologies to include nonhuman concerns. As we strive to be obedient to God's will, we need to learn to be more attentive in our daily lives to others in Earth community, including the fish, the worm, the plant, the wind, the sea, and cattle.

I want to close with some hermeneutical reflections on how I have vacillated in relationship to my own thesis. On the one hand, I have struggled with the idea that my thesis is simply so contemporary, that is, that it reflects our growing concern for how anthropocentrism is destroying the environment, that it cannot possibly be an accurate interpretation that would in any way relate to what the ancients understood from this text. I seem to be reading my own modern ideas into the ancient text.

On the other hand, the assumption behind this struggle is certainly ill-founded, that is, we cannot assume that we are the only humans in every time and place that have questioned the value of anthropocentrism. Here I seem to be reading our contemporary arrogance as valid and forcibly using this idea to filter out any possible similar interpretation of reality that the ancients may have had. Obviously, both of these perspectives must be avoided in order to allow the text to assert itself upon us and to challenge us with new ideas. I hope that that is where I have ended up: allowing the text to challenge my own culturally limited understandings of reality. As I understand the goals of ecological hermeneutics, that is what we all should strive to do in relationship to issues involving Earth community and our relationship to other members of this diverse community.

---

9. Phyllis Trible, *Rhetorical Criticism: Context, Method, and the Book of Jonah* (Minneapolis: Fortress, 1994), 223. Trible's interpretation (and by implication mine) is explicitly questioned as an "animal-rights-activist reading" in R. D. Moore, "'And Also Much Cattle?!': Prophetic Passions and the End of Jonah," *JPT* 11 (1997): 45.

Honey from the Rock: The Contribution of God as Rock to an Ecological Hermeneutic

Arthur Walker-Jones

"Back then things were different," said the Vuntut Gwich'in elder. "Back then people talked to caribou and caribou could talk to people."[1] Karsten Heuer was in Old Crow, a fly-in community in Canada's Yukon Territory to talk about his plans to follow—on foot, with his partner Leanne—the migration of the 123,000-member Porcupine caribou herd. The Gwich'in live on the northern edge of the caribou's winter range and have relied on the caribou for centuries.

As a scientist, Karsten was skeptical about such statements, but after months of traveling with the caribou, he tells of developing a different kind of knowing. Struggling to keep up with the caribou, repeatedly finding and losing them, they realized that the caribou were making a "thrumming" sound, barely audible near the lowest register of human hearing, that reverberated through the land and which they could follow.

Because the Porcupine caribou herd's future is endangered by oil development, Karsten and Leanne had decided to migrate with the caribou in order to tell their story. The caribou's summer calving grounds on Alaska's North Slope are in an area hotly contested by environmentalists and oil companies. The future of the caribou is interrelated with many other ecological and social issues. Foremost in the news as I write is that burning oil produces the greenhouse gases that contribute to climate change, which in turn threatens untold suffering from severe weather, rising sea levels, flooding in some areas, and drought and famine in others. Although we know from ecology that our life and well-being is interrelated with and dependent on Earth, the dangerous view persists in Western culture that humanity is separate from and superior to Earth perceived as an inanimate object.

In the search for new ways of being in Earth community, the way our society images God is important because images of God as separate from and superior

---

1. Karsten Heuer, *Being Caribou: Five Months on Foot with an Arctic Herd* (Toronto: McClelland & Stewart, 2006), 17.

to Earth reflect and support the belief that humanity is separate from and superior to Earth. While The Earth Bible series bracketed Godtalk in order to be in
conversation with ecologists, an ecological hermeneutic concerned with social
change toward a more ecological society needs to be concerned with understandings of God's relation to Earth. This article takes up the issue of metaphors for
God in the belief that they are particularly important for changing the Western
interpretation of the Judeo-Christian tradition that has legitimated exploitation
of Earth.

In *Beyond God the Father*, Mary Daly says: "When God is male, then male
is God. The divine patriarch castrates women as long as he is allowed to live on
in the human imagination."[2] When the dominant metaphor for imagining God
is male, it creates and sustains a patriarchal social structure. Similarly, when the
dominant metaphors for God are human, they tend to legitimate and sustain an
anthropocentric society. From the perspective of Earth, we could say: "When
God is human, the human is God. The divine human destroys Earth as long as
the divine human is allowed to live on in the human imagination." An ecological
hermeneutic, therefore, needs to deconstruct human metaphors for God and find
Earth metaphors to balance them.

As the introduction to the first volume of The Earth Bible series noted, eco-
feminists have pointed out that binary thinking in Western culture legitimates the
exploitation of women and Earth. Western language and culture maintains a network of dichotomies that include God and Earth, God and humanity, male and
female, rational and emotional, human and nonhuman, spirit and matter, animate and inanimate, subject and object. These dichotomies legitimate oppression
because the items on the left—God, male, human, rational, and spiritual—are
considered separate from and superior to those on the right.

In the typical logic then, male human metaphors are considered most appropriate for God. They are the metaphors that are considered "real." Even when
Earth metaphors are used for God, they may be considered poetic, beautiful, but
less "real." The anthropocentrism of human readers conditions what they consider real and what creates meaning for them. When the readers dare to live and
read as part of Earth community, however, Earth metaphors for God may take on
meaning as reflections of their reality.

This paper applies an ecological hermeneutic to one Earth metaphor for the
divine: God as Rock.[3] This metaphor for God appears frequently in the book of

---

2. Mary Daly, *Beyond God the Father: Toward a Philosophy of Women's Liberation* (Boston:
Beacon, 1973), 19.

3. Translations of the Bible capitalize some metaphors for God. For instance, Father is
often capitalized when it refers to God. Presumably the capitalization of Father, and not other
metaphors, is due to the importance of this metaphor in Christian theology and in patriarchal,
anthropocentric cultures. By way of contrast, the ecological hermeneutic of this paper chooses
to capitalize an ecocentric metaphor—God as Rock. In addition, the capitalization of Rock

Psalms—in fact, far more frequently than a metaphor that has been more influential in Christianity: God as father. References to God as father appear three times in the Psalter (Pss 68:5; 89:26; 103:13), but references to God as Rock occur twenty times (Pss 18:2 [2x], 31, 46; 19:14; 28:1; 31:2, 3; 42:9; 62:2, 6, 7; 71:3; 78:35; 89:26; 92:15; 94:22; 95:1; 144:1, 2). This is surprising given the pervasive use of Psalms in Judeo-Christian worship and prayer.

Appearances of God as Rock outside of the book of Psalms are relatively rare. There are a few scattered references in the Prophets (Isa 8:14; 17:10; 26:4; 30:29; 44:8; Hab 1:12); 2 Sam 22 is a parallel version of Ps 18. Deuteronomy 32, however, makes extensive and highly suggestive use of God as Rock (verses 4, 13, 15, 18, 30, 31).

The two Hebrew words that are translated by the English word "rock" are צור and סלע. In the majority of instances צור is used of God,[4] but occasionally סלע may be used.[5] צור has a broad range of meaning that runs all the way from pebble to mountain.[6] סלע has a similar range of meaning and the two words are twice used in parallel.[7] אבן, as the English translation "stone" indicates, has a different semantic domain and is only once applied to God (Gen 49:24).

1. Suspicion

Even though God as Rock is an Earth metaphor for God, an ecological hermeneutic begins with the suspicion that the use of the metaphor in biblical passages or in their interpretation may be anthropocentric. In the book of Psalms the image is characteristically used in psalms of individual lament and thanksgiving. The majority of occurrences appear in these genres where it is metaphorically related to a typical narrative: the psalmist is in danger of sinking down into Sheol or the pit, and God rescues the psalmist by placing him or her on solid ground or a rock.[8] As William Brown puts it, "whereas God's 'refuge,' the 'rock' of Zion, is the feature most elevated on the Psalter's theological landscape (Ps 61:2b–3), the 'pit'

---

sometimes follows the lead of the Earth Bible project by treating Rock as a proper noun and subject. The Earth Bible series capitalized "Earth" and removed the definite article to emphasize that, in these Earth readings, Earth is recognized as a subject and therefore its name, "Earth," is treated as a proper noun; consequently, its name is capitalized and never uses a definite/indefinite article.

4. Deut 32:4, 15, 18, 30, 31; 2 Sam 22:2, 3, 32, 47 (2x); 23:3; Pss 18:2 (2x), 31, 46; 19:14; 28:1; 31:2, 3; 42:9; 62:2, 6, 7; 71:3; 78:35; 89:26; 92:15; 94:22; 95:1; 144:1; Isa 8:14; 17:10; 26:4; 30:29; 44:8; Hab 1:12.

5. Pss 18:2; 31:4; 40:2; 42:9; 71:3; 144:2 (if emended).

6. Heinz-Josef Fabry, "צור," TDOT, 12:314.

7. Pss 18:3; 71:3.

8. In a forthcoming book, The Green Psalter, I present at greater length the evidence that genres in the Psalms use typical imagery and narrative patterns.

marks, as it were, the sinkhole in the psalmist's terrain, into which one descends to death."[9] Metaphorically, God as Rock is identified with the rock of refuge.

In this context, however, the concern may not be with humanity as an integral part of a larger Earth community, but with the individual and his or her human concerns. For example, Ps 71, an individual lament, appeals to "God, my rock" to be a "rock of refuge." The psalmist complains of enemies that plan to harm him or her and rejoices when God puts them to shame (Ps 71:10–11, 24).

> You who have made me see many troubles and evils will revive me again; from the depths of Earth you will bring me up again. (Ps 71:20)[10]

Far from identifying with Earth, the psalmist associates Earth with death and dishonor.

In some cases, the anthropocentric bias may reflect the interest of kings and priests who may be less connected with Earth community than commoners. There is some evidence that, while God as Rock was popular among the common people, the image was co-opted by royal and priestly elites. The image is ancient and widespread throughout the histories of Israel and Judah. The words הר, "mountain," and צור, "rock," are "frequent elements in Amorite names of the second millennium"[11] where they probably designate a god. The appearance of the names פדהצור, "Ransomed by the Rock" (Num 1:10; 2:20; 7:54, 59; 10:23), and, פדהאצר, "Ransomed by God" (Num 34:28) indicates that "rock" could represent "God" in Israelite names.[12]

The Hebrew Bible portrays a Canaanite religion with temples on mountains and high places. Judging by the polemic against them in the prophets, they remained popular among many Israelites. The Hebrew Bible also refers to the מצבה, a sacred stone or pillar that was part of Canaanite religion, and forbidden—at least officially—for Israelites (Exod 34:13; Deut 12:3). Nevertheless, there are a surprising number of cases where an experience of God is associated with a rock, or where a rock is used in worship. When Jacob had his vision at Bethel, he "rose early in the morning, and he took the stone (אבן) that he had put under his head and set it up for a pillar (מצבה) and poured oil on the top of it" (Gen 28:18;

---

9. William P. Brown, *Seeing the Psalms: A Theology of Metaphor* (Louisville, Ky.: Westminster John Knox, 2002), 26

10. Translations are mine, unless otherwise noted.

11. Frank M. Cross, Jr., "Yahweh and the God of the Patriarchs," *HTR* 55 (1962): 247. Cf. James B. Pritchard, *Ancient Near Eastern Pictures Relating to the Old Testament* (Princeton: Princeton University Press, 1954), pl. 490.

12. Rock is common as a name, or as an element of a name, in the P genealogies of Numbers: אליצור "Rock is God" (Num 1:5; 2:10; 3:35; 7:30, 35; 10:18), צורישדי "My Rock is Shadday" (Num 1:6; 2:12; 7:36, 41; 10:19), צור "Rock" (Num 25:15; 31:8 [also a Midianite chief in Josh 13:21]).

NRSV). Even Moses on Sinai is told that "there is a place by me where you shall stand on the rock (הצור); and while my glory passes by I will put you in a cleft of the rock" (Exod 33:21–22; NRSV). These are all evidence that the association between Rock and divinity was early and widespread.

As mentioned previously, God as Rock is a metaphor used most frequently in individual lament and thanksgiving psalms. Erhardt Gerstenberger has argued that laments have their origin in healing ceremonies in the family circle and were secondarily taken up in the national religion.[13] If this is the case, then God as Rock may have been part of the spirituality of many Israelite families. Among the reasons that God as Rock appears primarily in psalms and psalm-like literature may be that the priests felt the need to include in worship an image popular with the people and to some extent subsume it within the official cult.

In contrast to the widespread experience of the presence of divinity associated with rocks and use of sacred stones in worship recorded in the Hebrew Bible, some texts identify God as Rock with Sinai or Zion (Pss 27:5; 61:2; Isa 8:14; 30:29). This may represent the attempt of priestly and royal interests to control and limit an imagery perceived as subversive. Just as contemporary religious leaders may have a vested interest in limiting the presence of God to church and synagogue and, therefore, may be uncomfortable with the presence of God in Earth, Israelite kings and priests may have had a vested interest in limiting God to the central temple, and may have been uneasy with too readily identifying the presence of God in many rocks and stones throughout the countryside.

Michael Knowles thinks the number of times the image appears either at the beginning of a psalm (Pss 18:2; 28:1; 95:1; 144:1, 2), or in the introductory section (Pss 31:2, 3; 40:2; 61:2; 62:2; 71:3), or as part of a conclusion (Pss 18:46; 73:26; 94:22), or at the end (Pss 19:14; 92:15) indicates the significance of this metaphor.[14] A case can be made that it is the leading metaphor of these psalms. Often, however, Rock is clustered with a number of other epithets for God:

> The Lord is my Rock, my fortress, and my deliverer,
> my God, my Rock in whom I take refuge,
> my shield, and the horn of my salvation, my lofty refuge. (Ps 18:2)[15]

However, this clustering of God as Rock with metaphors of God as a fortress that is constructed by humans—as a shield, which is a human creation; as a deliverer, which could be a human image; and as salvation, an abstract concept—may shift

---

13. Erhard Gerstenberger, *Der bittende Mensch* (Neukirchener-Vluyn: Neukirchener, 1980).

14. Michael P. Knowles, "'The Rock, His Work is Perfect': Unusual Imagery for God in Deuteronomy XXXII," *VT* 39 (1989): 307.

15. Other examples with many of the same terms in parallel are Pss 62:6–7 and 71:3.

the focus away from an ecological metaphor and toward metaphors and concepts that are more anthropocentric.

Commentators seldom discuss Rock as an image for God at length, and, when they do, their interpretations tend to be conceptual reductions. Rock, they say, represents strength and protection, or the like. Ithamar Gruenwald claims that because the "understanding of these names, according to which God really is a 'rock' or a 'stone,' is viewed as running counter to customarily maintained theological beliefs and assumptions,"[16] commentators used a hermeneutical method, which he traces as far back as Maimonides, that provided conceptual reductions for mythological materials. He suggests that most secular scholars continue in the same hermeneutical tradition.[17] He makes this point in the course of arguing for the importance of God the Rock in a phenomenology of Israelite religion and post-biblical Judaism.[18] In addition to avoiding the mythological associations, however, conceptual reduction has the effect of avoiding the ecological associations.

In the psalms, "Rock" frequently appears with the possessive pronoun: "my Rock." On the one hand, this could subtly reflect or legitimate humanity's attempts to possess and own Earth. Private property is a pillar of the contemporary Western economy, and wars continue to be fought and natural habitats destroyed to control Earth's natural resources. On the other hand, the expression "my Rock" may speak of humanity's sense of identification and relationship with the rocks of Earth.

2. Identification

This chapter began by suggesting that Earth metaphors for God could play a role in breaking down the dichotomies that have legitimated exploitation of Earth in Western culture. This is supported by a number of psalms that speak of God as Rock and identify God with Earth, or identify humanity with Earth community. While I have suggested that these may go back to the spirituality of common Israelites, the important thing is not that they existed historically, but that they are available for the contemporary reader as resources to imagine a more ecological future.

Psalm 78 seems to connect the theme of water from the rock in the wilderness with God as Rock. Verses fifteen and sixteen recount the bringing of water from the rock—the other major use of "rock" in the Psalms. Later in Ps 78:35 the people remember that "God was their Rock . . . their redemption." God as Rock is

---

16. Ithamar Gruenwald, "God the 'Stone/Rock': Myth, Idolatry, and Cultic Fetishism in Ancient Israel," *JR* 76 (1996): 428–49.

17. Gruenwald, "Stone/Rock," 429.

18. Gruenwald, "Stone/Rock," 429.

the rock in the wilderness. God is in Earth and redemption comes through Earth, not from heaven.

Psalm 95 begins with a call "to make a joyful noise to the Rock of our salvation." This is followed by a section that portrays God as creator of the world and of humanity:[19]

> For the LORD is a great God,
> and a great king above all gods.
> In the LORD's hand are Earth's depths;[20]
> the mountain peaks are God's also.
> The LORD's is the sea, as the LORD made it.
> while the dry land God's hands have formed.
> O come, let us bow down that we may worship.
> Let us kneel before the LORD, our maker! (Ps 95:3–6)

If we take the imagery of God as Rock that opens the psalm seriously, and understand it as the introductory and organizing metaphor for God, then God is not separate from and above Earth. Rock creates Earth and is in Earth. Like all planets, Earth grew when stardust coalesced into larger and larger bodies of Rock. Rock forms both Earth and mountains. Lava from volcanoes creates land. Soil erodes from Rock and allows for the growth of plants. Animals are made up of minerals from Earth, and rely on minerals from plants and other animals. Rock surrounds and cradles the sea. In brief, Ps 95 identifies God with Earth and allows for an ecological understanding of the creator as part of creation, as God in Earth.

Psalm 92 concludes by addressing God as Rock. In the preceding verses, the psalmist is compared to a wild ox and the righteous to trees:

> But you have raised up my horn like that of the wild ox;
> I am drenched in luxurious oil.
> My eyes have seen the downfall of those who spy on me;
> Of the doom of the wicked who rise against me, my ears have heard.
> The righteous blossom like the date-palm,
> like a cedar in Lebanon they grow.
> Planted in the house of the LORD,
> in the courts of our God, they blossom.
> They still produce fruit in old age;
> they are healthy and flourish,

---

19. Claus Westermann and his students have shown that the creation of the world and the creation of humanity represent separate traditions. Psalm 92:3–4, which gives the reason for praise, uses the language of world creation; verse 5, which is a call to praise, uses the language of human creation.

20. David J. A. Clines, DCH, 5:228.

To show that the Lord is upright;
God is my Rock, and there is no injustice in God. (Ps 92:10–15)

An anthropocentric reading might understand these as merely poetic; an ecological interpretation might identify with the wild ox and the tress and hear intimations of the intrinsic value and interdependence of Earth community. The power of the wild ox comes from God. Palm and cedar trees are models of righteousness and abundance for humans. Like trees, humans require ample water and minerals to flourish and produce fruit. Humans are part of an Earth community in which the flourishing of all plants and animals defines righteousness. In short, the focus on wild ox and trees that conclude with praise of God as Rock suggests the identification of humanity with all Earth's creatures, and emphasizes the intrinsic value of all members of Earth community.

3. Retrieval

In addition to identification with Earth, there are a number of passages in which God as Rock can be read as treating Earth as a subject capable of hearing, speaking and acting.

Deuteronomy 32 begins with Moses addressing Earth as a subject:

Give ear, O skies, so that I may speak;
that Earth may hear the words of my mouth. (Deut 32:1)

Verse four addresses God as Rock, and verse six says:

With the Lord do you deal thus, O foolish people without wisdom?
Is not God your father, who created you,
who made you and established you?

The association between Rock and creation is even closer in verse eighteen:

Rock who bore you, you neglected;
you forgot the God who gave you birth.

In Deut 32, God is mother Rock who gave birth to Israel. The creator is identified with Earth. As in Ps 139, God is identified with Earth and Earth gives birth to humanity. The maternal imagery expresses the identification of humanity with Earth. This intimate imagery of identification might lead to reflection on how Rock gives birth to humans. Scientists now think variations in human skin color are a fairly recent development and debate whether this and other physical characteristics may have environmental causes.[21] To some extent, then, humans adapt to, and thus are created by, their geography.

Psalm 19, a psalm that concludes with an address to God as Rock (verse 14), begins with the skies speaking:

> The skies are telling the glory of God;
> The firmament proclaims the work of God's hands.
> Day to day pours out speech,
> and night to night declares knowledge. (Ps 19:1–2)

Yet this is not human speech. There is a mystery to this speech:

> There is neither speech, nor words;
> their voice is not heard;
> through all Earth their voice carries,
> and to the ends of the world their words. (Ps 19:3–4a)

Though clearly not human speech, it communicates knowledge. Like the "thrumming" of the caribou, it would require an identification with Earth and sensitivity in order to hear.

The next section of Ps 19 is dominated by praise of God's law (verses 7–11). Anthropocentric interpretations have identified this with the written law. Commentators often see this section as lacking coherence with what has preceded it and suggest that these verses originated separately and were attached at a later time. The word translated "law," however, might better be translated "instruction." From an ecological perspective—and especially in the context of the preceding verses—the instruction of God cannot be limited to an anthropocentric book. The Bible is only part of a larger revelation. All Earth is Scripture.

The mention of God as Rock at the end of the Ps 19 (verse 14) returns to the nature of the presence of God in creation. This creates a connection with the opening verses, and supports a broader understanding of God's presence in and communication through Earth.

In addition to addressing Earth as a subject, Deut 32 identifies God in Earth, and asserts Earth's resistance to exploitation. The Song of Moses identifies Rock as working in nature to provide abundantly for the people in a rocky land.

> [God] fed him with produce of the field;
> nursed him with honey from a cliff (סלע),
> with oil from flinty Rock (מחלמיש צור);
> curdled milk, and goat's milk,

---

21. Ann Gibbons, "European Skin Turned Pale Only Recently, Gene Suggests," *Science* 316 (2007): 364; Nicholas Wade, "Gene That Determines Skin Color Is Discovered, Scientists Report," *New York Times* 155 (2005): A36.

with fat of lambs and rams of Bashan;
and goats, with the choicest wheat,
and the blood of grapes, wine you drank. (Deut 32:13b–14)

The people of Israel, however, "abandoned God who made them, and treated as a fool their Rock (צוּר) of well-being" (Deut 32:15). They forgot Rock, the source of the bounty of Earth; denied their own dependence on Earth; and believed in gods with no connection to Earth. Reading in solidarity with Earth community, it is difficult not to hear the "revenge of Gaia"[22] in the passage that follows:

For a fire is kindled by my anger,
and burns to the bottom of Sheol;
it eats up Earth and its increase,
and sets ablaze the foundations of the mountains.
I will make evils sweep over them,
my arrows I will use up on them:
empty hunger, ravaging fire, bitter pestilence,
and the fang of wild animals I will send against them,
with venom of those who crawl in the dust. (Deut 32:22–24)

Rock works in Earth, bringing an end to the fertility of Earth. The result: famine, fires, disease, and war. These are the dire consequences that humanity now faces as Earth fights to restore the balance of nature.

Psalm 28 begins with a call for Rock to hear and respond:

To you, O Lord, I call;
my Rock, do not refuse to speak to me,
for if you are silent to me,
I shall be like those who go down to the pit. (Ps 28:1)

The request for Rock not to be silent seems to assume that Rock can speak. This raises the question of how Rock would speak and what Rock would say. Like many other individual laments, Ps 28 contains an abrupt shift from petition in verse five to thanksgiving in verse six. Joachim Begrich[23] explained this shift in mood by positing that, at this point in its ceremonial use, a priest or prophet provided an oracle of salvation (see 1 Sam 1:17, and Isa 41:8–13, 14–16; 43:1–7) to assure the person that their prayer had been heard.

We might, therefore, in reading Ps 28 and identifying with Earth community, write an oracle from Rock in the style of the prophets, in response to Earth's current distress.

---

22. James Lovelock, *The Revenge of Gaia: Earth's Climate Crisis and the Fate of Humanity* (New York: Basic, 2006).

23. Joachim Begrich, "Das priesterliche Heilsorakel," *ZAW* 52 (1934): 81–82.

Hear, O Earth, says Rock,
I am in you and you are in me.

The days are coming, are already here,
when you will fight to restore balance.

Climate change will cause flooding and drought.
Humans will fight wars over dwindling resources.

Do not be afraid, for there is still time
for humans to repent and return to you.

They will work to reverse climate change,
to preserve their Earth kin.

They will once again serve you with reverence
and respect the work of the hands of Rock.

They will discover that I, Rock, am in you,
and that they are in Earth.

Do not be afraid; I, Rock, gave birth to you.
I connect you with the universe.

Let humans hear your groaning,
your call to return to their Rock.[24]

4. Conclusion

This paper began by suggesting that the image of God as Rock could serve to subvert the dichotomies that have legitimated exploitation of Earth because it blurs the distinctions between God and Earth, God and humanity, humanity and Earth, spiritual and material.

Although Rock is an Earth metaphor, this chapter began with the suspicion that the texts and their interpreters might have an anthropocentric bias. Priestly and royal interests may have taken over an ancient belief in God as Rock, widespread among common people who lived closer to Earth. The image of "God as Rock" often appears in the introduction or conclusion of psalms. Though it is the leading image for God in these psalms, other more anthropocentric metaphors are often arranged around it. Interpreters often use a method of conceptual reduction that reduces the mythological and ecological associations of the image of God as Rock.

Nevertheless, some of the subversive potential of God as Rock is evident in a number of passages that identified God with Earth (Deut 32; Pss 78, 95), or

---

24. I would like to thank Norman Habel for his numerous contributions to the final form of this oracle.

humanity with Earth (Deut 32; Ps 92), or addressed Earth as a subject (Ps 19) capable of speaking (Ps 28) and resisting exploitation (Deut 32).

For centuries, Western culture has been imagining humanity as separate from and superior to Earth. This has deadly consequences for many species and, increasingly, for many human beings, too. God as Rock is a resource from the Hebrew Bible that represents a radical shift in perspective. It may help us to imagine a more liveable reality in which humanity is part of a sacred, interdependent and living Earth community made up of many diverse human and nonhuman subjects.

An Earthling's Lament: Hell on Earth

Alice M. Sinnott

Job in his first utterance, "Naked I came from my mother's womb, and naked shall I return there" (Job 1:21) asserts that he was born from mother Earth's womb, that he will "return there" to mother Earth at the end of his life, that he began life in a naked state like other Earth creatures, and that Earth is the location and source of all births and deaths.[1] With this threefold declaration, he identifies himself as a creature of Earth.

Although frequently interpreted as a claim by Job that he was born of woman in the manner of all human beings, Job's claim that he will "return there" indicates that he is speaking of Earth as "my mother's womb," as his mother. Job believes that at the end of his life he will return "there," that is, to Earth.

In his first speech to his visitors, Job returns to the notion of "there" to refer to mother Earth (Job 3:13) as his tomb, as a place of rest to which he longs to escape. Habel notes, "'There' is an obvious euphemism for the tomb or land of the dead in Job 3:17. Job cries out that 'there' is where the 'wicked cease raging' (Job 3:17), 'there both small and great are together' (Job 3:19)."[2]

As he expands on his identity as an Earth creature, and on his wish to return to mother Earth, Job envisages himself "lying in repose, asleep and at rest with kings and counselors of the Earth" (3:13–14), where "small and great alike are there and the slave is free of his master" (3:19b). In this instance, Job's desire to be at rest in mother Earth is strongly anthropocentric[3]—Earth is a resting place where he will be with other humans, and freed from the evils of the human condition: with kings and counselors, and free from the wicked, inequality, and suffering. Job's lamenting of his birth (3:1, 11, 12, 16, 20, 23) suggests that he

---

1. Job's reference to his nakedness echoes Gen 2:25, 3:7 and the notion common in the ancient world that naked or unclothed human beings were akin to the animals.

2. Norman C. Habel, "Earth First: Inverse Cosmology in Job," in *The Earth Story in Wisdom Traditions* (ed. Norman C. Habel and Shirley Wurst; The Earth Bible 3; Sheffield: Sheffield Academic Press, 2001), 66.

3. In this chapter, I use "anthropocentric" to denote interpretations and understandings that regard human beings, human values, and human experience as central or primary.

favors Earth as the mother and home of the dead rather than Earth as the mother and home of life. This is in sharp contrast to his references to light and day, darkness and night (3:3–10), which evoke Gen 1:3–5 where the creation of light and darkness is the prelude to the birth of Earth and the advent of Earth's fertility and life-giving abundance.

His depiction of himself as a creature of Earth, facing life as an Earthling whom "God has fenced in" (3:23, cf. 1:10) devalues Earth as a prison in which he is trapped. While his references to light and darkness and all they imply suggest that Job recognizes Earth as life-giving, he ignores, or cannot hear, the voice of Earth offering healing.

1. AN ECOLOGICAL APPROACH

My aim in this chapter is to use a contemporary ecological approach, which comprises a hermeneutics of suspicion, identification, and retrieval, to hear the voice of Earth in the book of Job. I am reading as an Earth creature: as a member of Earth community, in solidarity with Earth. I am reading from the standpoint that the text is likely to be inherently anthropocentric, valuing human concerns over those of Earth and other Earth creatures. While acknowledging my kinship with Job as an Earthling, I also seek to recognize Earth's voice and highlight some underlying assumptions about Earth and Earth community in the text of Job 7.

2. LIFE ON EARTH: PART ONE (JOB 7:1–8)

While he wishes that death would enable him to be "in Earth," as a child of Earth Job has to accept life "on Earth" (7:1b). He likens the lot of human beings to the futile toil demanded of hired laborers and slaves who never enjoy the fruits of their labors (7:3), who endure emptiness and misery, and, like slaves (שכיר), cannot escape their lot. Should Earth speak here she, too, could complain that her life-giving gifts are rendered futile when she is exploited and suffers at the hands of her children. The chiastic arrangement of Job 7:2–3 (2a parallels 3b; 2b parallels 3a), while ostensibly speaking of slaves and bonded workers who receive no return for their labor, by implication echoes the lost voice of an enslaved Earth who longs for shade, for relief from the burning heat and scorching sun, for fallow time to recover her fruitfulness, for water to relieve the drought that renders her soil barren.

Job's railing against his restlessness (נדדים) and his nights of toil (עמל) highlights the anthropocentric concerns of the text and Job's failure to recognize his kinship with Earth. From a human perspective he describes in horrific detail the visible symptoms of his physical condition: "worms, dust, wind;" and an endless cycle of sores, followed by apparent healing, followed by fresh outbreaks of the same condition (7:4–5). Job complains that "maggots and clods of Earth"—Earth elements associated with healing—cover his flesh. He denies or fails to notice that Earth, the bearer of sickness, misery, and hard labor, is also the bearer of life, healing, and cooling winds. Job is an Earth creature; he is one with worms, dust, and wind. His anthropocentric concerns with his own misery lead him to reject Earth as healer and comforter. He even appears to reject his earlier desire to return to mother Earth (3:17). From a human perspective, Earth's healing "worms, dust, and wind"—though integral components of Earth's cycle of fruitfulness—are more often harbingers of death and disintegration.

The perspectives of Earth and nonhuman Earth creatures do not enter into Job's considerations; his own disintegration and death are uppermost in his mind. Previously he wished for death (Job 3:21–23, 4:8–9, 11). Now he appears shocked by what he deems as the brevity of his life. This inexplicable change of attitude emerges in his personalized references to "my days" rather than the days allotted to Earth creatures generally. His concern about the fleeting nature of life does not include any concern for Earth or other creatures.[4]

Invoking a skillful craft image associated with human activity, he compares the swiftness of his life to the speed of the weaving shuttle. While translators usually take באפס תקוה to mean "without hope," a different translation is possible if we read תקוה as "thread" ("when the thread runs out"), which would continue the weaving imagery.[5] Job sees his life as reaching its end in the same way as a piece of woven fabric: when the weavers decide that the piece is complete, they cut the last thread or strand and free it from the loom.[6] This image sustains the view that Job's fourfold lament about the brevity of his life (7:7–8) is without a thought for the brevity of the lives of other Earth creatures. The Earthling Job laments "remember that my life is but a breath (רוח) . . . I shall never again see happiness," highlighting in a particularly poignant way his view of the brevity and fragility of his life. He does not draw any parallels with the unpredictability, brevity, and suffering of the lives of other Earth creatures. Job's triumphant assertion in the last section of the lament, "the eye that beholds me will see me no more; while your eyes are upon me I shall be gone" (7:8), is restated in verses 20–21 where he speaks of the dust (עפר) as a place away from the scrutiny of the "watcher of humans" (verse 20). He seems to relish the idea of escaping from God's sight, "You will seek me but I shall not be" (verse 21). Job's claim that God is so absorbed in spying on humans suggests an intensely anthropocentric view here.

---

4. Job uses many images to portray the speed of life's progress: cloud (7:9), wind or breath (7:7, 16), a shadow (8:9), a runner (9:25), reed boats, an eagle (9:26), a flower (14:2), a dream (20:8).

5. David J.A. Clines. *Job 1–20* (WBC 17; Dallas: Word Books, 1989), 186.

6. This image also appears in Isa 38:12: "You have folded up my life like a weaver who severs the last thread."

3. Life on Earth: Part Two (Job 7:9–16)

Job's second lament (7:9) begins "As the cloud fades and vanishes (כלה), so those who go down to Sheol do not come up." He notes the ephemeral nature of clouds and compares his own life to that of a cloud. This echoes Job 3:11–19 where he wishes he had not survived his birth but had returned "there" so he could be "lying in repose, asleep, and at rest" (3:13–17) in mother Earth. For Job in his second lament, Earth is again a place of rest or death and invisibility as he anticipates going down to Sheol.

In several texts, Job views Sheol, the abode of the dead (3:13–15, 11:8, 14:13,17:13, 16, 21:13, 24:19, 26:6), as a place of rest where all humans are equal. While death will entail the vanishing of his life (כלה) and the ending of all that is familiar—"his place knows him no longer" (7:10)—he does not see death as violent or painful.[7] Job assumes that God is not present in Sheol but as he does not regard the presence of God as unambiguously desirable, the notion that God will not find him in Sheol suggests freedom from surveillance and suffering.

Oddly, Job follows this apparently soothing reflection on death with bitter complaints expressed in a series of ironic rhetorical questions. "Am I the Sea or the Dragon that you muzzle me?" He wonders if God is treating him as if he were one of God's monstrous enemies with whom God engaged in primordial battles.[8] Casting himself as a creature of fleeting days, he sets up an ironic parallel (7:12) with the mythic opponents of God and implies a comparison between the perpetual captivity of the sea monster and Job's own incessant suffering as a creature trapped on Earth.[9] Job's identification of himself with the Sea and the Dragon, two dimensions of Earth usually perceived as negative, is ironic; Job's claim that God is treating him as one of God's monster enemies, is incongruous, since he considers himself as a "passing wind" (verse 7), a "cloud" (verse 9), or "mere breath" (verse 16). The image of the caged, imprisoned Sea (*Yam*) cannot but evoke the sympathy of the reader, as does the miserable Job.

His use of Earth likewise evokes our sympathy: "days" on Earth being but הבל, an illusion, or insubstantial breath of wind. If Earth's days are but a breath, Earth creatures are by analogy insubstantial and their lives fleeting.

---

7. The phrase is also used as an image for the brevity of human life in Ps 103:16.

8. While this image could have mythic allusions, in the book of Job this image seems more likely to represent Job's interpretation of his own situation (cf. Ps 74:13; Isa 27:1, 51:9). In the Enuma Elish, Marduk posts a guard or sentry to keep the waters of the sky in place. See Enuma Elish 4.139–40 (*ANET*, 67). Also D. A. Diewert, "Job 7:12: Yam, Tannin and the Surveillance of Job," *JBL* 106 (1987): 203–15.

9. Earlier commentators identified the mythical figures, Sea (Yam) and Dragon (Tannin) with Tiamat, the sea monster of Babylonian myth. More recently, the allusion is believed to be to a West Semitic cycle of myths telling how the Ugaritic high god Baal destroyed Yam the sea god.

Job claims God's surveillance, frightening nightmares and terrifying visions (7:12–14), and an inability to sleep or die as his lot. Earth would surely acknowledge that other Earth creatures suffer similar experiences. Does Job perhaps recognize something of this as his lament mocks a traditional psalm motif that portrays God as the comforter who hears and responds to grieving sufferers by bringing consolation and relief? Job's terrifying dreams and nightmares—forms of forced seeing experienced by humans—supplant the "comfort" (נחמל) he craves "till I prefer . . . death to my wasted frame" (7.15). Job's closing exclamation "let me alone!" (7:16) signals the omega point of Job's hostile portrayal of his life on Earth.

According to tradition, suppliants beseeched God to "see" (ראה) them (Pss 25:19, 59:4); "consider" (נבט) them (Pss 13:3, 80:14); "not to hide" (סתר פנים) from them (Pss 27:9, 69:17), whereas Job asks how long it will be before God looks away (שעה) from him.[10] By demanding that God withdraw God's sustaining power and presence, Job, the Earthling, asks for non-existence. He chooses (בחר) death in preference to weakness and frailty, distress of spirit (רוח), and bitterness of soul, the results of what Job perceives to be divine aggression (7:15–16; cf. 10:20). As an Earth creature, Job believes he cannot contend with the power God unleashed against him. He speaks ironically; he does not attempt to use conventionally devout language or praise to address the deity. Job once more looks to mother Earth not as the source of new life or birth but as his resting place in death.

Perhaps this dubious acknowledgment of Earth and Earth's capacity to provide him with rest is the seed that eventually takes root in Job and enables him to recognize his true place among Earth's creatures: "Therefore I sink (מאס) into the abyss, and I grieve over dry earth and ashes" (Job 42:6). However, at this point Earth's voice is lost and Earth and Earth creatures are silent as Job parodies the hierarchical structure of Ps 8, which lauds the position of human beings in relation to other Earth creatures.

4. LIFE ON EARTH: PART THREE (JOB 7:17–21)

Job begins his parody by satirizing Ps 8:4:

Job 7:17–18	Ps 8:4
What are human beings, that you make so much (גדל) of them,	What are human beings that you are mindful (זכר) of them,
that you set (שית) your heart (לבב) on them?	mortals that you care (פקד) for them?
visit (פקד) them every morning,	
test (בחן) them every moment?	

---

10. A similar plea appears in Job 10:20 and 14:6 (cf. Ps 39:13).

Psalm 8 praises God as Creator and claims that human beings—so insignificant when considered in relation to the whole universe—receive authority and power over the Earth and Earth creatures. Even the creatures of the deep are under human control. Why human beings, born of Earth, should receive a position of control and authority over the Earth is not explained. "What are human beings?" is the preface to Job's claim that, contrary to the statement in Ps 8 about the exalted position of humans, human beings are subjected to God's merciless scrutiny and perpetual examination—presented as "make so much of . . . set your heart on . . . visit . . . test." The silent moon and the stars may ask whether the psalmist's presentation of the insignificance of human beings vis-à-vis the moon and the stars serves as a foil for grateful recognition that God gave human beings authority over Earth and Earth creatures.

The phrases "make so much of . . . set your heart on . . . visit . . . test" (Job 7:17–18) echo the description of exaltation in Ps 8:5–6, but Job's ironic intent is unmistakeable as he questions God's sense of proportion. Where the psalmist marvels at God's care and mindfulness of human beings, Job reinterprets such divine attentiveness as unwelcome scrutiny (7:17b). Hebrew permits a clever word play here: the psalmist's "care for" (פקד) can also mean "inspect/call to account/muster" (Ps 8:5). Job 7:17–18 evokes the sentiments of the psalmist with ironic intent: the verb "raise up/cause to grow/give status" suggests God's strict accounting conveyed here by the verb "test." In this context, the term no longer refers to the status of human beings in God's eyes; rather it paints an image of an overseeing, demanding deity. Job perceives God's attention as testing. Thus, Job's irony acquires an edge that effectively subverts the psalmist's praise. Job begs God to desist from harassing him (7:19) and allow him to swallow his spittle in private.

While the psalm lauds God's exaltation of humankind and God's "mindfulness" of humans as inexplicable partiality, Job portrays God's "mindfulness" as incomprehensible interference and lack of prescience. He regards God's unsleeping care as spying and a source of harm, while the psalmist acclaims God's "visiting" as a sign of loving care. In many biblical texts, morning is precious as a time of God's deliverance (Pss 5:3, 45:5, 90:14, 143:8; Isa 33:2; Lam 3:23; Zeph 3:5); Job knows morning as a time of God's wrathful visitations. He resents such "testing" as he believes his sufferings indicate some indefensible failure in God's examination of him.

Earth's voice is striking in Job 7:16–19 where Job returns to the paradoxes of Earth-time first introduced in 7:1–3. As a human being (אנוש; Job 7:1, 17, 19) Job's Earth days are as transient as a breath of air, yet he would not choose to live forever (verse 16) because of God's unrelenting scrutiny—which he describes in decreasing units of Earth-time: "every morning . . . every moment" (verse 18).

When Job speaks of a period of relief he does so in terms of time as measured by an Earthling body: "long enough to swallow my spittle" (verse 19b). This image, like those of dreams, visions, and nightmares, suggests the invasive quality of divine scrutiny, which interferes with every minute aspect of an Earthling's life, even swallowing. Earth might contest the devaluing of Earth and Earth creatures in the exaltation of human beings and Job's obsessive belief that God focuses solely on human beings. Indisputably, Earth could ask why God should be concerned primarily with humans, by appointing them rulers as in Ps 8, thus oppressing the Earth and other Earth creatures; or by enslaving them and watching them incessantly as in Job 7, thus ignoring and devaluing Earth and Earth creatures. Earth might even consider such a God anthropocentric, pitiless, and ruthless.

Such a view seems possible if we consider the puzzling challenge Job next offers God: "If I have sinned, what have I done to you, watcher of humanity?" Although the Hebrew text has no word for "if," translators usually supply it. Even without "if," this statement poses a problem. As the author characterizes Job as a "just man" (1:1), we cannot question Job's righteousness. In addition, God declares that Job is "blameless and upright" (1:8, 2:3) and the narrator states that "Job did not sin with his lips" (2:10). Job also asserts that he has "not denied the words of the Holy One" (6:10). Neither is Job arguing that the sins of human beings are so trivial as to be beneath God's consideration.

Job might be arguing that, as his days are now so few, for God to seek retribution at this time is ridiculous—even if he had sinned; therefore, God should waive retribution. Why, Job wonders, does God continue to harass one human being who is dying anyway? Why has Job, whose days are a mere breath, become a target for God's wrath? Is God's fixation on Job out of proportion to Job's significance?

Job's use of the verb "keep watch" (נצר) once again gives an ironic twist to traditional language about God. Usually God's protection of the righteous and of all Earth creatures is apparent in God's "watching" (Pss 12:7, 31:23). Instead, Job characterizes God as a scrutinizer of humans (Job 7:12).

Some commentators have argued—incorrectly I believe—that Job admits guilt when he asks "Why do you not pardon my transgression and forgive my iniquity?" If Job believes he has sinned, surely he would have sought forgiveness sooner rather than begging for death and lamenting God's unjustified assaults against him. Anyone favoring the notion that Job acknowledges having sinned must explain why Job continues to assert that God must have something against him because of the suffering he is enduring.

It seems more in keeping with the context of the narrative that, in a desperate attempt to alleviate his suffering for the few days remaining to him, Job asks God to overlook and "lift up" a weak dying Earth creature. Job 7:20–21 surely go together with "if I have sinned," which sustains his plea for toleration as the verbs נשא ("lift up/tolerate"), עבר ("cause to pass away/overlook") suggest. Paramount for Job at this point is a reprieve from suffering and all the accompanying humiliations until death brings him to rest on the dust, which presumably means that he returns to dust in mother Earth. Soon (עתה), Job expects he will be in or on the dust, thus returning to the notion of Earth as resting place and receiver of the dead. Earth could challenge this claim by proclaiming that Earth is life-giver and sustainer of all living creatures.

Job's wish to "return to the dust" serves a twofold purpose: he reminds the audience of his desire to "return to the womb" and to the womb of mother Earth (1:21), and be "in Earth" when he lies in the dust (3:21). Interestingly, Job regards the dust (עפר) as a place where he can escape the scrutiny of the "watcher of humans" (7:20).

That Job is here using parody rather than prayer is evident in the epithet "watcher of humans," which parodies the sentiment commonly expressed in the psalms that address God as protector (Pss 12:8, 32:7, 40:12, 140:2, 5) and ignores any claims that Earth and Earth creatures might make that they, too, are "watched" by God. The strident theme of divine surveillance endows this title with a menacing tone. Certain that if God does not act soon it will be too late, Job ends his speech on what could be interpreted as a pleading note not unlike the ending of Ps 39:13: "Turn your gaze away from me, that I may smile again, before I depart and am no more." More likely this is a victory shout: "in Sheol I shall be out of your sight!" (cf. 7:8). Given what has gone before, it seems likely that Job is imitating the words of a plea but subverting their meaning.

One could also take the first two words as introducing a consequence "for then." Perhaps Job is suggesting that should God "lift him up," he might die, so that when God searches for him, Job will be beyond God's surveillance: he will no longer be an Earth creature but will be "in Earth," and beyond God's scrutiny. Such a conclusion would be apposite for Job's anti-psalm.

Rhetorically, Job's wordplay and irony provide the audience with persuasive and compelling reasons to agree with him and suspect some absurdity in the notion that the God of all creation would be so concerned with some possible transgression on Job's part. This dilemma provides a compelling reason for readers to follow the Joban arguments in the hope of discovering the outcome of Job's challenge.

5. CONCLUSION

The voice that speaks most clearly and at times stridently in Job 7 is that of Job the Earthling who intermittently—and at times by implication—identifies with Earth and Earth creatures, even the monsters. Job likens the lives of Earthlings—and by association the lives of all Earth creatures—to a kind of bondage or imprisonment in which the only escape is a return to the dust from which they came, that is, mother Earth. Although Job regards Earth as the dust or resting place for his inanimate remains, paradoxically he voices an Earth plea when he asks God to "remember" (זכר) that his life is but "breath" (7:7). He thus evokes two enigmatic constants in the Hebrew tradition: the brevity of all forms of Earth life (Pss 39:6, 12, 62:10, 78:39, 94:11, 103:14–18, 144:3–4; Qoh 2:1, 14–15); the wonder that Earth and Earth creatures are animated by the God-given breath of life, as suggested evocatively in the description of dying in Qoh 12:7: "the breath returns to God who gave it." Earth would surely agree but might contest the notion that a short life span is necessarily of little worth. Earth silently sustains, and thereby equally values, all life regardless of its duration.

Job's wish for death is at once a protest, a sardonic shout of triumph, and a lament—his life is about to end, but death will bring escape from the ever-watching eye of God. Yet he laments his parlous state. His reprise of the notion of life as "breath" (7:16) evokes Qoheleth (3:19, 11:5, 12:7), whose recurring theme *hebel* (הבל) designates, on the one hand, the futility and absurdity of human endeavors and wishes, and on the other hand, the fleeting and transitory nature of human life and indeed all life forms. Death is the definitive and irreversible end of all life.

In contrast to Job's expressed wish to "be in Earth," Qoheleth exhorts his audience to cherish the life they have as a gift of God and to live life to the full every day. Job, however, welcomes death as his escape from the "watcher of humans."

For the most part, Earth is silent in Job 7; nevertheless, Earth is an abiding presence throughout the text. While the audible voice of the Earthling Job spells out many disturbing aspects of his inexplicable suffering, by association, the questions he raises are also questions that address the plight of Earth and Earth creatures. Job's laments over his life as an Earthling, while bearing the hallmarks of anthropocentrism, do challenge a tradition that lauded the notion of the superiority and authority of humans within creation. Job continues throughout his debates with his visitors to expand on his plight by moving away from his focus on anthropocentric concerns to describe God's cruel treatment of Earth and Earth creatures. Job 12:7–15 commands Job's audience to "ask the beasts and let one of them teach you, also the birds of the air . . . or speak to the Earth and let it teach you and let the fish of the sea declare to you . . . who does not know that the hand of the Lord has done this." Job goes on to detail one Earth catastrophe after another.[11]

A clear pattern emerges in this reading of Job 7. Prior to chapter 7, Job speaks optimistically of mother Earth and the world of mother Earth to which he will return. Chapter 7 portrays life on that same Earth as tormented and nightmarish under the pitiless eye of God the spy. Job uses the images air/breath, maggots, and clods of Earth—symbols and healing elements of Earth—as repulsive and detrimental to life and fails to acknowledge their healing qualities. Death is equated with Sheol and being in the dust of Earth.

Unexpectedly, thoughts about death in mother Earth occasion a lament about the brevity and unpredictability of life. This may be strategic—a sort of

---

11. See A. M. Sinnott, "Job 12: Cosmic Devastation and Social Turmoil," in Habel and Wurst, *The Earth Story in Wisdom Traditions*, 78–91.

backing down from his earlier bravado about his wish to die. However, death in the dust of mother Earth is still preferable to life on Earth under the cruel spying eye of God. The voice of mother Earth is suppressed because of Job's self-obsession, though Job uses Earth as a compelling symbol to illustrate God's injustice towards creation. As a reader sensitive to Earth, I hear the suppressed voice of Earth singing a song of consolation:

MOTHER EARTH'S SONG OF CONSOLATION FOR JOB

> Job, my Earthling, my delight,
> in the fullness of time
> you will return to my womb in death.
> Your cruel suffering and your hounding
> under the inescapable eye of God
> is ever-present to me.
>
> Job, my Earthling, life is for living,
> for celebrating the skies, the clouds,
> the clods, and dirt, and wild sea monsters
> that YHWH forms and delights in every day.
> Rejoice in life-giving air, wild wind, breath of YHWH—
> a mystery surpassing your wretched state!
> Cease being God's victim—you are my cherished child!

The Spirit of Wisdom in All Things: The Mutuality of Earth and Humankind

Marie Turner

1. Introduction: the Promise

In Wis 12:1, the sage claims that God's immortal Spirit is present in all things. The sage's statement encourages us to expect a consistent theology of God's presence that encompasses the whole of creation. In this anticipated theology, the ecological reader is attentive to the voice of Earth as Earth seeks recognition as a bearer of the divine presence, that is, the Spirit of Wisdom. The author raises our expectations of Earth in solidarity with human creation as Wisdom maintains her presence in τα παντα, all things.

Yet a careful examination of the text of the Wisdom of Solomon confirms a suspicion that the sage's focus on nonhuman creation is not consistent throughout the book. This chapter argues that in spite of its radical claim of the presence of God's Spirit in the whole of creation, the Wisdom of Solomon first acknowledges and then marginalizes nonhuman creation in favor of human creation.

In the first two chapters of the book, the author sets the scene for an inclusive theology. He[1] claims that God created everything for existence but that the ungodly are responsible for the death of creation. Cognizant of the fleeting nature of human and nonhuman life, the ungodly make a speech in Wis 2:1–20 that indicates their decision to exploit nonhuman and human creation and bring death to the cosmos by inviting an envious devil on to Earth. As they ponder the brevity and fragility of life, they chronologically prioritize exploitation of nonhuman creation. Yet at the end of the second chapter (Wis 2:23–24) nonhuman creation drops out of view: human creation and its promised immortality through Wisdom dominates the remainder of the book.

This marginalization of nonhuman creation is not total throughout the book. Several texts attest to the presence of God's Spirit in all things. Integral to this

---

1. I am presuming male authorship since this was the more likely sex of a sage in an Alexandrian wisdom school.

presence is the role of Wisdom; the sage refers to Wisdom when he claims, in 12:1, that God's immortal Spirit is in all things.

In the hymn of praise to Wisdom in Wis 6:12–9:18, a significant aspect of her role is as the cause and fashioner of all things. Within these chapters, however, an anthropocentrism overshadows her and she is transformed from an active and free cosmic agent whose domain is the whole of creation to a bride sitting waiting for the return of the monarch at the end of his day's work. In this eloquent poem that offers so much promise, Wisdom's relationship with the whole cosmos is narrowed and Wisdom becomes an object to be possessed by humankind, rather than the free and gracious presence of God in all creation.

This introduction is intended to alert the reader that, in spite of the book's radical claim of the intrinsic worth of Earth, in the final analysis the sage betrays an anthropocentric mindset. His vision of a cosmos in which all things are created for existence and share in the immortal Spirit of God, gives way to a curtailed vision of humankind alone sharing God's immortal Spirit. Likewise, his perception of the universal presence of God gives way to a narrowed vision. In this vision, the Spirit of Wisdom is relegated to a subordinate role: King Solomon and God cooperate to curtail Wisdom as she moves freely in a loving relationship with all creation.

2. Suspicion: Narrowing the Vision of Creation

The expression, τα παντα, "all things," is first used in Wis 1:7 where the sage says that "the Spirit of the Lord has filled the world and that which holds all things together knows what is said." The neuter-gender term τα παντα "all things" includes nonhuman creation. The reader knows from the parallelism in Wis 1:4–5 that Wisdom, Sophia, and the Spirit are identified with each other:

[4]Wisdom will not enter a deceitful soul	ὅτι εἰς κακότεχνον ψυχὴν
or dwell in a body enslaved to sin	οὐκ εἰσελεύσεται σοφία οὐδὲ
for a holy and disciplined Spirit will flee from deceit	κατοικήσει ἐν σώματι κατάχρεῳ ἁμαρτίας
	ἅγιον γὰρ πνεῦμα παιδείας
	φεύξεται δόλον καὶ
[5]and will leave foolish thoughts behind	ἀπαναστήσεται ἀπὸ λογισμῶν
	ἀσυνέτων καὶ ἐλεγχθήσεται
and will be ashamed at the approach of unrighteousness.	ἐπελθούσης ἀδικίας

By force of parallelism Sophia is here equated with Spirit. The identification is spelled out more clearly in Wis 1:6:

⁶for Wisdom is a kindly spirit
but will not free blasphemers from
   the guilt of their words
because God is witness of their
   inmost feelings,
and a true observer of their hearts
and a hearer of their tongues.
	Φιλάνθρωπον γὰρ πνεῦμα σοφία
	καὶ οὐκ ἀθῳώσει βλάσφημον ἀπὸ
	χειλέων αὐτοῦ ὅτι τῶν νεφρῶν
	αὐτοῦ μάρτυς ὁ θεὸς καὶ τῆς
	καρδίας αὐτοῦ ἐπίσκοπος ἀληθὴς
	καὶ τῆς γλώσσης ἀκουστής

In Wis 1:7 the spirit is the Spirit of the Lord:

⁷Because the Spirit of the Lord has
   filled the world
And that which holds all things
   together knows what is said.
	ὅτι πνεῦμα κυρίου πεπλήρωκεν
	τὴν οἰκουμένην καὶ τὸ συνέχον τὰ
	πάντα γνῶσιν ἔχει φωνῆς

The movement is thus from Wisdom to Spirit; then to Wisdom as a kindly spirit; and then to the Spirit of the Lord. Accepting the association of Wisdom and the Spirit, Pneuma, the Pneuma/Wisdom has filled the world. Wisdom of Solomon 1:7 is ambiguous because it is not clear what "holds everything together." The formulaic phrase, "holds all things together," expresses a concept, possibly from Stoicism,[2] of a divine bond that unifies the world. The sage, in using the person of divine Wisdom, unites the Hellenistic intellectual tradition of a unified cosmos with the biblical faith in the Spirit of God active in the world. In the very first chapter of the book, therefore, the sage affirms that all creation is the locus of God's presence. According to Wis 1:13–14, God's creative act is directed towards life for all creation—nonhuman and human:

¹³God did not make death and does
   not delight in the death of the
   living
but created all things so that they
   might exist;
¹⁴the generative forces of the world
   are wholesome, and there is no
   destructive poison in them,
and the dominion of Hades is not
   on Earth.
	ὅτι ὁ θεὸς θάνατον οὐκ ἐποίησεν
	οὐδὲ τέρπεται ἐπ' ἀπωλείᾳ ζώντων
	ἔκτισεν γὰρ εἰς τὸ εἶναι τὰ πάντα
	καὶ σωτήριοι αἱ γενέσεις τοῦ
	κόσμου καὶ οὐκ ἔστιν ἐν αὐταῖς
	φάρμακον ὀλέθρου οὔτε ᾅδου
	βασίλειον ἐπὶ γῆς

---

2. Ernest G. Clarke, *The Wisdom of Solomon* (Cambridge: Cambridge University Press, 1973), 18.

Scholars debate whether these lines refer to physical or spiritual death.[3] At least on one level the sage is referring to physical death, because nonhuman creation is clearly included. According to these lines, Hades, a metonym for death, is an alien presence on Earth. As the ultimate "other" in regards to creation, death has no place in the sage's theology of the creator. As the sage claims in Wis 2:22–24:

[22][the ungodly] did not know the mysteries of God, nor hoped for the wages of holiness, nor discerned the prize for blameless souls;	καὶ [ἀσεβεῖς] οὐκ ἔγνωσαν μυστήρια θεοῦ οὐδὲ μισθὸν ἤλπισαν ὁσιότητος οὐδὲ ἔκριναν γέρας ψυχῶν ἀμώμων
[23]for God created us for incorruption, and made us in the image of God's own eternity,	ὅτι ὁ θεὸς ἔκτισεν τὸν ἄνθρωπον ἐπ' ἀφθαρσίᾳ καὶ εἰκόνα τῆς ἰδίας ἀϊδιότητος ἐποίησεν αὐτόν
[24]but through the devil's envy death entered the world, and those who belong to his company experience it.	φθόνῳ δὲ διαβόλου θάνατος εἰσῆλθεν εἰς τὸν κόσμον πειράζουσιν δὲ αὐτὸν οἱ τῆς ἐκείνου μερίδος ὄντες

Here the sage has shifted nonhuman creation to the margins in his use of the *imago aeternitatis* (the image of God's eternity) to apply only to humankind, whereas a few verses earlier he had spoken of "all things" being created for existence. In so doing, he has also narrowed the concept of the term "mysteries of God" (translated as the "secret purposes of God" in the NRSV) to apply to humankind alone.

Celia Deutsch points out that at Qumran the term "mystery" referred to the principle of order behind the phenomena of weather and heavenly bodies, to the creation of humankind, and to principles of poetry and music. Mystery is used at Qumran in 1QH1 to refer to the hidden order behind certain features of the created world. These mysteries are the work of God's Wisdom (1QH1:7, 14, 19) and are understood through insight.[4] In Wis 2:23 the sage's understanding of "mysteries" is clearly stated: "the creation of humankind into incorruption." "Mysteries" has therefore been narrowed to apply only to the creation of human beings. There

---

3. For a discussion of this topic, see in particular Michael Kolarcik, *The Ambiguity of Death in the Book of Wisdom 1–6: A Study of Literary Structure and Interpretation* (Rome: Editrice Pontificio Istituto Biblico, 1991).

4. Celia Deutsch, *Hidden Wisdom and the Easy Yoke: Wisdom, Torah and Discipleship in Matthew 11:25–30* (JSNTSup 18; ed. D. Hill; Sheffield: JSOT Press, 1987), 76.

is thus an inherent anthropocentrism in the sage's argument, since the "mysteries of creation" does not appear to refer to nonhuman creation.

2. Suspicion: Narrowing the Vision of Wisdom

A reading of the texts dealing with nonhuman creation reveals that God's presence is in all creation, human and nonhuman. These texts attest to a graced creation that includes the nonhuman. God's Spirit of Wisdom actively and pervasively loves all creation, human and nonhuman. Chapters 6:12–9:18 clearly assert the relationship between Wisdom, the immortal Spirit of God, and nonhuman creation. The narrator, King Solomon, says in the hymn of praise to Wisdom (Wis 7:17–22):

[17]For it is God who gave me unerring knowledge of what exists, to know the structure of the world and the activity of the elements; [18]the beginning and end and middle of times, the alternations of the solstices and the changes of the seasons, [19]the cycles of the year and the constellations of the stars,	αὐτὸς γάρ μοι ἔδωκεν τῶν ὄντων γνῶσιν ἀψευδῆ εἰδέναι σύστασιν κόσμου καὶ ἀνέργειαν στοιχείων ἀρχὴν καὶ τέλος καὶ μεσότητα χρόνων τροπῶν ἀλλαγὰς καὶ μεταβολὰς καιρῶν ἐνιαυτοῦ κύκλους καὶ ἄστρων θέσεις
[20]the natures of animals and the tempers of wild animals, the powers of spirits and the thoughts of human beings, the varieties of plants and the virtues of roots; [21]I learned both what is secret and what is manifest,	φύσεις ζῴων καὶ θυνοὺς θηρίων πνευμάτων βίας καὶ διαλογισμοὺς ἀνθρώπων διαφορὰς φυτῶν καὶ δυνάμεις ῥιζῶν ὅσα τέ ἐστιν κρυπτὰ καὶ ἐνφανῆ ἔγνων
[22]for wisdom, the fashioner of all things, taught me.	ἡ γὰρ πάντων τεχνῖτις ἐδίδαξέν με σοφία

In Lester Grabbe's summation, these verses contain a list of characteristics of the natural world, and references to plants and animals and the workings of the cosmos.[5] The final line, "for wisdom, the fashioner of all things, (τὰ πάντα), taught me," reaffirms the mutuality of human and nonhuman creation. Wisdom

---

5. Lester L. Grabbe, *Wisdom of Solomon* (Sheffield: Sheffield Academic Press, 1997), 65.

is the creative agent responsible for the nature of all things in the cosmos, and the one who educates humankind about the cosmos. She is creator and sustainer of all things, human and nonhuman. Her positive relationship with nonhuman creation is expressed in Wis 7:24, 27 and in 8:1, 4–5 where Solomon says:

7:24Because of her pureness she pervades and penetrates all things . . . 27and while remaining in herself, she renews all things.	δὲ καὶ χωρεῖ διὰ πάντων διὰ τὴν καθαρότητα . . . μία δὲ οὖσα πάντα δύναται καὶ νένουσα ἐν αὐτῇ τὰ πάντα καινίζει
8:1She reaches mightily from one end of the earth to the other, And she orders all things well . . .	διατένει δὲ ἀπὸ πέρατος ἐπὶ πέρας ευρώστως καὶ διοικεῖ τὰ πάντα χρηστῶς . . .
4For she is an initiate in the knowledge of God and an associate in God's works . . .	μύστις γάρ ἐστιν τῆς τοῦ θεοῦ ἐπιστήμης καὶ αἱρετὶς τῶν ἔργων αὐτοῦ . . .
5what is richer than Wisdom, the active cause of all things?	τί σοφίας πλουσιώτερον τῆς τὰ πάντα ἐργαζονένης

In Wis 9:1–2 Solomon addresses God as the God of the ancestors and the Lord of mercy,

1who have made all things by your word, 2And by your Wisdom have formed humankind	ὁ ποιήσας τὰ πάντα ἐν λόγῳ σου καὶ τῇ σοφίᾳ σου κατασκευάσας ἄνθρωπον

According to this poetic parallelism, God makes things through the word (*logos*) and has formed humankind through Wisdom. The purpose and effect of the synonymous parallelism is not to differentiate between word and Wisdom or between humankind and "all things," but to associate them. Word and Wisdom and human and nonhuman creation are interconnected. Further, it is out of love that this interconnectedness is established (Wis 11:24–26, 12:1):

11:24For you love all things that exist, and detest none of the things that you have made, for you would not have made anything if you had hated it.	ἀγαπᾷς γὰρ τὰ ὄντα πάντα καὶ οὐδὲν βδελύσσῃ ὧν ἐποίησας οὐδὲ γὰρ ἂν μισῶν τι κατεσκεύασας

11:25How would anything have endured if you had not willed it? Or how would anything not called forth by you have been preserved?	πῶς δὲ διέμεινεν ἄν τι εἰ μὴ σὺ ἠθέλησας ἢ τὸ μὴ κληθὲν ὑπὸ σοῦ διετηρήθη
26You spare all things, for they are yours, O Lord, you who love the living.	φέδῃ δὲ πάντων ὅτι σά ἐστιν δέσποτα φιλόψυχε
12:1For your immortal Spirit is in all things.	τὸ γὰρ ἄφθαρτόν σου πνεῦμά ἐστιν ἐν πᾶσιν

In spite of these verses establishing the relationship between Wisdom and all creation, when we look at 7:22–8:21, which falls within the hymn in praise of Wisdom in 6:12–9:18, we find a movement from Wisdom's freely given presence in τὰ πάντα to Solomon's pursuit and eventual possession of her.

The section begins by asserting Wisdom's radiance and includes Solomon's claim that she is easily found by those who love her. Wisdom takes the initiative in making herself known to those who desire her. She is found sitting at the gates, a stance that indicates her availability to the public (Wis 6:12–14). She seeks out those who are worthy of her, and she chooses graciously to appear to people and encounters them in their thoughts (6:16). She interacts with humankind, but her presence is freely given. In 6:22 Solomon embarks on an account of her course from the beginning of creation. His speech focuses on the necessity of being a wise ruler. He calls on God for help and the Spirit of Wisdom comes to him.

The sage begins Wis 7:22–8:21 with an affirmation of Wisdom's autonomous relationship with all things within Earth's boundaries. In 7:22 Solomon remarks that "Wisdom the fashioner of all things, taught me." There is a supporting statement in 8:1; Solomon says of Wisdom, "She reaches mightily from one end of the Earth to the other and she orders all things well." From 8:2–21, however, the reader can detect a narrowing from the self-directed activity of Wisdom to a Wisdom who is controlled by God at the request of the human being, Solomon. The scene is set in Wis 7:15–21 where it is God who guides Wisdom. In 8:2–21 the emphasis on Wisdom as a free subject who gives herself graciously recedes into the background; she becomes an object to be pursued and possessed:

8:2I loved her and sought her from my youth: I desired to take her for my bride, And became enamoured of her beauty.	ταύτην ἐφίλησα καὶ ἐξεζήσα ἐκ νεότητός μου καὶ ἐζήτησα νύμφην ἀγαγέσθαι ἐμαυτῷ καὶ ἐφαστὴς ἐγενόμην τοῦ κάλλους αὐτῆς
8:9Therefore I determined to take her to live with me, Knowing that she would give me good counsel	ἔκρινα τοίνυν ταύτην ἀγαγέσθαι πρὸς συμβίωσιν εἰδὼς ὅτι ἔσται μοι σύμβουλος ἀγαθῶν καὶ παραίνεσις φροντίδων καὶ λύπης

And encouragement in cares and
  grief .

8:16When I enter my house I shall   εἰσελθὼν εἰς τὸν οἶκόν μου
  find rest with her   προσαναπαύσομαι αὐτῇ οὐ γὰρ
For companionship with her has no   ἔχει πικρίαν ἡ συναναστροφὴ
  bitterness,   αὐτῆς οὐδὲ ὀδύνην ἡ συμβίωσις
And life with her has no pain but   αὐτῆς ἀλλὰ εὐφροσύνην καὶ
  gladness and joy.   χαράν

8:21But I perceived that I would not   γνοὺς δὲ ὅτι οὐ ἄλλως ἔσομαι
  possess Wisdom unless God   ἐγκρατής ἐὰν μὴ ὁ θεὸς δῷ καὶ
  gave her to me—   τοῦτο δ' ἦν φρονήσεως τὸ εἰδέναι
and it was a mark of insight to   τίνος ἡ χάρις ἐνέτυχον τῷ κυρίῳ
  know whose gift she was—   καὶ ἐδεήθην αὐτοῦ καὶ εἶπον ἐξ
so I appealed to the Lord and   ὅλης τῆς καρδίας μου
  implored him.

While Wisdom's gifts of good governance, courage in war, and immortality are
more than those of the average human wife, she has nevertheless been presented
here as the dutiful wife. She is waiting to fulfill Solomon's needs regardless of
how noble his needs are in relation to his righteous rule. She is a possession to
be gained by humankind. Her mobility throughout Earth where she renews all
things has been curtailed: she sits in Solomon's palace waiting for him to cease
from his kingly activity so that she can serve him as a wife.

4. The Interpreters: Acknowledging Mutuality

Three writers from three different periods of biblical studies illustrate that the
sage's insights on the mutuality of human and nonhuman creation have not gone
unremarked. Writing in 1901, Tennant recognizes a level of ambiguity in the
death associated with nonhuman creation. He points out that in Wis 1:14a τα
παντα is "at least as comprehensive as the world of animate beings and that εἶναι
in 1:14 is equivalent to the ζῆν of 1:13. Thus God's creation of all things "to be"
includes nonhuman creation.[6] Tennant goes on:

> It is by no means necessary to assume that the author of Wisdom, in such pas-
> sages as these, must needs have been confronted with all the consequences of his
> statement, or have been careful to clearly and accurately expound his thought,
> or even have been absolutely consistent with himself . . . all that the passage

---

6. F. R. Tennant, "The Teaching of Ecclesiasticus and Wisdom on Sin and Death," *JTS* 2
(1901): 219.

need be taken to mean is something such as this: just as God appointed to man [*sic*] a destiny of happy immortality and did not Himself [*sic*] ordain the eternal death by which that destiny is forfeited, so the world of lower created things was endowed with the power to perpetuate and maintain itself, each thing enjoying its natural span, without any inherent element of destruction to disturb the creator's original appointment. It would seem that any other explanation of this verse involves the necessity of charging Pseudo-Solomon with serious confusion and looseness of thought; a charge which has indeed been made by more than one commentator, but perhaps a little hastily.[7]

Yet Tennant undermines his own valuable insight regarding the claim that the sage makes in reference to the inclusion of nonhuman creation in God's plan of life for all things by remarking in a footnote,

> it is difficult to see how this verse could . . . be introduced otherwise than as an illustration of the general principle that the creation, as it left the hand of God, did not contain within itself the germ of its own destruction. The verse is valid as an illustration, and was hardly intended to be a complete analogy or a major premiss.[8]

In 1979 Yehoshua Amir's insights reflected a balanced view that acknowledges both human and nonhuman creation: "Every being in the created world is made for sustaining its vital power; but in a very special sense that is said of man [*sic*]."[9] The ungodly are said to be Thanatos'[10] portion, just as the people of God are said to be the Lord's portion (Deut 32:9). Indeed, Amir suggests that it is not only humankind that fits into this dualistic pattern, but the whole of creation. If humankind is said to be "of" the portion of Thanatos, he argues that it may be the world at large that is divided into this dualistic pattern. Although Amir's perception of the sage's dualism may be open to challenge, he is accurate understanding of the sage's theology of creation as holistic.

As a final example of interpreters who go some way towards retrieving the sage's inclusive vision, Barbara Green indicates an awareness of the sage's interest in the creation of all things for existence. She acknowledges the cosmos in Wis 11–19 in particular as a character in the book that actively assists the just and thwarts the ungodly.[11]

---

7. Tennant, "Ecclesiasticus and Wisdom," 219.

8. Tennant, "Ecclesiasticus and Wisdom," 219 n. 1.

9. Yehoshua Amir, "Figure of Death in the Book of Wisdom," *JJS* 30 (1979): 154–78.

10. That is, Death. I use the Greek term *Thanatos* in the manner of a proper name to remind the reader that Death was often personified, sometimes as a beautiful young man.

11. Barbara Green, "The Wisdom of Solomon and the Solomon of Wisdom: Tradition's Transpositions and Human Transformation," *Horizons* 30 (2003): 41–66, 55.

5. Conclusion: Anthropocentric Blindness and Retrieving the Insights

These interpreters are examples of those who acknowledge the sage's concern with nonhuman creation. In each case, however, their major emphasis falls on human creation. This is not the fault of the interpreters—I have also argued that the sage himself loses sight of nonhuman creation in his anthropocentrism. After the sage's initial focus on the plan of God for the existence of all creation and the subsequent exploitation of that creation by the ungodly his focus shifts to the incorruption of all humankind. He narrows the term "mysteries" of God to apply only to human creation. In the hymn to Wisdom, he depicts Wisdom as the autonomous Spirit of God who is the creator and sustainer of the cosmos, only to straitjacket her into the dutiful bride waiting at home for Solomon.

In defence of the sage, however, we need not be limited by Tennant's caution that the sage's focus on nonhuman creation was not intended as a major focus. At the same time, there is so much in the Wisdom of Solomon that is radically positive in regards to nonhuman creation that ecological hermeneutics encourages us to take the sage seriously as having a pro-Earth orientation.

Intentionally or unintentionally, the sage initiates a radical theology that encompasses the whole of creation. In this theology, the Earth is a mutual partner with humankind as the locus of God's presence. In listening to the voice of Earth, the ecological reader is reminded that Earth, too, is a beloved child of Wisdom, who comes into being before humankind. She dwells in the Cosmos, and is as much a spiritual expression of Wisdom as humankind. If the sage all too quickly loses sight of the implications of his claim, the positive attitude in relation to creation nevertheless pervades the book, including sections I have not discussed. This attitude is open to retrieval by the discerning reader.

The sage himself may not have realized the potential inherent in his claim that God's immortal Spirit is in all things. It is ironic that he claims the ungodly are blind to the mystery of God in creation (Wis 2:21–22). The sage himself may have underestimated the mysteries of God by confining God's purpose to the immortality of humankind and by not allowing Wisdom her free rein throughout the cosmos. It is an anthropocentric blindness that may have infected all of us and prevented us from appreciating the comprehensive mysteries of God in regards to the whole of creation.

THE DESCENT OF DARKNESS OVER THE LAND: LISTENING TO THE VOICE OF EARTH IN MARK 15:33

Susan Miller

In the Passion Narrative of the gospel of Mark, darkness covers the land for a three-hour period preceding the death of Jesus. The darkness ends at the ninth hour when Jesus cries out in abandonment to God, but no human being appears to be aware of the darkness. This raises questions about the significance of the descent of darkness in Mark's gospel.

The SBL Consultation for Ecological Hermeneutics (2004–2006) developed a methodology seeking to discern the voice of Earth. In this approach Earth is interpreted as the total ecosystem, the web of life. The interpretative strategy involves a hermeneutics of suspicion, identification, and retrieval. To what extent have biblical interpreters silenced the voice of Earth? In what ways may we identify with Earth? Are there passages in which we may uncover traces of the voice of Earth, and gain new insights into our understanding of the relationship between biblical interpretation and current ecological debates?

This paper aims to read Mark's account of the descent of darkness from the perspective of the Earth. I will begin by assessing commentators' analyses of this passage, and then explore the narrative by the method of identification with Earth. Scholars have attempted to interpret the description of darkness in the gospels in terms of natural phenomenon such as a storm or a black sirocco.[1] The orderly timing of the darkness into a three-hour period, however, has led other commentators to discern a possible theological or symbolic interpretation of the darkness. Ched Myers cites Exod 10:22, which describes a period of darkness lasting three days in the land of Egypt.[2] In Exodus, God brings about the darkness because Pharaoh refuses to permit the Israelites to go out to the desert to worship God. An allusion to Exod 10:22 is supported by the timing of Passover

---

1. C. E. B. Cranfield, *The Gospel According to St Mark* (Cambridge: Cambridge University Press, 1959), 457–58.

2. Ched Myers, *Binding the Strong Man. A Political Reading of Mark's Story of Jesus* (New York: Orbis, 1988), 389.

in both Exodus and Mark. In this interpretation, darkness is a sign of the judgment of God upon the enemies of Israel. In Exodus, however, the darkness does not affect the Israelites, whereas in Mark, Jesus' cry of dereliction suggests that he also experiences darkness.

Other scholars, such as Raymond Brown, note the similarities between Mark's account of the crucifixion and Amos 8:9–10.[3] Both passages refer to the darkness at the time of noon, and they associate darkness with the mourning of an only son. Amos 8:9–10 describes events that take place on the Day of the Lord, and darkness is linked with the Day of the Lord in a range of texts (Jer 13:16; Joel 2:2, 10; Amos 5:20; Zeph 1:15). In these passages, darkness is related to the advent of God in judgment on the world on account of the oppression and injustice carried out by the people. Morna D. Hooker suggests that the descent of darkness in Mark's gospel is a sign of judgment upon Israel because they have not accepted Jesus as the Messiah.[4] Craig A. Evans, moreover, proposes that the darkness on the land is an indication of the judgment that falls upon Jesus.[5] These interpretations highlight the role of God in bringing about darkness over the land, and Earth is depicted as an object that suffers the judgment of God on account of the actions of human beings. A hermeneutics of suspicion observes that Earth becomes an innocent recipient of God's wrath.

In Mark's account, however, we are not told who is the agent or the cause of the darkness. To what extent may we discover an alternative interpretation if we recognize Earth as a subject in the narrative? What new insights may be gained by interpreting the descent of darkness from the point of view of Earth?

1. Identification

The interpretative strategy of identification involves readers taking the side of Earth, and seeking to empathize with Earth during the events described in the gospel. Mark contains few detailed descriptions of landscapes or locations, and the gospel tends to refer to places in a general way, such as the desert, the sea, and the land. Mark, however, does locate the crucifixion in a particular setting, Golgotha, the place of the skull (Mark 15:22). The name of this place may derive from the formation of the land in the shape of a skull or it may have been named after the executions carried out in that location. This name has anthropocentric associations because the land is defined in terms of its similarities to the human form. The setting, however, may also be linked with impurity and death on account of the crucifixions carried out there (cf. Deut 21:23). A hermeneutics of suspicion

---

3. Raymond E. Brown, *The Death of the Messiah: From Gethsemane to the Grave* (2 vols.; New York: Doubleday, 1994), 2:1035.

4. M. D. Hooker, *The Gospel According to St Mark* (London: A&C Black, 1991), 376.

5. C. A. Evans, *Mark 8:27–16:20* (WBC 34B; Nashville: Thomas Nelson, 2001), 507.

highlights the ways in which the land has been regarded as impure on account of the actions of human beings.

In Roman times, people were crucified near a road outside the city of Jerusalem. All the people entering and leaving the city were reminded of the power of Rome, the occupiers of the land. Crucifixion was reserved for rebels against the state and for slaves. It was used to deter anyone from taking on the might of the Roman authorities. In seeking to empathize with Earth, we become aware of the atrocities carried out upon the land. Earth is unable to prevent these crucifixions but must remain as a witness to the horrific events that are carried out by humanity.

In the Passion Narrative, Jesus is arrested, and he is subject to the actions of the religious and political authorities. He is tried before the Sanhedrin and then taken to Pilate before being handed over to the Roman soldiers who lead him out to be executed. Jesus is placed on the cross at the third hour; he is mocked for three hours before his death. The passersby deride him; the chief priests and scribes mock him; those crucified along with him revile him (Mark 15:29–32). The mockeries focus on Jesus' inability to save himself from death (15:30–32). Jesus does not attempt to prevent his crucifixion but he stands firm before his opponents. In this way Jesus is aligned with Earth: Earth is also unable to intervene to halt the events taking place but remains as a suffering witness.

Human opposition to Jesus culminates at the sixth hour when darkness descends over the land. When we listen to Earth as a subject in the passage, darkness may be interpreted as a response of the natural world to the voices of opposition and mockery raised against Jesus. Darkness descends upon the land aligning the natural world with the suffering of Jesus. During this period of three hours no human voice is heard. This portrayal contrasts with the voices of mockery that dominate the preceding three hours. Amos 8:9–10 associates darkness with a time of mourning, but in this text those who mourn are human. In Mark, Jesus is betrayed by one of his twelve chosen disciples (Mark 14:10–11); he is abandoned by his disciples at his arrest (14:50); even his women followers stand at a distance (15:40–41). The absence of human mourners stands in stark contrast to the mourning of Earth.

Mark's portrayal of Earth corresponds to other accounts of Earth in passages from the Old Testament in which Earth is presented as a subject (Jer 4:27–28, 12:11; Hos 4:3; Joel 1:10, 20). In Jer 4:27–28 darkness is linked with the mourning of Earth: "The earth shall mourn and the heavens above grow black." Joel 1:10 states: "The fields are ruined, the ground mourns; for the grain is ruined, the new wine has come to naught, the oil has failed." In 2 Bar 10:12 the darkness of the sun and moon reflects the suffering of Zion: "For why should the light rise again, where the light of Zion is darkened?" In these passages Earth responds to human suffering. In Jer 4 the mourning of Earth is a response to the devastation of the land by war. The fertile land has become a wilderness and towns are deserted. In Joel 1 the mourning of Earth is associated with the failure of the harvest and the land's lost fertility. These calamities have been caused by human crimes and perse-cution. Similarly, in Mark, Earth mourns the suffering of Jesus caused by human violence and oppression. Jeremiah 5:25 notes that human wrongdoing has "upset nature's order." In Mark, Earth also suffers from the injustice of human beings, and identifies with Jesus in his anguish.

The interpretation of the mourning of Earth is supported by the description of the tearing of the temple veil at the death of Jesus: the tearing of material such as clothes was a sign of mourning. The high priest tears his robe when he con-victs Jesus of blasphemy (Mark 14:63), and mourning is indicated by the action of Elisha who tears his garments at the passing of Elijah (2 Kgs 2:12). Josephus notes that the temple veil was made up of material of four colors representing the four elements of the universe (*J. W.* 5.212–215). In this way the tearing of the temple veil may allude to the mourning of the whole of creation.

Dale C. Allison notes that the descent of darkness is associated with the deaths of Roman rulers.[6] Cicero describes the darkening of the sun at the death of Romulus who disappears from the Earth and becomes a god (*Resp.* 2.10, 6.21). Virgil records a period of darkness at the death of Julius Caesar: "He (the sun) and no other was moved to pity Rome on the day that Caesar died, when he veiled his radiant face in gloom and darkness, and a godless age feared everlasting night" (*Georg.* 1.466–467). The eclipse of the moon is associated with the death of Car-neades: "At the time he died the moon is said to have been eclipsed, and one might well say that the brightest luminary in heaven next to the sun thereby gave token of her sympathy" (Diogenes Laertius 4.64).

In some texts of the Pseudepigrapha the mourning of Earth is related particu-larly to the death of prominent figures. Darkness is also associated with mourning in the account of the death of Adam (*T. Adam* 3:6; *L.A.E.* 46:1–3) and the depar-ture of Enoch (*2 En.* 67). The *T. Adam* describes the darkening of the sun for seven days following the death of Adam alluding to the seven-day period of cre-ation. Earth returns to chaos after the death of Adam, the first human being. In *2 En.* 67 the Lord sends darkness onto the Earth, and angels carry Enoch to heaven. In *2 En.* light returns after Enoch has departed, and there is a striking similarity with Mark's gospel, which mentions that the darkness comes to an end at the very point when Jesus dies. A similar tradition is associated with Jesus in *Ps.-Clem. Rec.* 1.41, which describes the darkening of the sun at the suffering of Jesus because "all the world suffered with him." In Mark, the voice of Earth is raised in mourning at the suffering of Jesus. But does the Earth mourn only Jesus? What of the two men crucified with him? Or the many others crucified in the same place over the years by the Roman authorities?

---

6. D. C. Allison, *The End of the Ages Has Come: An Early Interpretation of the Passion and Resurrection of Jesus* (Edinburgh: T&T Clark, 1985), 27–28.

In Mark, Jesus is condemned on account of his claim to kingship (15:2), and he is mocked as a king by the Roman soldiers. Jesus, however, is not acknowledged as a king on earth, and he is crucified as a slave and rebel to the state. Jesus defines his mission in terms of coming not to be served but to serve and to give his life as a ransom for many (10:45). In this way the purpose of the death of Jesus is intended to bring life to others. The term λύτρον may be translated as "ransom" or the "price required to redeem a slave." In his death Jesus is aligned with the least in society, and he is portrayed as a representative of the suffering of humanity. Earth is therefore aligned with all who suffer. This portrayal of Earth emphasizes the interrelationship between human beings and the natural world. Earth is not impassive but bears witness to these events.

2. Protest

In Mark's account of the crucifixion, the response of Earth is contrasted with the actions of the human beings who crucify Jesus and those who abandon him. Earth's sympathetic response thus raises questions about the nature of human actions. The darkness may also be interpreted as a protest against these atrocities. The descent of darkness is a disruptive action because human beings and the natural world depend upon a cycle of light and darkness in order to sustain life. When this cycle is broken, there can be no growth of plants or harvests of crops. The darkness over the land reminds humans of their powerlessness in the face of disruptions in the natural world and its cycles.

The darkness at the cross, moreover, is reminiscent of the loss of the light of the sun and of the moon at the *parousia* (Mark 13:24). Jesus prophesies that the sun will be darkened, and the moon will not give its light. The stars will fall from the heavens, and the powers of the heavens will be shaken (Mark 13:25). For Ched Myers, this description is an indication that the present world order is coming to an end.[7] The dissolution of the sun, moon, and stars points to the end of the world. Dennis E. Nineham proposes that Mark interprets the sun, moon, and stars as personal powers in opposition to God; their dissolution thus highlights the greater power of God.[8]

Linking the darkness at the crucifixion with the *parousia*, however, raises questions about Jesus' cry of dereliction. Did Jesus believe that the descent of darkness indicated the imminent intervention of God? Does his cry of dereliction imply that he felt abandoned by God in the midst of this darkness?

In the account of the crucifixion, the land is covered in darkness. However, no human being acknowledges this event; no help comes to Jesus. In contrast, according to Mark's account, human beings will respond to the signs in nature that

---

7. Myers, *Binding*, 389.
8. D. E. Nineham, *Saint Mark* (London: SCM, 1963), 357.

accompany the *parousia* of the Son of Man. At the crucifixion, Earth responds, mourning the death of Jesus by darkening the sky. At the *parousia* the heavens are again darkened. Jesus' prophecy depicts wars and rumors of wars, and asserts that the violence of human beings corresponds to the disruption of nature illustrated by earthquakes and famines. During this period there will be greater suffering than at any time since the beginning of creation (Mark 13:19).

Keith D. Dyer points out that apocalyptic accounts of the end of the world have been interpreted by some Christians as a reason to devalue the earth and to seek salvation in heavenly terms.[9] In Dan 7, the Son of Man ascends to heaven; but in Mark's gospel, the Son of Man descends to Earth indicating that salvation concerns the whole of creation (Mark 13:27). When we read this account identifying with Earth, the darkening of the heavens may be interpreted as the participation of Earth with the intention of bringing the suffering of the end time to a close. Mark 13 ends with the parable of the fig tree whose tender branches indicate that summer is near (13:28). This parable's focus on a fragile symbol of growth contrasts with the preceding cataclysmic and destructive images of wars, earthquakes, and famines (Mark 13:8).

The darkness at the crucifixion, moreover, is reminiscent of the darkness at the beginning of creation. In Genesis the world is described in darkness before God brought light into being (σκότος ἐπάνω τῆς ἀβύσσου; Gen 1:2, LXX). Dominic Rudman notes the association of darkness with the forces of chaos and death (cf. Job 10:21, 17:11–16; Eccl 11:8).[10] He points out that this darkness recalls the darkness that occurs during the boat journeys when storms arise (Mark 4:35–41, 6:45–52). For Rudman, this is a sign of the victory of the forces of chaos at the crucifixion, and vindication only comes with the resurrection of Jesus. In Mark, however, the darkness ends with Jesus' death. That light returns when Jesus dies indicates that the normal cycle of light and darkness has resumed. In Jer 4:23 and in other apocalyptic writings, the world returns to chaos and darkness before the new age begins (cf. *4 Ezra* 6:39, 7:30; *L.A.E.* 46:1–2).

In Genesis, God creates the sun, moon, and stars, and separates light from darkness. The purpose of creation is to provide a sustainable environment in which humanity and the natural world may flourish. Without the boundaries of light and darkness, the land cannot bear fruit. In Mark the descent of darkness indicating a return to the state of chaos and darkness before God brings an ordered environment into existence. The Gen 1 creation account does not express a doctrine of *creatio ex nihilo* but describes conditions of chaos from which the

---

9. K. D. Dyer, "When Is the End Not the End? The Fate of Earth in Biblical Eschatology (Mark 13)" in *The Earth Story in the New Testament* (ed. Norman C. Habel and Vicky Balabanski; The Earth Bible 5; London: Continuum, 2002), 44–56.

10. D. Rudman, "The Crucifixion as Chaoskampf: A New Reading of the Passion Narrative in the Synoptic Gospels," *Bib* 84 (2003): 102–7.

Earth emerges. In this way darkness and chaos are depicted not as negative states, but as the conditions from which creation emerges.

Why should Earth seek to return to the conditions before creation? At the Last Supper, Jesus identifies the bread as his body and the wine as his blood of the covenant poured out for many (Mark 14:22–24). Jesus is therefore identified with the produce of the natural world. He gives his life as the covenant between God and humanity and also with the whole of creation. The bread and wine are signs of the covenant that will be ratified in the last days (cf. Jer 31:31–34). This covenant establishes the relationship between God, humanity, and the natural world. It promises a sustaining order in a world of chaos, and brings reassurance and security to the whole Earth community. Jesus states that he will not drink wine until he drinks it new in the kingdom of God (Mark 14:24). His words point to the continuity of the natural world when the kingdom comes.

Following the death of Jesus, the temple veil is torn in two from top to bottom. The tearing of the veil (ἐσχίσθη; Mark 15:38) recalls the tearing apart of the heavens in the prologue to Mark's gospel (σχιζομένους τοὺς οὐρανούς; 1:10). The opening of the heavens indicates a time of revelation, and God declares Jesus to be the beloved Son (1:11).

The crucifixion is also a time of revelation because the Roman centurion is depicted as the first human being to recognize Jesus as the Son of God (Mark 15:39). A group of women is described standing at a distance (15:40–41). They have followed and served Jesus in Galilee before accompanying him to Jerusalem. These women will be the first witnesses to the resurrection when they visit the empty tomb, and they offer hope of the emergence of a new community on Earth.

3. Retrieval

What features of Earth may be retrieved form Mark's account of the descent of darkness over the land from this analysis? A hermeneutics of suspicion has highlighted the ways in which Earth has been silenced by biblical interpretation. Earth has been regarded as an object that suffers the judgment and wrath of God on account of the actions of humans. When we seek to identify with Earth, and interpret the Markan account of the descent of darkness from the perspective of the Earth, new insights emerge. Earth speaks in mourning and empathizes with the suffering of Jesus. This portrayal of Earth retrieves both biblical traditions and Hellenistic texts, which present Earth as a subject who mourns the death of human beings. In Mark, Earth mourns Jesus not only as Son of God but as the representative of the least in society. Earth responds in solidarity with oppressed and suffering human beings.

The descent of darkness over the land is not anthropocentric for several reasons. First, it expresses the mourning of Earth, and indicates the interrelationships of human beings and the natural world. Second, the presentation is not anthropocentric because Earth not only mourns human beings, but also raises a voice in protest against injustice. The darkness over the land speaks for the land and for human beings who endure oppression. Human beings are silent while Earth speaks in protest against the injustice being carried out. In this way Earth is not a passive backdrop to the events of the Passion Narrative. Finally, the descent of darkness is also a voice of protest because it calls into question all human power and authority, and speaks in judgment against aggressors and those who commit acts of violence. Not only the perpetrators of injustice but all human beings depend on the cycle of light and darkness for life. The voice of Earth is an empowerment of those who suffer injustice. Even when human beings ignore the suffering of others, Earth is not silent. Earth bears witness to the events taking place. This analysis of Mark's gospel thus reveals a holistic understanding of the relationship between human beings and Earth.

Healing Ointment/Healing Bodies: Gift and Identification in an Ecofeminist Reading of Mark 14:3-9

Elaine Wainwright

As a feminist interpreter, I have worked for two decades with a hermeneutics of suspicion and hermeneutics of retrieval, the latter being named and nuanced in many different ways.[1] Over that time, however, my feminist frame of analysis has become more multidimensional to include other critical perspectives that were demanding ethical attention when interpreting biblical texts, in particular, the postcolonial and ecological.[2] Within the feminist paradigm, gender functioned as a vehicle of "implicit identification" with the female biblical characters[3] until postcolonial interpretations and the voices of women of color began to be heard globally. Identification became much more nuanced and specific although not

---

1. Elizabeth Schüssler Fiorenza has developed and nuanced this basic paradigm in *In Memory of Her: A Feminist Reconstruction of Christian Origins* (New York: Crossroad, 1983); *Bread not Stone: The Challenge of Feminist Biblical Interpretation* (Boston: Beacon, 1984); *But She Said: Feminist Practices of Biblical Interpretation* (Boston: Beacon, 1992); and *Wisdom Ways: Introducing Feminist Biblical Interpretation* (Maryknoll, N.Y.: Orbis, 2000). See my own particular construction of such a hermeneutic in *Towards a Feminist Critical Reading of the Gospel according to Matthew* (BZNW 60; Berlin: de Gruyter, 1991), 44–55; and *Shall We Look for Another: A Feminist Rereading of the Matthean Jesus* (Maryknoll, N.Y.: Orbis, 1998), 9–32.

2. In the opening chapter of my most recent book, *Women Healing/Healing Women: The Genderization of Healing in Early Christianity* (London: Equinox, 2006), 11–23, I explored such a multidimensional hermeneutic for my study of gender and healing in the Greco-Roman world and early Christianity. I highlighted four areas as informing the ecological aspect of reading: attentiveness to the material, the Earth, the body, and space.

3. Initially within feminist biblical studies, as in feminist studies generally, it was assumed that "woman" as a category included all women, hence identification was considered implicit. As the disciplines developed and the voices of women of color and of women claiming gendered differences were raised critically, what was assumed as implicit identification became much more nuanced.

necessarily named in this way. One of the challenges, therefore, proposed by the Earth Bible team that initiated the Earth Bible project,[4] and by Habel in his introduction to this volume, is that *identification* is a key hermeneutical moment and movement within an ecological reading.

Identification will function, therefore, as a very explicit lens in this paper. An ecofeminist reading of Mark 14:3–9 will demonstrate that such identification needs to be multidimensional, with all members of Earth community—the other-than-human as well as the human—in order that ethical readings be as inclusive as possible of that entire community. Within such a perspective, there remains the need to be attentive to particular categories such as gender and colonization. This is to shift our reading lens to include the other-than-human, the materiality of bodies, and physical space in the meaning-making process that is the interpreting of texts—but in that shift to continue to read with the lens of gender and postcolonialism. The category of *gift* will provide a second interpretive grid that will assist in further exploring webs of relationships within the text toward an ecofeminist reading.

The *Australian Oxford Dictionary* provided me with two possible meanings as I began to explore *identification*: to regard oneself as sharing characteristics of, or to associate oneself with (another person or thing).[5] The *Encarta World English Dictionary* tool on my computer amplified this to include "a powerful feeling of affinity with another person or group, which sometimes involves regarding somebody as a model and adopting his or her beliefs, values, or other characteristics."[6] Each of these definitions seems to assume a network or web of relationships within which *identification* takes place. It recognizes the "otherness" of the person or the other-than-human, but also the sharing of characteristics. The other is one with whom I associate and with and for whom I feel a strong sympathetic or imaginative bond. It does not collapse difference but allows for it within relationship. Val Plumwood says in this regard that "two movements are therefore required to overcome dualistic constructions of self/other—recognizing kinship and recognizing difference."[7] Keeping in mind these two movements should help to avoid one of the inherent dangers in *identification*: one can so identify with the other that the otherness of the self or, more likely of the other, is lost and sameness cloaks difference.

---

4. See Earth Bible Team, "Guiding Ecojustice Principles," in Habel, *Readings from the Perspective of Earth*, 38–53.

5. "Identify," in *The Australian Concise Oxford Dictionary* (ed. J. M. Hughes, P. A. Mitchell and W. S. Ramson; 2d ed.: Melbourne: Oxford University Press, 1992), 558.

6. "Identification" in *Encarta® World English Dictionary* © 1999 Microsoft Corp. Developed for Microsoft by Bloomsbury Publishing Plc.

7. Val Plumwood, *Feminism and the Mastery of Nature* (Feminism for Today; London: Routledge, 1993), 155.

In turning toward Mark 14:3–9, the pouring out of healing ointment, I want to look to the web of relationships constructed in this text. In reviewing my previous readings of this text,[8] I have noted that while I recognized both the presence of the *muron* or healing ointment in the text, and its capacity to turn attention to the other-than-human, I did not explore its place within the web of relationships established in the text. My focus was more explicitly directed to the human-to-human relationships within that web. It is to the human-to-"other-than-human" relationships that I turn explicit attention in this paper, drawing these, however, into the more inclusive web of identification within Earth community.

The reader, on entering this narrative in Mark 14:3, is drawn into a web of relationships: introduced to Jesus and his location in a particular space, a space into which a woman comes with an alabaster flask of costly ointment (pure nard), which she pours over the head of Jesus. At this point in the narrative, the reader knows much about Jesus from the previous thirteen chapters of the gospel narrative, and nothing of the woman who is simply called *gynē*, but is given a rich description of the ointment. The action of the woman in breaking the flask and pouring the ointment or *muron* over the head of Jesus focuses our attention on this web of relationships.

The text directs the reader's attention first to the space in which the woman's action takes place. It is in Bethany and in a house, that of Simon the leper. In the Markan text, Bethany is discursively constructed as a place away from the threat of arrest in Jerusalem (Mark 14:1–2).[9] The house as context for Jesus' reclining at table was both gendered and colonized space. Although the "private" space of the household was associated with women, it was male activity and definitions that determined how such space within the house was gendered. Reclining at table was constructed as male space even if women were present.[10] Material space and human processes intertwine in these opening phrases of the Markan text in ways that have overlaid the material with the social to the point of rendering the material invisible, more invisible indeed than the ancient gendering process seeks to

---

8. Elaine Wainwright, "The Pouring out of Healing Ointment: Rereading Mark 14:3–9," in *Toward a New Heaven and a New Earth: Essays in Honor of Elisabeth Schüssler Fiorenza* (ed. Fernando F. Segovia; Maryknoll, N.Y.: Orbis, 2003), 157–78; idem, *Women Healing/Healing Women*, 131–37.

9. Jorunn Økland, *Women in Their Place: Paul and the Corinthian Discourse of Gender and Sanctuary Space* (JSNTSS 269; London: T&T Clark, 2004), 58–77, discusses how space is discursively constructed but she also notes, quoting Foucault, that discourse points beyond itself to become historical (see 39).

10. John J. Winkler, *The Constraints of Desire: The Anthropology of Sex and Gender in Ancient Greece* (New York: Routledge, 1990), 8, says of this construction of gendered space that "when women are active, they are trouble. Since a man does not want to invite trouble, it is prudent for him and other men to assume, until forced to do otherwise, that the women of his household are invisible, obedient, and industrious."

render woman. The evocation of material space in the text can, however, alert the ecologically attentive reader to such space as gift.[11]

In this space that the narrative creates, attention is drawn both to the woman and to the alabaster jar of ointment of pure nard. The naming of the *alabastron* turns our attention toward Earth and the stalagmitic deposits from which this transluscent marble called *alabastros* was obtained. It was often used for decorative vases to hold perfumes or perfumed oils because it was believed to preserve them.[12] Earth has given of its resources to provide the woman with an appropriate container for the costly ointment or perfumed oil. Traces of the flask's origins remain, however, in the beautiful lines and patterns in the alabaster. Earth and the material of Earth are drawn into relationship with the human and invite the human person to be attentive to the gift.[13]

Into the *alabastron* has been placed very costly ointment (*muron*) of pure nard. *Muron* is a general word used to describe a wide range of perfumed ointments or oils both of which are prepared from plant substances grown in the Earth. What distinguishes this particular ointment is the descriptor νάρδου πιστικῆς. Nard or spikenard is generally associated with the *Nardostachys jatamansi* grown in the soil of India and imported throughout the ancient Near East. Houghton describes it as having an "aromatic odour" and as being used as "an ingredient in ointment and as a stimulant medicine."[14] It is the root of the plant that is used for its aroma and it is this which renders expensive the ointment or oil to which it is added. The adjective πιστικῆς is generally assumed to be a derivative of πιστός and hence is translated as pure or genuine. Houghton argues that it is derived from the Sanskrit name for the *Nardostachys jatamansi, pisita*, which came to be associated with the fleshiness of the root. This particular ointment of νάρδου πιστικῆς would, therefore, have been expensive because of this imported substance, the most valued part of the plant. In this short descriptive phrase we

---

11. Mark Manolopoulos, "If Creation is a Gift: Towards an Eco/Theo/Logical Aporetics" (Ph.D. diss., Monash University, 2003), explores the material as gift in dialogue with many contemporary philosophers for whom *gift* has been a significant category of analysis.

12. F. Bechtel, "Alabaster," in *The Catholic Encyclopedia* (vol. 1; Robert Appleton, 1907. Online ed., 2003. Cited 9 November 2005. Online: http://www .newadvent.org/cathen/01244b.htm on 9 November 2005.

13. Anne Primavesi, *Sacred Gaia: Holistic Theology and Earth System Science* (London: Routledge, 2000), 160, says that "to see life as a gift event is to see that I am alive because I am continuously gifted with what I need to live. I am gifted because other organisms and species have not evaded or ignored the demands I make on them. Ultimately, this fact does not allow me to evade or ignore my dependence on the earth. Or to ignore my responsibility to return it, at the very least, the gift of gratitude."

14. William Houghton, "The Pistic Nard of the Greek Testament," *Proceedings of the Society of Biblical Archaeology* (1888): 145.

are introduced to the process by which different materials of Earth[15] are skill-fully combined by human ingenuity to provide aromatic oils or ointments that are medicinal[16] but which also give refreshment and enjoyment to the human body in a gift event. Again, we see the aspect of gift as the plants yield up their life to the human community in relationship.

Returning to the web of relationships in the text, we have noted that the woman enters the space, the house, having an alabaster jar, or with an alabaster jar as the NRSV translates it. She is identified with the nardic ointment, and her action invites identification. Her breaking of the stem of the flask and pouring out of the ointment on the head of Jesus is an act of giving. She is the instrument of the giving, of the gifting, through her identification with the ointment—but the ointment is the gift (it has been received by her as gift and will be given to Jesus as gift). Jesus as recipient freely receives the gift. As Anne Primavesi says:

> These interactive relationships between giver and receiver, between giver and gift, and between gift and receiver link them openly, materially, sensually, with the link made tangible (usually) in some object passed by one to the other, chosen by one for the other, and received by one from the other.[17]

Returning to the web of relationships of the gift event, "the donor is assumed to have power to bestow something . . . which the other lacks. When the gift is received, the perceived deficiency is remedied," according to Primavesi.[18] Power is in the gift, in the *muron*, a power to bestow something that is lacking. The context, Mark 14:1–2, points readers toward the lack: it is two days before the Passover and the chief priests and scribes are seeking to arrest Jesus and kill him. Jesus is "facing into death" with all the emotional turmoil that would entail (Mark 14:32–35). *Muron* poured over the head would put "good odours to the brain" Athenaeus says in the *Deipnosophistae*, and this, he affirms, is "a highly impor-tant element of health."[19] He goes on to say that "the sensations of the brain are soothed by sweet odours and cured [or healed] besides."[20] The healing power of the *muron* of pure nard, this *pharmakon*, remedies the lack in Jesus so that he is able to face death: "she has ointmented my body . . . for burying" (Mark 14:8). His need has been met by the generosity of the woman and the power of the oint-

---

15. Theophrastus, *Enquiry into Plants*, 9:7:3, explains that it is the "roots, bark, branches, wood, seeds, gum or flowers which in different cases yield the perfume."

16. Theophrastus, *Enquiry into Plants*, 9:8:2, describes the "plants in Syria which have remarkable fragrance" as "somewhat medicinal."

17. Primavesi, *Sacred Gaia*, 156.

18. Primavesi, *Sacred Gaia*, 156.

19. Athenaeus, *Deipnosophistae*, 15:687 d.

20. Athenaeus, *Deipnosophistae*, 15:687 d.

ment. Had the gift been withheld as the indignant ones would have wished, the deficiency in Jesus would have been felt more acutely.

Jesus' allusion to his burial and hence his death in this context of the gift event draws the attention of readers to the giving and the taking, the life and the death organically linked in life as gift event. Just as the *Nardostachys jatamansi* and other plants constituting the healing ointment of nard gave up their life to give life-enhancing and life-strengthening healing to Jesus as he "faced into death," so too will the one who "gives his life as a ransom for many" (Mark 10:45) give life-enhancing and life-strengthening healing to those many.[21] Jesus, too, is identified with the *muron*, the healing ointment. Both share characteristics and Jesus claims this identification when he associates the healing ointment with his body beyond death: μυρίσαι τὸ σῶμά μου εἰς τὸν ἐνταφιασμόν (Mark 14:8). The other-than-human and the human are drawn into the life-cycle of giving and taking, into life as gift event. As ointment is poured down over the head of Jesus (κατα-χέω; Mark 14:3) so will his blood—the blood of the covenant—be poured out for many (εκ-χέω; Mark 14:24).

The giver of this gift does not turn attention to himself as giver in a way that destroys the gift event but rather points to another giver and, identified with her, another gift. Her pouring out of the healing ointment and the healing ointment poured out or given will be told *in memory* wherever the gospel is preached in the whole world, in the cosmos (Mark 14:9). Just as in ancient Greece *pharmakon* was both healing remedy and death-dealing poison, so too does life as gift event in all its excess hold together the ambiguity of life and death: the giving up and the giving to. Male and female and the other-than-human give and receive in this interchange of identifications so that no one alone is linked to giving and sacrifice.[22] Identification within the web of relationships in this story of healing ointment enables this more global story to be given and to be received, making possible the healing of relationships within our *EarthScape*, to borrow a word from Primavesi.[23]

There is, however, another character set in the web of relationships: the indignant ones who say to themselves, "why was this ointment wasted in this way" (verse 4). They are indignant in the face of the gift event; they name the gift or

---

21. Primavesi, *Sacred Gaia*, 161–67, situates the two-edged nature of the scapegoat, the *pharmakos*, within her exploration of the gift event of life. Rita Nakashima Brock and Rebecca Ann Parker, *Proverbs of Ashes: Violence, Redemptive Suffering, and the Search for What Saves Us* (Boston: Beacon, 2001), provide a radical critique of the Christian theology of atonement, which emphasizes the giving unto death to the exclusion of the giving unto life of the Christian tradition and of the gift event.

22. See Morny Joy, "Beyond the Given and the All-giving: Reflections on Women and the Gift," *Australian Feminist Studies* 14 (1999): 315–32.

23. Primavesi, *Sacred Gaia*, 158.

the giving of the gift as waste, and they reproach the giver (verse 5). They negate the gift and the life-enhancing aspect of the gift. They name it as "destruction,"[24] and in their very act of naming they cause a destruction of their relationship to the *muron*. They are unable to enter into a relationship with the *muron*, unable to identify with it, or with the woman who pours out the *muron*, or with Jesus on whom it is poured out. They place themselves completely outside the web of relationships of the gift event by naming it annihilation or destruction.

Such words are evocative for the ecological reader. They herald descriptions of the heavy human ecological footprint that is now constantly being drawn to our attention. The indignation of the *tines* or unnamed ones therefore deserves specific attention. They are indignant in the face of the gift event, of the healing woman's identification with the healing ointment, the giver with the gift, and the receiving of the giver and the gift into the web of relationships by Jesus. They place themselves outside the gift event. They negate the gift event by naming it as waste: superfluity serving no purpose, or useless remains, or by-product.[25] They fail to identify in any way with the healing ointment, fail to recognize its power, its function in the gift event in the web of relationships. Rather, they cut across the process of gift event with that of commodity exchange: why wasn't the ointment sold for three hundred denarii and given to the poor? (Mark 14:5).

At the heart of not only this gifting that is the central focus of this Markan text, but of all gifting is "dependence." We have already noted the woman's dependence on Earth to give up its *pharmakon* and Jesus' dependence on the woman's gift to prepare him for burial. The indignant ones, however, seem to want to reject any appearance of dependence in Jesus, and therefore in themselves as disciples of Jesus. It is such rejection that Primavesi says turns gift-giving into commodity exchange.[26] A denial of dependence means an inability to recognize dependence on the Earth and its gifts in a web of relationships, contrary to what the woman and Jesus knew. There is no ability to identify with the power of the healing ointment and its crucial place in the life–death event into which they are being drawn with Jesus. Rather, the *muron* is commodified. It is a means of exchange and it is into this web of exchange that they draw giving to the poor. They render the poor dependent on their commodity exchange but they themselves reject any form of dependence or interdependence within the web of relationships between the woman, the healing ointment, and Jesus.

24. Walter Bauer, William F. Arndt, F. Wilbur Gingrich and Frederick W. Danker, eds., *A Greek-English Lexicon of the New Testament and Other Early Christian Literature* (2d ed.; Chicago: University of Chicago Press, 1958), 103, gives "destruction" or "annihilation" as the dominant meaning for the Greek text. The NRSV translates it as "waste."

25. Hughes *et al.*, *Australian Concise Oxford Dictionary*, 1318.

26. Primavesi, *Sacred Gaia*, 157.

The indignant ones may, however, be read from another perspective. Their question "why was this *muron* wasted or destroyed?" can function repetitively and radically in the contemporary ecological crisis. They draw attention to the excessive nature of the gift event, to what seems to be the squandering of Earth's resources by some so that others are rendered poor, so that they become the scapegoats whose lives are given up for the many who live beyond their means. The gift and gift-giving is tensive in nature and identification with the poured-out *muron* enables the reader to explore both aspects of the gift.

Jesus, however, rescues the giving to the poor from the commodity-exchange model that the indignant ones signify. He returns it to the gift-event process and in that move also acknowledges the significance of time in this process. The woman and her healing ointment poured out have done a "good work in/for Jesus" at this most appropriate time as he faces death (Mark 14:6–7). This is not to take away from the needs of the poor, those whom the commodity-exchange model renders of no account, without life's resources, and who are given up or made into scapegoats for the many who participate in gift exchanges beyond their needs. Rather, Jesus invites the indignant ones into a new mode of gifting: whenever they "will" they are able to do good for the poor, just as the woman did a good thing for Jesus. They are invited to learn to participate in the gift event rather than the commodity exchange. They will need to learn dependence on the Earth and its gifts, and accept dependence and interdependence within the web of Earth relationships if they are to become givers rather than exchangers.

Identification with the other-than-human is more than sharing characteristics with, associating with, or even feeling a strong sympathetic or imaginative bond with the other. It is recognition of and participation in the play of dependence and interdependence in the web of relationships in which the other-than-human, the human, and the divine live out the unfolding gift event. It is the recognition that both the gift and the giving are for life enhancement not death dealing first and foremost. But this also needs to be coupled with the awareness that the point of giving for the other/s even to death is an integral part of life as gift event. This is the gospel, the good news that is to be preached in the whole cosmos, the ὅλον τὸν κόσμον (Mark 14:9). This is the *basileia* of God come near (Mark 1:15).

In this final proclamation, Jesus returns the gift, the healing that the woman and the poured out *muron* had wrought together. In verse 7, Jesus drew the indignant human ones into the web of the gift exchange, inviting them to be gift-givers to the poor—and by establishing relationships between themselves, the scapegoats, and the resources offered to them, enabling them to do among those without gifts whatever they wish to do (δύνασθε αὐτοῖς εὖ ποιῆσαι). The verb ἐποίησεν in the phrase "she did what she could" of verse 8 links Jesus' explanation of what she has done in her gift exchange with what the indignant ones will be able to do, namely, to honor resources and themselves in the dynamic of gift event. The weaving of the web of relationships is completed in verse 9 when what she has done (ὅ ἐποίησεν αὕτη) in receiving and giving the perfumed ointment, identifying with the ointment in her self gift, and enabling Jesus to likewise identify with it in his self gift is to be told in *her* memory. The action of the woman is no longer colonized in the house/cosmos nor are these space gendered. The woman, however, does not stand alone but is the one having an alabaster jar of pure or precious ointment. To tell this story in memory of her and all whom she represents is also to tell it in memory of the *muron* and the other-than-human that this *muron* signifies.

Reading with the other-than-human, with the body given up to life and given up to death within the space of the house and the cosmos filled with the fragrance of healing ointment poured out, is to undertake an ecological reading. I have not here given extended attention to the feminist or the postcolonial readings that intersect significantly with the ecological. There have been moments within this reading when the three have intersected and there are other places in the text when they cry out for further attention. The challenge of reading through the lens of identification has turned me toward the other-than-human in a way that has brought these to the center of my reading lens. The challenge beyond this is how better to integrate such a reading with readings shaped by other ethical perspectives so that healing can happen in the multidimensional ways that are needed in our world today.

CREATION GROANING IN LABOR PAINS

Sigve Tonstad

In Romans, Paul takes the modern reader by surprise when he suddenly turns the pulpit over to nature. Not only does nonhuman creation speak as subject in the text, but the voice is that of a pregnant woman (Rom 8:22). It is a startling sight and an arresting sound: the pregnant woman, while standing in the Pauline pulpit, goes into labor and wails in labor pain. This poignant passage in Rom 8:19–22 invites an ecological hermeneutic, speaking explicitly in support of the ecojustice principles[1] of interconnectedness, voice, and purpose. Implicitly the passage also echoes the principle of nature's worth: nature is humanity's partner in redemption. Trends in Pauline scholarship serve to broaden, stabilize, and embolden an ecologically sensitized reading along these lines.

1. PERTINENT READINGS OF PAUL

Richard B. Hays opens up new territory in Paul's letters by showing that they should be read as an extension of an underlying narrative to which the letter alludes and upon which it freely draws.[2] In the letter, Paul does not presume to introduce Christianity to his readers from scratch. The Roman church, one that Paul did not found or visit in person, takes the prior narrative for granted. Paul emphasizes and explicates, but he works from a core of assumptions that he holds in common with his readers. We see the prior narrative coming into play in the present passage, "for we know that the whole creation groans and labors with birth pangs together until now" (Rom 8:22). The giveaway is the claim "we know," indicating that Paul is not introducing a new and unfamiliar subject. Instead, he rehearses and reaffirms a known story and theme, harnessing "a widespread

---

1. Cf. Habel, *Readings from the Perspective of Earth*, 25–53.
2. Richard B. Hays, *The Faith of Jesus Christ: An Investigation of the Narrative Substructure of Galatians 3:1–4:11* (SBLDS 56; Chico: Scholars Press, 1983; repr. Grand Rapids: Eerdmans, 2002), 33–117.

knowledge and use of Jewish apocalyptic traditions within the earliest Christian congregations," according to James D. G. Dunn.[3]

Allowing the prior narrative to come to the surface helps correct distortions in our reading. The letters are not in themselves exhaustive statements of Paul's message. Even when a statement in his letters is brief or singular, tempting us to prioritize a given subject on the basis of the quantity of the text, the link to an underlying narrative changes the map as to the assumed importance of the subject in question. Brendan Byrne points out that Paul's reference to the hope and the plight of nature is unique and that the passage in Romans is perhaps the first and "only time in his extant letters Paul considers human beings in relation to the nonhuman created world."[4] However, we need to realize that nature's voice is already a part of the ideological and theological narrative of the Roman church and not make too much of the singularity of the topic in the book of Romans. Nature's voice is not alien to the Christian witness. To the extent that this outlook is eclipsed, it represents a lost treasure, a contraction of the Christian vision, and a spiritual hearing loss. Retrieving nature's voice must be seen as a profoundly biblical enterprise.

Hays also heightens our awareness of echoes of and allusions to the Old Testament in Paul's letters.[5] This feature is an extension of the underlying narrative because Paul counts on awareness of Scripture in his argument, and the Old Testament is the most important substrate upon which he draws. "Paul is seeking to ground his exposition of the gospel in Israel's sacred texts," writes Hays.[6] He does indeed. "For the creation was subjected to futility, not willingly, but because of him who subjected it in hope," Paul says (Rom 8:20). There is virtual unanimity among scholars that Paul in this text is alluding to the Genesis story of the Fall.[7] "Cursed is the ground because of you," God says to Adam in Genesis (Gen 3:17), indicating the consequences for nature of the choice made by humans. The original relationship of interdependence is not invalidated, but there is nevertheless

---

3. James D. G. Dunn, *Romans 1–8* (WBC; Dallas: Word Books, 1988), 410.

4. Brendan J. Byrne, *Reckoning with Romans: A Contemporary Reading of Paul's Gospel* (GNS 18; Wilmington, Del.: Michael Glazier, 1986), 165

5. Richard B. Hays, *Echoes of Scripture in the Letters of Paul* (New Haven: Yale University Press, 1989).

6. Hays, *Echoes of Scripture*, 34.

7. C. E. B. Cranfield, *A Critical and Exegetical Commentary on the Epistle to the Romans* (2 vols.; ICC; Edinburgh: T&T Clark, 1979), 1:413; Dunn, *Romans 1–8*, 470; Joseph A. Fitzmyer, *Romans. A New Translation with Introduction and Commentary* (AB; London: Geoffrey Chapman, 1993), 505; A. Katherine Grieb, *The Story of Romans: A Narrative Defense of God's Righteousness* (Louisville, Ky.: Westminster John Knox, 2002), 80; Edward Adams, "Paul's Story of God and Creation: The Story of How God Fulfils His Purposes in Creation," in *Narrative Dynamics in Paul* (ed. Bruce W. Longenecker; Louisville, Ky.: Westminster John Knox, 2002), 28–29.

an element of disruption. With the prediction that the ground shall bring forth "thorns and thistles," we are warned that nature will be less pliant toward human beings (Gen 3:18). The "thorns and thistles" may even be seen as the outward expression of inward resistance.

It is a case in point in this respect that creation "was subjected to futility" (Rom 8:20). Here Paul resorts to the Greek word *mataiotēs*, a word that carries with it the distant drumbeat of the wisdom literature in the Old Testament: the "vanity of vanities" that the ancient wisdom seeker pronounced on his quest for meaning (see, for example, Ecc 1:2).[8] In the context of Paul, nature does not relish the burdensome role assigned to it. As the *Good News Bible* translation asserts, "creation was condemned to lose its purpose" (Rom 8:20).[9] While the unenviable condition that came about could not be avoided, it pointedly exists "not of its [nature's] own will" (Rom 8:20). Again, a disposition of inward resistance is implied.

Most importantly, however, the fact that creation comes into view in Romans serves as a forceful reminder that God is not the God of human beings only. The story in the Bible is also a story for and about Earth. In the words of Rolf Knierim,

> Yahweh is not the God of creation because he is the God of the humans or of human history. He is the God of the humans and of human history because he is the God of creation. For the Old Testament, just as for the New Testament, the most universal aspect of Yahweh's dominion is not human history. It is the creation and sustenance of the world.[10]

In the creation account, humanity receives a blessing and a commission on the sixth day of creation (Gen 1:28), but the blessing that comes to humanity is worded almost identically to the blessing that is pronounced on the birds and the creatures of the sea on the fifth day (Gen 1:22). Of the three explicit blessings in the Genesis creation account, the human mandate on the sixth day and the blessing of the seventh day, receive a fair measure of attention, while the equally weighty and identically worded blessing on nonhuman creation is rarely noted. Paul's New Testament witness reveals that there is a purpose for nature, too: a God-ordained bill of rights. Even if the purpose is temporarily thwarted by human sin, nature is not left without hope (Rom 8:20). Paul affirms the worth

---

8. William Sanday and Arthur C. Headlam, *A Critial and Exegetical Commentary on the Epistle to the Romans* (5th ed.; Edinburgh: T&T Clark, 1901; repr. 1992), 205.

9. Byrne, *Romans*, 260. Otto Michel, *Der Brief an die Römer* (KEK 4; Göttingen: Vandenhoeck & Ruprecht, 1978), 267, sees Paul referring to "the transitoriness, the emptiness, and the nothingness, perhaps also the perversion and the disorder of the world."

10. Rolf Knierim, *The Task of Old Testament Theology: Substance, Method and Cases* (Grand Rapids: Eerdmans, 1995), 13.

of nonhuman creation and Earth. Nature's impassioned speech in Romans is a reflection of nature's value in the Christian outlook.

Hays makes a third contribution, one relating to the import of the faith-language of Paul.[11] This takes us to one of the most hallowed areas in the study of Paul's letters, an area posting signs that "violators will be prosecuted" to discourage anyone from infringing on the Protestant doctrine of justification by faith alone and its traditional formulations.[12] Hays' contention, now enjoying such wide support to the point that Stanley Stowers hails it as a paradigm change of rare and exceptional importance,[13] holds that when Paul's link to the Old Testament is kept in focus, his emphasis is not exclusively on the believers' faith in Jesus but on the faithfulness of Jesus Christ.[14] At a semantic level, in the original Greek there is a shift from an objective to a subjective genitive reading of *pistis Christou*. This leads, in turn, from an emphasis on human faith as the means to divine faithfulness as the basis for the believer's confidence. Paul's message of salvation for human beings thus belongs inside the broader framework of a sustained theodicy.

What at first sight seems like a small step for semantics becomes a giant leap for interpretation, opening the door to consider the full range of God's faithfulness to all of God's creation. Creation "was subjected to futility," but nature is not left out or left in limbo with respect to God's redemptive purpose (Rom 8:20). The terms of nature's involuntary exile are defined; it was subjected "in hope" (Rom 8:20). Thus, Paul does not strike an alien or dissonant chord when he brings nature into the picture in Romans because the broadening horizon is part and parcel of his underlying theme. The plight of nature lines up alongside human plight, and the expectation of nature, like human hope, rests on the affirmation of God's faithfulness. This is a ringing affirmation of God's purpose, including God's purpose for the nonhuman creation.

A fourth characteristic of Paul's letters that is now widely recognized is their pervasive apocalyptic outlook and undercurrent. Perhaps no one has emphasized this as much as J. Christiaan Beker, who argues that "the apocalyptic world view

---

11. Hays, *The Faith of Jesus Christ*, 119–207. For a review of some of the issues raised in the debate, see also Sigve Tonstad, "πίστις Χριστοῦ: Reading Paul in a New Paradigm," *AUSS* 40 (2002), 37–59. The key passages for this phrase are Gal 2:16, 20; 3:22, 26; cf. Rom 3:22, 25, 26; Phlm 3:9.

12. As Brendan Byrne points out in "Creation Groaning: An Earth Bible Reading of Romans 8.18–22," in Habel, *Readings from the Perspective of the Earth*, 194, interpreters in the traditional paradigm "were engaged in a virtually exclusive preoccupation with relations between human beings and God."

13. Stanley Stowers, *A Rereading of Romans: Justice, Jews, and Gentiles* (New Haven: Yale University Press, 1994).

14. Hays, *Echoes of Scripture*, 36–41.

is the fundamental carrier of Paul's thought."[15] The term "apocalyptic" includes the following elements: special revelation; insight into otherworldly phenomena; the end of the present age; a circumscribed cosmic dualism; and belief in the resurrection of the body. Beker is no doubt correct that in relation to these points there is no difference between Paul the Pharisee and Paul the believer in Jesus.[16] Paul's attention to nature in Romans is also spurred on by apocalyptic concerns. When creation "waits with eager longing for the revealing of the children of God" (Rom 8:19), it is understood that the apocalyptic, ultimate hope, is in view.[17] When, too, we are told that "the whole creation has been groaning in labor pains until now" (Rom 8:22), Paul is referring to an apocalyptic insight.[18] Recalling that this is a view he holds in common with other believers does not detract from the fact that their shared insight belongs to the awaited apocalyptic unveiling and is not merely common knowledge throughout the Roman Empire. These verses, says C. E. B. Cranfield, "are certainly not to be understood as merely an inference from the observable and generally recognized fact of the prevalence of suffering in nature."[19]

Even more to the point, perhaps, is the apocalyptic temperament of the passage, its verbal body language. Paul is at pains to find words that are up to the task. The "eager longing" of creation conjures up the image of "spectators straining forward over the ropes to catch the first glimpse of some triumphal pageant."[20] Nature has caught a glimmer of hope on the horizon;[21] indeed, a certain hope has come into view toward which nature turns with "confident expectation."[22] Likewise, the perception that "the whole creation has been groaning in labor pains" conveys an apocalyptic stirring within nature, its very groaning intensified by the conviction that the tide has turned and that relief long-awaited is within sight. Interest in nature is not unique to apocalyptic writings. Nature also has a voice in the prophetic books of the Old Testament.[23] It can hardly be denied that in Paul's

---

15. J. Christiaan Beker, *Paul the Apostle: The Triumph of God in Life and Thought* (Philadelphia: Fortress Press, 1980), 181; cf. also Klaus Koch, *The Rediscovery of Apocalyptic* (trans. Margaret Kohl. London: SCM Press), 1972; John J. Collins, *The Apocalyptic Imagination* (2d ed.; Grand Rapids: Eerdmans, 1998).

16. Beker, *Paul the Apostle*, 144.

17. Ulrich Wilckens, *Der Brief an die Römer*, (3 vols.; EKKNT; Neukirchen-Vluyn: Benziger Verlag, 1980), 2:152; Byrne, *Romans*, 256–57.

18. Michel, *Der Brief an die Römer*, 2:269.

19. Cranfield, *Romans*, 410.

20. Sanday and Headlam, *Romans*, 204–5.

21. Ernst Käsemann, *Commentary on Romans* (trans. Geoffrey W. Bromiley; Grand Rapids: Eerdmans, 1994), 235.

22. Cranfield, *Romans*, 410.

23. See e.g. Terence E. Fretheim, "The Earth Story in Jeremiah 12," in Habel, *Readings from the Perspective of Earth*, 96–110.

apocalyptic outlook, nature's voice is raised to a higher pitch, whether in voicing its plight or its hope.

But this view of nature leads naturally to a fifth contemporary current in the field of Pauline studies. Paul, this view maintains, is also providing a critique of the Roman Empire and its self-professed image as the provider of peace and benign prosperity.[24] The present passage, allowing nature to state its case, strips away the imperial pretense and the veneer of a golden age that the imperial cult is foisting on the citizens of the empire. Paul's epistle to the Romans depicts nature gasping under the iron heel of an oppressive and exploitative master, reflecting the early Christian conviction that "a peaceful, magically prosperous golden age is illusory."[25] In reference to the Roman Empire, nature voices resistance.

A final proposal, suggested by E. P. Sanders, holds that Paul's argument does not run from plight to solution but from solution to plight.[26] Putting this proposition to the test in the present passage, the result is affirmative. In Romans, Paul states the plight of nature twice (Rom 8:20, 22), each time foregrounding the solution (Rom 8:19, 21). This sequence of ideas may seem incidental, but it draws attention to Paul's view that the solution is ascendant.

Each of these six propositions contributes in one way or another to refute the supposition that "nature plays a very small role for the apostle."[27] C. H. Dodd, who writes eloquently and admiringly of how Paul in Romans is "declaiming against the vices of the age like a satirist, speculating on the knowledge of God and the conscience of . . . [human beings] like a philosopher, arguing from Scripture like a rabbi, and analysing experience like a psychologist," finds him here speaking "with the vision of a poet."[28] But his accolade misses the mark because Paul is not speculating or waxing lyrical; he is spelling out the implications of the apocalyptic hope in ways that even some of the greatest Pauline scholars have not acknowledged. For those who have wondered why Paul brings up the subject of nature at all, the answer might be that on this issue Paul is not the kind of thinker many would like him to be. He is certainly not the kind of detached desk theologian that he is often made out to be. This view is a far cry from his activist vision and persona in his letter to the Romans.

---

24. Klaus Wengst, *Pax Romana and the Peace of Jesus Christ* (trans. John Bowden; London: SCM Press, 1987), 7–37, gives a representative account of the imperial self-perception of *Pax Romana*.

25. Robert Jewett, "The Corruption and Redemption of Creation: Reading Rom 8:18–23 within the Imperial Context," in *Paul and the Roman Imperial Order* (ed. Richard A. Horsley; Harrisburg: Trinity Press International, 2004), 32.

26. E. P. Sanders, *Paul and Palestinian Judaism* (Minneapolis: Fortress, 1979), 443.

27. Käsemann, *Commentary on Romans*, 233; cf. also Jan Lambrecht, *The Wretched "I" and Its Liberation: Paul in Romans 7 and 8* (Louvain: Peeters, 1992), 131.

28. C. H. Dodd, *The Epistle to the Romans* (MNTC; London: Hodder & Stoughton, 1932), 133.

2. APPLICATION

How does this remarkable and singular text touch our time and reflect our reality? Space allows only three extrapolations in the light of the emphases sketched above.

Following the trajectory of Paul's argument, the perception of what is wrong and the prescription for what will set things right are both conceived within an apocalyptic frame of reference. Only the ear sensitized by revelation truly hears the groaning of nature; only the eye touched by the eschatological unveiling sees nature convulsed in agony. What does the believer's ear hear today? What does the believing eye see? On this point it is fair to say that if nature is to have any hope, it will be on the basis of an apocalyptic intervention. As Marie Turner has shown in her comment on this passage in The Earth Bible series, the faith that is in view is at its innermost core a resurrection faith,[29] and resurrection faith rises within the framework of an apocalyptic view of reality.

On the other hand, however, an apocalyptic perspective is fast becoming dispensable for perceiving nature's plight. Nature's wail is now audible even to the dull and desensitized ear that is unfamiliar with apocalyptic perspectives and uneasy about its outlook. Perhaps we hear the wail of nature nowhere more piercingly than in the agonized squealing of pigs, turkeys, and chickens that lead the line of victims of modern factory farming in the Western world. These animals, in descending order, are the most abused animals of our time. They testify, each in their own distinctive voice,[30] that the relationship between human and nonhuman creation fractured by the Fall has in our time become unhinged and intolerable. It must suffice to mention only one contemporary account of this abusive reality, Matthew Scully's book, Dominion: The Power of Man, the Suffering of Animals, and the Call to Mercy.[31] Surely the reality depicted in Scully's book has the fervency and the time-turning connotation of an apocalypse without wearing its mantle. Recalling the blessing on nonhuman creation in Genesis and hearing the labor pangs of nature in the New Testament, it misses the mark to see the call to mercy as a generous concession on the part of human beings. The call to mercy reflects nature's worth. Mercy is the God-given right of nonhuman creation.

---

29. Marie Turner, "God's Design: The Death of Creation? An Ecojustice Reading of Romans 8.18–30 in the Light of Wisdom 1–2," in Habel and Wurst, The Earth Story in Wisdom Traditions, 168–78.

30. This is Isaac Bashevis Singer's perception in his short story "The Slaughterer," in The Collected Stories of Isaac Bashevis Singer (New York: Farrar, Straus & Giroux, 1996), 209.

31. Matthew Scully, Dominion: The Power of Man, the Suffering of Animals, and the Call to Mercy (New York: St. Martin's Press, 2002).

As contemporary readings of Paul bring to light, the apocalyptic perception of reality also exposes the guile of political illusions, both past and present. The imperial authority and its religious cult seek to cultivate an image of peace and prosperity that, from the apocalyptic point of view—from nature's perspective, as voiced by nature—is seen as a cunning propaganda ploy. If nature wails in agony against the abuses of the Roman Empire, what must nature, and the apocalyptic voice of nature, be saying today? If the imperial political mantra of Paul's time is refuted when nature calls its bluff, what must nature be saying in our time, in its apocalyptic voice, when it is subjected to abuses both unimagined and unimaginable in Paul's day, in a cultural setting that claims to honor the legacy of Paul?

Finally, what does Paul have in mind when he writes in Rom 8:19 (NJB) that "the whole creation" waits with intense and expectant longing "for the revealing of the children of God"? Does he expect action in the present that will transform imperial policy and, in turn, have a trickle-down benefit to nature? Or, sensing that an intervention in the present will only have a limited, temporizing effect, is nature's longing of necessity a vision deferred that cannot begin in the present? Does Paul's remedial vision on this point lie closer to that of the Old Testament prophets who, in H. H. Rowley's view, "foretold the future that should arise out of the present, while the apocalyptists foretold the future that should break into the present."[32]

When Robert Jewett answers that the responsibility and obligation of "the children of God" begin in the present, he has not misread Paul, but it seems curiously removed from contemporary reality to believe that "the entire creation waits with bated breath for the emergence and empowerment of those who will take responsibility for its restoration."[33] To believe that the forces of exploitation and oppression will at last be tamed by the action of "the children of God"—in the sense that "their altered lifestyle and revised ethics begin to restore the ecological system"[34]—seems to overestimate the impact of God's children whether in the light of the biblical or the contemporary evidence.

For Paul, however, prophecy and apocalyptic are not mutually exclusive options. The view he holds, in common with companies of scattered believers in the first century C.E., envisions urgent and responsible action in the present, according to the pattern of Old Testament prophecy *and* divine intervention configured according to the scale of apocalyptic beliefs. Nature keeps a vigilant watch for "the revealing of the children of God" because the believers offer hope even though they may be few in number, and they offer hope because their existence is proof of a greater hope. A secret, implied reciprocity is in view. Nature will accept

---

32. H. H. Rowley, *The Relevance of Apocalyptic: A Study of Jewish and Christian Apocalypses from Daniel to the Revelation* (London: Lutterworth, 1944), 51.

33. Jewett, "Corruption and Redemption," 35.

34. Jewett, "Corruption and Redemption," 35.

as children of God those who "demonstrate" they are God's children by "exercising the kind of dominion that heals rather than destroys."[35] The children of God will give nature a brief foretaste of the more permanent relief that is to come. Indeed, as Philip Esler perceives the context of the book of Romans, nature swells the ranks of the believers: it is "aligned with, and supportive of, the tiny minority constituting the Christ-movement."[36]

And then, too, hope is ascendant. As is often the case in Paul's writings, his argument in Rom 8:19–22 runs from solution to plight—both in the structure of his presentation and at the core of his thinking. To the entire creation, the long shadow of its plight is receding in the face of the reality of the solution that has come to light in the unveiling of the faithfulness of God.

---

35. Jewett, "Corruption and Redemption," 46.

36. Philip Esler, *Conflict and Identity in Romans: The Social Setting of Paul's Letter* (Minneapolis: Fortress, 2003), 262.

CRITIQUING ANTHROPOCENTRIC COSMOLOGY: RETRIEVING A STOIC "PERMEATION COSMOLOGY" IN COLOSSIANS 1:15–20

Vicky Balabanski

In February 2004, the *New Scientist* journal had an article about the Rocky Mountain locusts,[1] a particularly beefy species of grasshopper that devastated the American frontier in the mid 1870s. Even as an Australian, I had heard of the way in which the newly settled pioneers in Minnesota, Nebraska, Iowa, and the Dakotas had been beset by locust plagues of biblical proportions: the swarm of 1875 reliably estimated to have been almost 3000 kilometers long and 180 kilometers wide.

What caught my eye about this article were the ecological and theological problems it posed. On 26 April 1877, the governor of Minnesota, John Pillsbury, called for a day of prayer to intercede for deliverance from the locusts. A few days later, the insects rose up and left, and were never to plague Western farmers again. In fact, within thirty years this species was extinct. The article describes the research of Jeffrey Lockwood, an insect ecologist who traced the geography of the extinction to the surprisingly small home base of the locusts in the river valleys of Montana and Wyoming. This was where the locusts buried their eggs, and by ploughing and watering these fertile spots, the incoming settlers were the insects' own nemesis. The last living Rocky Mountain locust was found on the Canadian prairie in 1902.

Theologically, a Christian might be inclined to celebrate the providence of God and the spectacular success of the day of prayer. Ecologically, one might be inclined to see this extinction as a warning rather than a victory, noting how vulnerable species are to the disruption of their habitat.

The challenge is to bring these perspectives together into an ecological theology. This article seeks to do this by rethinking the *cosmology* implicit in how these events were interpreted, and showing that an anthropocentric cosmology

---

1. Sharon Levy, "Last Days of the Locust," *New Scientist* 2435 (2004): 48–49.

is neither the most legitimate interpretative framework nor even necessarily the cosmology of early Christian interpreters.

1. Recognizing Our Perspective

We can see that in the 1870s there was a pattern of sudden migration in two species: Rocky mountain locusts and human settlers. These sudden migrations interacted with one another, perhaps even precipitated one another. There were winners and losers. When we do theology from an anthropocentric point of view, and the winners are the humans, there doesn't appear to be a problem. God's provenance is on our side. It's only when we recognize God's concern for and presence in the whole of creation that it becomes imperative to find more inclusive ways of doing theology.

Can an ecological perspective enable us to recognize and critique our anthropocentric bias that when humans are the winners and the biosphere is expendable? Can adopting an ecological ideology give us a framework *both* for critiquing our narrow perspective that the biosphere is here, first and foremost, for human well-being, *and* yet enable us to continue to assert that God cares for human beings in a special way?

2. The Colossians Hymn

I want to explore what bringing these questions to the biblical text of the Colossians hymn, Col 1:15–20, may contribute to this discussion. This passage formulates a christological cosmology. If we understand cosmology to be the "theory of the universe as an ordered whole, and of the general laws that govern it,"[2] a christological cosmology lays claim to Christ playing a pivotal role in how the universe is ordered. Such a cosmology could not have been formulated in a vacuum. In order to understand what claims are being made for Christ, I want to explore the resonances between Col 1:15–20 and other ancient cosmological frameworks. What similarities are there? What differences? These similarities and differences may shed light on how some early Christian communities understood the salvation offered to them. If Christ is indeed pivotal to the whole cosmos—as the Colossians hymn claims—the fate of the Rocky Mountain locusts, as well as the fate of the pioneers, is significant to God.

15. He is the image of the invisible God, the firstborn of all creation;
16. for in him all things in heaven and on earth were created, things visible and invisible, whether thrones or dominions or rulers or powers—all things have been created through him and for him.

---

2. OED, *ad loc.*

17. He himself is before all things, and in him all things hold together.
18. He is the head of the body, the church; he is the beginning, the firstborn from the dead, so that he might come to have first place in everything.
19. For in him all the fullness of God was pleased to dwell,
20. and through him God was pleased to reconcile to himself all things, whether on earth or in heaven, by making peace through the blood of his cross.

This hymnic material presents a very striking cosmology. First, the invisible aspects of reality are given great prominence: the invisible God, the invisible thrones, dominions, rulers and powers, and even the dead. It is as though the invisible dimensions of reality are pressing in upon the visible. Second, there is great attention to origin as a signifier of rank of precedence. This is a highly nuanced cosmology of rank and status. Third, this cosmological picture asserts a fundamental interconnection between all things, an interconnection that has not only a unified origin, but also a unified *telos,* or goal, namely, the reconciliation of all things. Fourth, the invisible God is equated with "the whole fullness" in verse 19, but is otherwise articulated only through the visible image of Christ. And finally, the cosmology is outrageously christocentric: he is the expression of God, the origin, the means, the goal, the purpose, the sustainer, the reconciler. And he is these things not just as the cosmic Christ, but as the one who died on the cross.

The anthropocentricity of a cosmology that proclaims a human being as divine mediator and savior is clear. A mediator/savior who is aligned with humanity first and foremost sets up a hierarchy within the *bios,* implying that salvation for the rest of creation is necessarily secondary to human salvation and derivative of it. Just as feminist scholarship has posed the question of whether a male savior can save women, we ask whether a human savior can be salvific for other species as well.

The Colossians hymn claims that this is indeed the case and that the cosmic Christ is not only instrumental in the existence of all creation, but the means whereby God has reconciled all things, *ta panta.* There is some ambiguity in verse 20 as to whether this reconciliation is to God's Self, or whether it should be translated as "the whole fullness was pleased to reconcile all things to him," that is, Christ. This latter interpretation is favored by C. Breytenbach in his book on reconciliation,[3] and seems in keeping with the christocentricity of the rest of the hymn.

In examining the Colossians hymn, it is customary to begin with an analysis of the structure and form with the intention of discerning the "original"—perhaps

---

3. C. Breytenbach, *Versöhnung: Eine Studie zur paulinischen Soteriologie* (WMANT 60; Neukirchen-Vluyn: Neukirchener, 1989), 190–91.

even pre-Christian—hymn, and defining those elements that may best be under-stood as glosses.[4] It's then common to examine the key terms and phrases, seeking to analyze the extent to which they reflect Platonic elements, Jewish wisdom spec-ulation, as well as Hermeticism and early Gnosticism. But, as Schüssler Fiorenza[5] has pointed out, the hymn's statements of exaltation and pre-existence use the "language and elements of various myths and mythologies," and it's difficult, if not impossible, to draw lines of clear demarcation between the philosophical streams by means of semantic association. What I mean is that the word *eikon* "image" could be Platonic, or Hermetic, or reflect Philo's wisdom speculation. Similarly, *pleroma* "fullness" could be early Gnostic, or Hermetic, or neither. By the first century c.e., many of these boundaries were fluid.[6]

3. The Cosmology of the Colossians Hymn

I propose a simpler way of gaining a sense of the intellectual context of the Colos-sians hymn: namely, via the cosmology that it evokes. If I may paint with broad brushstrokes for a moment, the cosmology of middle Platonism—and those streams of thought that stand in continuity with it—propound a cosmology of distance. The divine, however that is construed, is at a distance from humanity and the material world, and there is need of an intermediary, or intermediaries, to bridge the chasm. For Platonists, the sage sought to bear this role. For Jewish wisdom speculation, that intermediary was Sophia wisdom; for Philo, it was Logos wisdom. In the first hermetic tractate the revealer is called Poimandres, "the Mind of the Sovereignty." Whatever their particular soteriology, they all presuppose a cosmology of distance.

This is the framework within which we have always sought to interpret the christological claims of the Colossians hymn, and indeed the other christological

---

4. For a discussion of whether it is possible to reconstruct an earlier hymn, see George H. Van Kooten, *Cosmic Christology in Paul and the Pauline School* (WUNT 171; Tübingen: Mohr Siebeck, 2003), 115–19. Van Kooten concludes that the author of Colossians can most plausibly be taken to be the author of the hymn.

5. E. Schüssler Fiorenza, "Wisdom Mythology and the Christological Hymns of the New Testament," in *Aspects of Religious Propaganda in Judaism and Early Christianity* (ed. R. Wilken; Studies in Judaism and Christianity in Antiquity 2; Notre Dame: University of Notre Dame Press, 1975), 38.

6. So Hans-Friedrich Weiss, *Untersuchungen zur Kosmologie des hellenistischen und palästinischen Judentums.* (TUGAL 97; Berlin: Akademie-Verlag: Texte und Untersuchungen zur Geschichte der altchristlichen Literatur, 1966) 253–54, with particular reference to Poseidonios, Philo and Plutarch. For a detailed treatment of the cosmology of Colossians against the backgrounds of Stoic and Middle Platonist physics, see Van Kooten, *Cosmic Christology.*

hymns of the Christian Scriptures. A cosmology of distance requires an intermediary to bridge that distance who is none other than Christ.

However, in the Colossians hymn we also have echoes of another framework: Stoicism. Against the background of the cosmology of distance, it is the odd one out. By contrast with the contemporary cosmologies of distance, Stoic cosmology proposes quite a different model for divine/human connection.

Stoics understand Nature, *physis*, to be what holds the world together, a rational agent that is the ultimate cause of all things. As such, Nature is another way of referring to God. Far from holding a cosmology of distance, Stoics perceive the world to have divine purpose, *logos*, immanent within it and that this divine purpose is working for the benefit of rational beings. So Nature or God is the active principle in the world, interacting with inert matter. As one Stoic put it, "God is mixed with matter, penetrates the whole of matter and shapes it."[7]

We could therefore call this cosmology panentheistic *par excellence*. I am aware that Stoics often present themselves as pantheistic—they readily make reference to the gods, and understand the individual gods of the Olympic pantheon as the natural phenomena whose names they have been given.[8] The Stoics perceived Nature/God as a creating or artistic "fire" with material substance that pervades all things and accounts for their persistence and their change.

So we have on the one hand various cosmologies of distance that see the divine separated from humanity. On the other we have the Stoic cosmology of divine permeation.

What if we suspended the cosmology of distance with which we generally approach the Colossians hymn, and tried to hear the hymn against a background of Stoic cosmology? There are two main reasons for doing so. First, to quote David Hahm, "more people in the Mediterranean world would have held a more or less Stoic conception of the world than any other" from the third century B.C.E. to the second century C.E.[9] As Hahm states, in this period, Stoicism was very likely the most widely accepted worldview in the Western world, and "it appealed to all classes, attracting slaves and laborers as well as kings and emperors. Its ideals infiltrated religion and science, medicine and theology, poetry and drama, law and government."[10] So it is highly likely that many of the people who heard and/or used the Colossians hymn in praise were familiar with the Stoic turns of phrase and had an understanding of Stoic cosmology.

---

7. In H. von Arnim, ed., *Stoicorum Veterum Fragmenta* (Leipzig, 1903–24; repr., Stuttgart: Teubner, 1964), 2:310.

8. Hera or Juno is "air." Stoics held that there was one ultimate deity, Nature, whose name is also Zeus. See A. A. Long, *Hellenistic Philosophy: Stoics, Epicureans, Sceptics* (London, Duckworth, 1974), 150.

9. David E. Hahm, *The Origins of Stoic Cosmology* (Ohio: Ohio State University Press, 1977), xiii.

10. Hahm, *Stoic Cosmology*, xiii.

Second, the hymn itself invites us to do so. The repeated use of *pan/ panta eis* evokes the Stoic praise of the self-contained harmony of all things. In verse 16 we hear that *en autō ektisthē ta panta* (in him all things were created), and then, in the same verse, an even more vivid expression of this notion: *ta panta di'autou kai eis auton ektistai* (all things have been created through him and for him). It has long been recognized that these are strongly Stoic formulations. Marcus Aurelius' words are a classic Stoic formulation of this notion: "All things come from you, subsist in you, go back to you" (*ek sou panta, en soi panta, eis se panta*).[11]

Furthermore, verses 17–18 speak of Christ as a cosmic body, which resonates with the Stoic view of nature as being filled with the deity. In verse 17, the verb *sunestēkenai* (to be established; to continue, exist, endure) is a word that is used in Stoic philosophy to denote the unity of the entire world.[12] For these reasons, Eduard Lohse pointed out the following in his commentary on Colossians: "From the Hellenistic synagogue, this confession of God the creator, *formulated in Stoic phrases*, was appropriated by the Christian community and joined together with its confession of Christ."[13] But why did the Christian community formulate their confession in Stoic phrases? Was it because the Stoic cosmological framework lent itself to Christological reflection? I suggest that this is the case, though our Aristotelian and Platonic heritage has since obscured or subsumed the Stoic cosmology in this hymn.

4. CHRISTOLOGY AND STOIC COSMOLOGY

Those who thought in terms of Stoic cosmology already believed that the world is permeated with *pneuma*. They believed that not everything has equal amounts of this *pneuma*, though. It is most "densely" situated in the human sage. However, though they believed the "Good Man" is fully in harmony with spirit/Nature/God, some had reservations about the actual existence of any human who has "made the grade."[14] It is here that christology comes into play. If you come to accept that there was but one person who was Good, and in whom *Logos* was fully present, namely the Christ, cosmologically, it is straightforward to accept that "his" *logos* is through all and in all.

Because the Stoics confined "existence" to bodies[15] (which was justified by the assumption that for something to exist it must be capable of producing or experiencing some change, and that this condition is only satisfied by bodies), the

---

11. C.f. Marcus Aurelius 4.23.2. In Marcus Aurelius' writings, this is addressed to Nature ("*physis*").

12. E. Lohse, *Colossians and Philemon* (Philadelphia: Fortress, 1971), 52. This word was also current in Platonic philosophy.

13. Lohse, *Colossians and Philemon*, 50. Italics mine.

14. Long, *Hellenistic Philosophy*, 204.

15. E.g., von Arnim, *Stoicorum Veterum Fragmenta*, 2:525.

earthly Jesus' bodily existence was in continuity with the bodily permeation of the *logos* within the whole of creation.

Thus the shift between historical particularity of Jesus and cosmological permeation of the risen Christ is relatively straightforward within a Stoic framework because spirit is necessarily embodied, and necessarily one. With *logos*, distinctions between the universal and the particular are unnecessary.

Thus a Stoic cosmology lent itself smoothly to the Colossians hymn's Christological affirmation that this human person was a visible, embodied expression of God.

Moreover Stoics held a utopian vision of community life: all distinctions based on sex, birth, nationality, and property are dispensed with. Something of this vision found actual expression in the Christian church, the *ekklesia*. In the church, people were able to experience a heightened density of *pneuma* and move towards *eudaimonia* (happiness, as a "favor" or gift of the divinity).

The religious affirmation that salvation was to be found in the one in whom and through whom all things exist must have been appealing to those who accepted the cosmological framework of Stoicism, but found the ethical idealism of Stoicism too hard to attain or who could not perceive any salvation in the Stoic teaching that willing acceptance of the external situation constitutes freedom.

By formulating a christological confession in Stoic categories, this hymn makes a synthesis of Hellenistic thought and Christian experience and reflection. The writings of Philo some decades earlier demonstrate that such syntheses between Jewish and Hellenistic categories were a contemporary phenomenon.

5. Towards a Permeation Cosmology

In what way does the discussion of a Christological cosmology in Colossians 1:15–20 assist us in forging an ecological theology capable of enabling us to recognize and critique our anthropocentric bias? Does recovering a cosmology of permeation drawn from Stoic thought make a difference? It is clear that we cannot simply adopt an ancient cosmology like that of the Colossians hymn with its hierarchies of angelic powers. Nevertheless, the affirmation of interconnection between all things—so common in ancient cultures, yet surprisingly difficult for those who are shaped by the binary nature of much Western thought—is vital for our shared future.

If we work within a framework of a cosmology of distance, with a mediator/savior who is aligned with humanity first and foremost, the rest of creation is necessarily secondary and derivative. So when we hear the affirmation in Colossians 1:20 that "through him God was pleased to reconcile to God's self *all things*," we might hear "all things" to mean "all things pertaining to humans." We certainly do not hear "through him God was pleased to reconcile to God's self all things, including Rocky Mountains locusts."

However if we work with a Stoic cosmology of God permeating Nature, we can affirm that the nonhuman *bios* has value and worth because it is permeated by the very same *pneuma* that was fully expressed in Christ. This means that the Colossians hymn expresses soteriology not only for humans but for the whole of creation.

An example of the tendency towards anthropocentricity in reading the Colossians hymn is found in E. Lohse's commentary. He states: "The great drama, wherein the principalities are stripped of their power and the reconciliation of all things has taken place, *is for the sake of man alone.*"[16] A cosmic human is the savior of humans first and foremost.

What about *ta panta*?

My proposal is that it is possible to read the hymn to the cosmic Christ in a way that moves beyond anthropocentrism, and understands *ta panta* to include the whole biosphere. To do so, however, we need a cosmology of divine permeation, not a cosmology of distance.

If the divine *logos*/wisdom permeates the whole of creation, and was most fully embodied in Christ, the same impulse towards life that motivated the pioneers also motivated the locusts. The voice of Earth is heard in the impulse to life that motivated both locusts and settlers. Yet their respective impulses towards life meant that the interests of the two species came into conflict. In what sense then can we claim, along with Col 1:20, that through Christ, God has reconciled *ta panta* to himself, given that competition between species seems to belong to the very principle of life, or *logos*, itself?

As scientist Donald A. Windsor has argued that, while conflict between species harms individual organisms in an ecosystem, it is beneficial at the species level.[17] Conflict regulates ecosystems and thereby enables species to survive and coexist. In a comparable way, the locust swarms sent many pioneers off the land, and this also moderated the impact of the sudden change in the ecological balance that the pioneers' agricultural practices had introduced.

The reconciliation that the Colossians hymn claims is located in Christ is of a spiritual order. By bringing our contemporary ecological concerns into dialogue with this claim, I am asking whether we can discern any impulse towards reconciliation between species in the Christ event. After all, if *ta panta* in the Colossians hymn is not deemed to embrace more than humans and higher species of life, angels, and heavenly powers, then the Christological vision of Col 1 proclaims anthropocentric hegemony over creation and belies its own affirmation of reconciliation.

---

16. Lohse, *Colossians and Philemon*, 61. Italics mine.

17. Donald A. Windsor, "Equal Rights for Parasites (Call for Protection of Parasites Against Extinction)," *Perspectives in Biology and Medicine* 40 (1997): 222–29.

I propose that if there is a reconciliation or peace between all things through the cosmic wisdom of Christ, it is through a renewed perspective on the species' respective impulses towards life. Reconciliation and peace-making processes validate the worth of all things, thereby asserting the right of both Rocky Mountain locusts and the pioneers to live.

The cosmic Christ who spilt his blood on the cross, and was emptied of power, is the icon of God in the sense that he did not prioritize his life and his power over others. In doing so, Christ demonstrated that there is more to existence than power clashing against power and competition between those who become winners at the expense of those who are rendered losers. There is the possibility of respecting the impulse to life in the other as being in continuity with one's own impulse to life, and also choosing to forego power for the sake of the kinship of the *pneuma* we share.

But as humans, we stand in a privileged position, and with that privilege of both perspective and means, we can no longer deny the validity of the life claims of other species. Yet such a perspective cannot simply be adopted as though it were a single act or decision. It must constantly be chosen, and be motivated by the deepest impulses by which we make meaning. For Christians, the peace-making through Jesus' blood on the cross is a dynamic process. It is not a single event. It enables us to move towards a bio-centric cosmology, learning and relearning respect for the impulse towards life in all creation.

In this essay I have sought to bring ecological issues, an ancient Christological hymn, and the Stoic cosmology of permeation into a creative dialogue. In doing so, I have shown the tendency towards anthropocentric readings in the tradition, and, in contrast, I have proposed a theology of reconciliation. The ecojustice principle of interconnectedness[18] is fundamental to this reading, and is further explicated by it.

In conclusion, I recognize that this theology would have had very little resonance with the settlers at the time of the locust plague: salvation for them was divine intervention to save their livelihood, not the fortitude to participate in a painful process of ecological change.

Yet Christ's death on the cross as the icon of God is less about divine intervention and more about self-limitation and participation in powerlessness. When it comes to ecological matters, Christians are yet to become truly cruciform in their thinking. Perhaps by finding a renewed perspective towards other species, Christ will indeed be experienced as the icon of God and the one reconciling all things.

---

18. "Earth is a community of interconnected living things that are mutually dependent on each other for life and survival," the second of six ecojustice principles undergirding the Earth Bible approach (see p. 2).

Bibliography

Adams, Edward. "Paul's Story of God and Creation: The Story of How God Fulfils His Purposes in Creation." Pages 19–43 in *Narrative Dynamics in Paul: A Critical Assessment.* Edited by Bruce W. Longenecker. Louisville, Ky.: Westminster John Knox, 2002.

Ahlström, G. W. *Joel and the Temple Cult of Jerusalem.* VTSup 21. Leiden: Brill, 1971.

Alexander, Philip S. "Jerusalem as the Omphalos of the World: On the History of a Geographical Concept." Pages 104–19 in *Jerusalem: Its Sanctity and Centrality to Judaism, Christianity, and Islam.* Edited by Lee I. Levine. New York: Continuum, 1999.

Allison, D. C. *The End of the Ages Has Come: An Early Interpretation of the Passion and Resurrection of Jesus.* Edinburgh: T&T Clark, 1985.

Amir, Yehoshua. "Figure of Death in the Book of Wisdom." *JJS* 30 (1979): 154–78.

Andersen, Francis I., and David Noel Freedman. *Hosea: A New Translation with Introduction and Commentary.* AB 24. Garden City, N.Y.: Doubleday, 1980.

Arnim, H. von, ed. *Stoicorum Veterum Fragmenta.* 4 vols. Leipzig, 1903–24. Repr., Stuttgart: Teubner, 1964.

Athenaeus. *The Deipnosophists.* Translated by Charles Burton Gulick. 7 vols. Loeb Classical Library. London: Heinemann, 1916.

Barstad, Hans M. "After the 'Myth of the Empty Land': Major Challenges in the Study of Neo-Babylonian Judah." Pages 3–20 in *Judah and the Judeans in the Neo-Babylonian Period.* Edited by Oded Lipschitz and Joseph Blenkinsopp. Winona Lake, Ind.: Eisenbrauns, 2005.

Barton, John. "Natural Law and Poetic Justice in the Old Testament." *Journal of Theological Studies* 30 (1979): 1–14. Repr. pages 32–44 in: *Understanding Old Testament Ethics: Approaches and Explorations.* Louisville, Ky.: Westminster John Knox, 2002.

Bauer, Walter, William F. Arndt, F. Wilbur Gingrich, and Frederick W. Danker, eds. *A Greek-English Lexicon of the New Testament and Other Early Christian Literature.* 2d ed. Chicago: University of Chicago Press, 1958.

Bechtel, F. "Alabaster," *The Catholic Encyclopedia,* Volume I. New York: Robert Appleton, 1907. Online ed., 2003. Cited 9 November 2005. Online: http://www.newadvent.org/cathen/01244b.htm.

Bechtel, L. M. "Rethinking the Interpretation of Genesis 2.4b–3.24." Pages 77–117 in *A Feminist Companion to Genesis.* Edited by A. Brenner. Sheffield: Sheffield Academic Press, 1993.

Begrich, Joachim. "Das priesterliche Heilsorakel." *ZAW* 52 (1934): 81–82

Beker, J. Christiaan. *Paul the Apostle: The Triumph of God in Life and Thought*. Philadelphia: Fortress, 1980.

Berlin, Adele. *Zephaniah: A New Translation with Introduction and Commentary*. AB 25A. New York: Doubleday, 1994.

———. *Lamentations: A Commentary*. OTL. Louisville, Ky.: Westminster John Knox, 2002.

Birch, Charles. *On Purpose*. Sydney: University of New South Wales Press, 1990.

Botterweck, G. Johannes., Helmer Ringgren, and Heinz-Josef Fabry, eds. *Theological Dictionary of the Old Testament*. 12 vols. Grand Rapids: Eerdmans, 1974–2006.

Braaten, Laurie J. "Earth Community in Hosea 2." Pages 185–203 in Habel, *The Earth Story in Psalms and Prophets*, 2001.

———. "All Creation Groans: Romans 8:22 in Light of the Biblical Sources." *HBT* 28 (2006): 131–51.

Breytenbach, C. *Versöhnung: Eine Studie zur paulinischen Soteriologie*. WMANT 60. Neukirchen-Vluyn: Neukirchener, 1989.

Brock, Rita Nakashima and Rebecca Ann Parker. *Proverbs of Ashes: Violence, Redemptive Suffering, and the Search for What Saves Us*. Boston: Beacon, 2001.

Brown, Raymond E. *The Death of the Messiah. From Gethsemane to the Grave*. 2 vols. New York: Doubleday, 1994.

Brown, William P. *Seeing the Psalms: A Theology of Metaphor*. Louisville, Ky.: Westminster John Knox, 2002.

Brueggemann, Walter. *Genesis*. IBC. Atlanta: John Knox, 1982.

———. "The Uninflected Therefore of Hosea 4:1–3." Pages 231–49 in *Social Location and Biblical Interpretation in the United States*. Vol. 1 of *Reading from this Place*. Edited by Fernando F. Segovia and Mary Ann Tolbert. Minneapolis: Fortress, 1995.

Byrne, Brendan J. *Reckoning with Romans: A Contemporary Reading of Paul's Gospel*. Good News Studies 18. Wilmington: Michael Glazier, 1986.

———. "Creation Groaning: An Earth Bible Reading of Romans 8.18–22." Pages 193–203 in Habel, *Readings from the Perspective of Earth*, 2000.

Cassuto, Umberto. *From Adam to Noah*. Jerusalem: Magnes Press, Hebrew University, 1961.

Childs, Brevard S. "The Enemy from the North and the Chaos Tradition." *JBL* 78 (1959): 187–98.

Clark, W. M. "The Animal Series in the Primeval History." *VT* 18 (1968): 433–49.

Clarke, Ernest G. *The Wisdom of Solomon*. Cambridge: Cambridge University Press, 1973.

Clements, R. E. *God and Temple*. Oxford: Blackwell, 1965.

Clines, David J.A. *Job 1–20*. WBC 17. Dallas: Word Books, 1989.

———. "Was There an *'bl* II 'Be Dry' in Classical Hebrew?" *VT* 42 (1992): 1–10.

———. ed. *The Dictionary of Classical Hebrew*. 5 vols. Sheffield: Sheffield Academic Press, 1993–.

Coats, George W. *Genesis, with an Introduction to Narrative Literature*. FOTL 1. Grand Rapids: Eerdmans, 1983.

Collins, John J. *The Apocalyptic Imagination*. 2d ed. Grand Rapids: Eerdmans, 1998.

Conradie, Ernst M. "Toward an Ecological Biblical Hermeneutics: A Review Essay of the Earth Bible Project." *Scriptura* 85 (2004): 123–35.

Cooper, Alan. "The Message of Lamentations." *JANES* 28 (2001): 1–18.

Craig, Kenneth M., Jr. *A Poetics of Jonah: Art in the Service of Ideology.* 2nd ed. Macon, Ga.: Mercer University Press, 1999.

———. "Questions Outside Eden (Genesis 4.1–16: Yahweh, Cain and Their Rhetorical Interchange)." *JSOT* 86 (1999): 107–28.

Cranfield, C. E. B. *The Gospel According to St Mark.* Cambridge: Cambridge University Press, 1959.

———. *A Critical and Exegetical Commentary on the Epistle to the Romans.* 2 vols. International Critical Commentary. Edinburgh: T&T Clark, 1979.

Cross, Frank Moore, Jr. "Yahweh and the God of the Patriarchs." *HTR* 55 (1962): 225–59.

———. *Canaanite Myth and Hebrew Epic.* Cambridge, Mass.: Harvard University Press, 1973.

Daly, Mary. *Beyond God the Father: Toward a Philosophy of Women's Liberation.* Boston: Beacon, 1973.

Daniels, Dwight. "Is there a 'Prophetic Lawsuit' Genre?" *ZAW* 99 (1987): 339–60.

Deist, Ferdinand E. "Parallels and Reinterpretation in the Book of Joel: A Theology of the Yom Yhwh?" Pages 63–79 in *Text and Context: Old Testament and Semitic Studies for F. C. Fensham.* JSOTSup 48. Edited by W. Claassen. Sheffield: Sheffield Academic Press, 1988.

DeRoche, Michael. "The Reversal of Creation in Hosea." *VT* 31 (1981): 400–409.

Deutsch, Celia. *Hidden Wisdom and the Easy Yoke: Wisdom, Torah and Discipleship in Matthew 11:25–30.* JSNTSup 18. Edited by D. Hill. Sheffield: JSOT Press, 1987.

Diewert, D. A. "Job 7:12: Yam, Tannin and the Surveillance of Job." *JBL* 106 (1987): 203–15.

Dobbs-Allsopp, F. W., and Todd Linafelt. "The Rape of Zion in Thr (Lamentations) 1,10." *ZAW* 113 (2001): 77–81.

———. *Lamentations.* IBC. Louisville, Ky.: Westminster John Knox, 2002.

Dodd, C. H. *The Epistle to the Romans.* Moffatt New Testament Commentary. London: Hodder & Stoughton, 1932.

Driver, G. R. "Confused Hebrew Roots." Pages 73–82 in *Occident and Orient, Being Studies in Semitic Philology and Literature, Jewish History and Philosophy and Folklore in the Widest Sense, in Honor of Haham Dr. M. Gaster's 80ᵗʰ Birthday. Gaster Anniversary Volume.* Edited by B. Schindler and A. Marmorstein. London: Taylor's Foreign Press, 1936.

Driver, S. R. *The Book of Genesis: With Introduction and Notes.* London: Methuen, 1904.

Dunn, James D. G. *Romans 1–8.* WBC. Dallas: Word Books, 1988.

Dyer, K. D. "When Is the End Not the End? The Fate of Earth in Biblical Eschatology (Mark 13)." Pages 44–56 in *The Earth Story in the New Testament.* Edited by Norman C. Habel and Vicky Balabanski. The Earth Bible 5. London: Continuum, 2002.

Earth Bible Team. "Guiding Ecojustice Principles." Pages 38–53 in Habel, *Readings from the Perspective of Earth*, 2000.

Eidevall, Göran. *Grapes in the Desert: Metaphors, Models and Themes in Hosea 4–14.* Stockholm: Almqvist & Wiksell International, 1996.

Encarta® World English Dictionary © 1999 Microsoft Corporation. Developed for Microsoft by Bloomsbury Publishing Plc.

Esler, Philip. *Conflict and Identity in Romans: The Social Setting of Paul's Letter*. Minneapolis: Fortress, 2003.

Evans, C. A. *Mark 8:27–16:20*. WBC 34B. Nashville: Thomas Nelson, 2001.

Fitzmyer, Joseph A. *Romans: A New Translation with Introduction and Commentary*. Anchor Bible. London: Geoffrey Chapman, 1993.

Follis, Elaine R. "The Holy City as Daughter." Pages 173–84 in *Directions in Biblical Hebrew Poetry*. Edited by Elaine R. Follis. JSOTSup 40. Sheffield: JSOT Press, 1987.

Fretheim, Terence E. *The Suffering of God: An Old Testament Perspective*. OBT. Philadelphia: Fortress, 1984.

——. "The Plagues as Ecological Signs of Historical Disaster." *JBL* 110 (1991): 385–96.

——. "The Book of Genesis: Introduction, Commentary, and Reflections." Pages 319–674 in *General Articles on the Bible, General Articles on the Old Testament,Genesis, Exodus, Leviticus*. Vol. 1 of *The New Interpreter's Bible*. Edited by Leander E. Keck. Nashville: Abingdon, 1994.

——. "The Earth Story in Jeremiah 12." Pages 96–110 in Habel, *Readings from the Perspective of Earth*, 2000.

——. *God and World in the Old Testament: A Relational Theology of Creation*. Nashville: Abingdon, 2005.

Gaster, T. H. *Myth, Legend, and Custom in the Old Testament*. New York: Harper & Row, 1969.

Gerstenberger, Erhard. *Der bittende Mensch*. Neukirchener-Vluyn: Neukirchener, 1980.

Gibbons, Ann. "European Skin Turned Pale Only Recently, Gene Suggests." *Science* 316 (2007): 364.

Gillingham, Susan. "'Who Makes the Morning Darkness': God and Creation in the Book of Amos." *SJT* 45 (1992): 165–84.

Grabbe, Lester L. *Wisdom of Solomon*. Sheffield: Sheffield Academic Press, 1997.

Green, Barbara. "The Wisdom of Solomon and the Solomon of Wisdom: Tradition's Transpositions and Human Transformation." *Horizons* 30 (2003): 41–66.

Grieb, A. Katherine. *The Story of Romans: A Narrative Defense of God's Righteousness*. Louisville, Ky.: Westminster John Knox, 2002.

Gruenwald, Ithamar. "God the 'Stone/Rock': Myth, Idolatry, and Cultic Fetishism in Ancient Israel." *JR* 76 (1996): 428–49.

Guest, Deryn. "Hiding Behind the Naked Women in Lamentations: A Recriminative Response." *BibInt* 7 (1999): 413–48.

Gunkel, Hermann. *Genesis übersetzt und erklärt*. Göttingen: Vandenhoeck & Ruprecht, 1902.

——.Introduction to *Die Grossen Propheten*, by Hans Schmidt. SAT 2/2. Göttingen: Vandenhoeck & Ruprecht, 1923.

Gunkel, Hermann, and Joachim Begrich. *Einleitung in die Psalmen: Die Gattungen der religiösen Lyrik Israels*. HKAT Abt. 2 Supp. Göttingen: Vandenhoeck & Ruprecht, 1933.

Habel, Norman C. "The Challenge of Ecojustice Readings for Christian Theology." *Pacifica* 13 (2000):125–41.

——. "Geophany: The Earth Story in Genesis One." Pages 34–48 in Habel and Wurst, *The Earth Story in Genesis*, 2000.

——. "Guiding Ecojustice Principles." Pages 38–53 in Habel, *Readings from the Perspective of Earth*, 2000.

——. "Introducing the Earth Bible." Pages 25–37 in Habel, *Readings from the Perspective of Earth*, 2000.

——, ed. *Readings from the Perspective of Earth*. The Earth Bible 1. Sheffield: Sheffield Academic Press, 2000.

——. "Earth First: Inverse Cosmology in Job." Pages 65–77 in Habel and Wurst, *The Earth Story in Wisdom Traditions*, 2001.

——, ed. *The Earth Story in Psalms and Prophets*. The Earth Bible 4. Sheffield: Sheffield Academic Press, 2001.

——. "The Origins and Challenges of an Ecojustice Hermeneutic." Pages 141–59 in *Relating to the Text: Interdisciplinary and Form-Critical Insights on the Bible*. Edited by Timothy Sandoval and Carleen Mandolfo. London: T&T Clark, 2003.

——. "Playing God or Playing Earth? An Ecological Reading of Genesis 1.26–28." Pages 33–41 in *"And God Saw That It Was Good." Essays on Creation and God in Honor of Terence Fretheim*. Edited by Frederick Gaiser and Mark Throntveit. WWSup 5. St. Paul: Luther Seminary, 2006.

Habel, Norman C., and Shirley Wurst, eds. *The Earth Story in Genesis*. The Earth Bible 2. Sheffield: Sheffield Academic Press, 2000.

Habel, Norman C., and Shirley Wurst, eds. *The Earth Story in Wisdom Traditions*. The Earth Bible 3. Sheffield: Sheffield Academic Press, 2001.

Hahm, David E. *The Origins of Stoic Cosmology*. Ohio: Ohio State University Press, 1977.

Hayes, Katherine M. *"The Earth Mourns": Prophetic Metaphor and Oral Aesthetic*. SBLAcBib 8; Atlanta, Ga.: Society of Biblical Literature, 2002.

Hays, Richard B. *Echoes of Scripture in the Letters of Paul*. New Haven: Yale University Press, 1989.

——. *The Faith of Jesus Christ: An Investigation of the Narrative Substructure of Galatians 3:1–4:11*. SBLDS 56. Chico: Scholars Press, 1983. Repr., Grand Rapids: Eerdmans, 2002.

Heim, Knut M. "The Personification of Jerusalem and the Drama of Her Bereavement in Lamentations." Pages 129–69 in *Zion, City of Our God*. Edited by R. S. Hess and Gordan J. Wenham. Grand Rapids: Eerdmans, 1999.

Heuer, Karsten. *Being Caribou: Five Months on Foot with an Arctic Herd*. Toronto: McClelland & Stewart, 2006.

Hooker, M. D. *The Gospel According to St Mark*. London: A&C Black, 1991.

Houghton, William. "The Pistic Nard of the Greek Testament." *Proceedings of the Society of Biblical Archaeology* (1888): 144–46.

Huffmon, Herbert B. "The Covenant Lawsuits in the Prophets." *JBL* 78 (1959): 285–95.

Hughes, J. M., P. A. Mitchell, and W. S. Ramson, eds. *The Australian Concise Oxford Dictionary*. 2d ed. Melbourne: Oxford University Press, 1992.

Jacob, Edmond. *Osée*. 3d ed. CAT 11a. Geneva: Labor et Fides, 1992.

Jeremias, Jörg. *Der Prophet Hosea*. Das Alte Testament Deutsch 24/1. Göttingen: Vandenhoeck & Ruprecht, 1983.

Jewett, Robert. "The Corruption and Redemption of Creation: Reading Rom 8:18–23 within the Imperial Context." Pages 25–46 in *Paul and the Roman Imperial Order*.

Edited by Richard A. Horsley. Harrisburg, Pa.: Trinity Press International, 2004.

Jobling, David, and Nathan Loewen. "Sketches for Earth Readings of the Book of Amos." Pages 72–85 in Habel, *Readings from the Perspective of Earth*. Edited by Norman Habel. The Earth Bible 1. Sheffield: Sheffield Academic Press, 2000.

Joy, Morny. "Beyond the Given and the All-giving: Reflections on Women and the Gift." *Australian Feminist Studies* 14 (1999): 315–32.

Kaiser, Barbara Bakke. "Poet as 'Female Impersonator': The Image of Daughter Zion as Speaker in Biblical Poems of Suffering." *JR* 67 (1987): 164–82.

Käsemann, Ernst. *Commentary on Romans*. Translated by Geoffrey W. Bromiley. Grand Rapids: Eerdmans, 1994.

Knierim, Rolf. *The Task of Old Testament Theology: Substance, Method and Cases*. Grand Rapids: Eerdmans, 1995.

Knowles, Michael P. "'The Rock, His Work Is Perfect': Unusual Imagery for God in Deuteronomy XXXII." *VT* 39 (1989): 307–22.

Koch, Klaus. *The Rediscovery of Apocalyptic*. Translated by Margaret Kohl. London: SCM Press, 1972.

——. "Is There a Doctrine of Retribution in the Old Testament?" Pages 57–87 in *Theodicy in the Old Testament*. Edited by James L. Crenshaw. Philadelphia: Fortress, 1983.

Koehler, L., W. Baumgartner, and J. J. Stamm. *Hebräisches und aramäisches Lexikon zum Alten Testament*. 5 vols. Leiden: Brill, 1967–95.

Kolarcik, Michael. *The Ambiguity of Death in the Book of Wisdom 1–6: A Study of Literary Structure and Interpretation*. Rome: Editrice Pontificio Istituto Biblico, 1991.

Kugel, James L. *The Idea of Biblical Poetry: Parallelism and Its History*. Baltimore: John Hopkins University Press, 1981.

——. "Cain and Abel in Fact and Fable: Genesis 4:1–16." Pages 167–90 in *Hebrew Bible or Old Testament? Studying the Bible in Judaism and Christianity*. Notre Dame: University of Notre Dame Press, 1990.

Kusher, Harold. *How Good Do We Have to Be?* Boston: Little, Brown, & Co., 1996.

Lambert, W. G., ed. *Babylonian Wisdom Literature*. Oxford: Oxford University Press, 1960.

Lambrecht, Jan. *The Wretched "I" and Its Liberation: Paul in Romans 7 and 8*. Louvain: Peeters, 1992.

Lanahan, William F. "The Speaking Voice in the Book of Lamentations." *JBL* 93 (1974): 46–56.

Levenson, Jon D. "The Temple and the World." *JR* 64 (1984): 275–98.

——. *Sinai & Zion: An Entry into The Jewish Bible*. San Francisco: HarperCollins, 1985.

——. *Sinai and Zion: An Entry into the Jewish Bible*. San Francisco: HarperSanFrancisco, 1987.

Levy, Sharon. "Last Days of the Locust." *New Scientist* 2435 (2004): 48–49.

Lichtheim, Miriam. *The Old and Middle Kingdoms*. Vol. 1 of *Ancient Egyptian Literature*. Berkeley and Los Angeles: University of California Press, 1973.

Linafelt, Todd. *Surviving Lamentations: Catastrophe, Lament, Protest in the Afterlife of a Biblical Book*. Chicago: University of Chicago Press, 2000.

Litke, Joel. "The Messages of Chapter 4 of Genesis." *JBQ* 31 (2003): 197–200.

Lohse, E. *Colossians and Philemon*. Philadelphia: Fortress, 1971.

Long, A. A. *Hellenistic Philosophy: Stoics, Epicureans, Sceptics*. London: Duckworth, 1974.

Lovelock, James. *The Revenge of Gaia: Earth's Climate Crisis and the Fate of Humanity*. New York: Basic, 2006.

Manolopoulos, Mark. "If Creation is a Gift: Towards an Eco/Theo/Logical Aporetics." Ph.D. diss., Monash University, 2003.

Mays, James Luther. *Hosea: A Commentary*. Old Testament Library. Philadelphia: Westminster, 1969.

Meadowcroft, Tim. "Some Questions for the Earth Bible." Paper presented at the ANZATS Conference. Christchurch, New Zealand, July 2000.

Meier, Samuel A. *Speaking of Speaking: Marking Direct Discourse in the Hebrew Bible*. VTSup 46. Leiden: Brill, 1992.

Michel, Otto. *Der Brief an die Römer*. KEK 4. Göttingen: Vandenhoeck & Ruprecht, 1978.

Middlemas, Jill. *The Troubles of Templeless Judah*. OTM. Oxford: Oxford University Press, 2005.

Miller, Charles W. "Reading Voices, Personification, Dialogism, and the Reader of Lamentations 1." *BI* 9 (2001): 393–408.

Moberly, R. W. L. "Preaching for a Response? Jonah's Message to the Ninevites Reconsidered." *VT* 53 (2003): 156–68.

Möller, Karl. *A Prophet in Debate: The Rhetoric of Persuasion in the Book of Amos*. Sheffield: Sheffield Academic Press, 2003.

Moore, Rickie D. "'And Also Much Cattle?!': Prophetic Passions and the End of Jonah." *Journal of Pentecostal Theology* 11 (1997): 35–48.

Mulzer, Martin. "Die Buße der Tiere in Jona 3,7f. und Jdt 4,10." *BN* 111 (2002): 76–88.

Myers, Ched. *Binding the Strong Man. A Political Reading of Mark's Story of Jesus*. New York: Orbis, 1988.

Newsom, Carol A. "Response to Norman K. Gottwald, 'Social Class and Ideology in Isaiah 40-55.'" *Semeia* 59 (1992): 73–78.

———. "Common Ground: An Ecological Reading of Genesis 2–3." Pages 60–72 in Habel and Wurst, *The Earth Story in Genesis*, 2000.

Nielsen, Kirsten. *There is Hope for a Tree: The Tree as Metaphor in Isaiah*. Sheffield: Sheffield Academic Press, 1989.

Nineham, D. E. *Saint Mark*. London: SCM, 1963.

Ogden, Graham S. "Joel 4 and Prophetic Responses to National Laments." *JSOT* 26 (1983): 103–5.

Økland, Jorunn. *Women in Their Place: Paul and the Corinthian Discourse of Gender and Sanctuary Space*. JSNTSup 269. London: T&T Clark, 2004.

Olyan, Saul M. *Biblical Mourning: Ritual and Social Dimensions*. Oxford: Oxford University Press, 2004.

Paas, Stefan. *Creation and Judgment: Creation Texts in Some Eighth Century Prophets*. OTS 47. Leiden: Brill, 2003.

Parker, Simon B. *The Pre-Biblical Narrative Tradition*. SBLRBS 24. Atlanta: Scholars Press, 1989.

Paul, Shalom M. *Amos: A Commentary on the Book of Amos*. Minneapolis: Fortress, 1991.

Person, Raymond F., Jr. *In Conversation with Jonah: Conversation Analysis, Literary Criticism, and the Book of Jonah.* JSOTSup 220. Sheffield: Sheffield Academic Press, 1996.

Pfeifer, Gerhard. "Jahwe als Schopfer der Welt und Herr ihrer Machte in der Verkundigung des Propheten Amos." *VT* 41 (1991): 475–81.

Pham, Xuan Huong Thi. *Mourning in the Ancient Near East and the Hebrew Bible.* JSOTSup 302. Sheffield: Sheffield Academic Press, 1999

Plumwood, Val. *Feminism and the Mastery of Nature.* Feminism for Today. London: Routledge, 1993.

Primavesi, Anne. *Sacred Gaia: Holistic Theology and Earth System Science.* London: Routledge, 2000.

Pritchard, James B. *Ancient Near Eastern Pictures Relating to the Old Testament.* Princeton: Princeton University Press, 1954.

———. ed. *Ancient Near Eastern Texts Relating to the Old Testament.* Princeton: Princeton University Press, 1969.

Provan, Iain. "Reading Texts Against an Historical Background: The Case of Lamentations 1." *SJOT* 4 (1990): 130–43.

———. *Lamentations.* NCBC. Grand Rapids: Eerdmans, 1991.

Rowley, H. H. *The Relevance of Apocalyptic: A Study of Jewish and Christian Apocalypses from Daniel to the Revelation.* London: Lutterworth, 1944.

Rudman, D. "The Crucifixion as *Chaoskampf*: A New Reading of the Passion Narrative in the Synoptic Gospels." *Bib* 84 (2003): 102–7.

Sanday, William, and Arthur C. Headlam. *A Critial and Exegetical Commentary on the Epistle to the Romans.* 5th ed. International Critical Commentary. Edinburgh: T&T Clark, 1901. Repr. 1992.

Sanders, E. P. *Paul and Palestinian Judaism.* Minneapolis: Fortress Press, 1979.

Sasson, Jack M. *Jonah.* AB 24B. Garden City: Doubleday, 1990.

Savran, G. "Beastly Speech: Intertextuality, Balaam's Ass and the Garden of Eden." *JSOT* 64 (1994): 33–55.

Schmidt, H. H. "Creation, Righteousness, and Salvation: 'Creation Theology' as the Broad Horizon of Biblical Theology." Pages 102–17 in *Creation in the Old Testament.* Edited and translated by Bernard W. Anderson. IRT 6. Philadelphia: Fortress, 1984.

Schüssler Fiorenza, Elizabeth. "Wisdom Mythology and the Christological Hymns of the New Testament." Pages 17–41 in *Aspects of Wisdom in Judaism and Early Christianity.* Edited by R. L. Wilken. Center for the Study of Judaism and Christianity in Antiquity 1. Notre Dame: University of Notre Dame Press, 1975.

———. *In Memory of Her: A Feminist Reconstruction of Christian Origins.* New York: Crossroad, 1983.

———. *Bread not Stone: The Challenge of Feminist Biblical Interpretation.* Boston: Beacon, 1984.

———. *But She Said: Feminist Practices of Biblical Interpretation.* Boston: Beacon, 1992.

———. *Wisdom Ways: Introducing Feminist Biblical Interpretation.* Maryknoll, N.Y.: Orbis, 2000.

Scully, Matthew. *Dominion: The Power of Man, the Suffering of Animals, and the Call to Mercy.* New York: St. Martin's Press, 2002.

Shields, Mary E. *Circumscribing the Prostitute: The Rhetorics of Intertextuality,*

Metaphor and Gender in Jeremiah 3:1–4:4. JSOTSup 387. Edited by D. J. A. Clines and P. R. Davies. London: T&T Clark, 2004.

Singer, Isaac Bashevis. *The Collected Stories of Isaac Bashevis Singer.* New York: Farrar, Straus & Giroux, 1996. First pub. 1953.

Sinnott, Alice M. "Job 12: Cosmic Devastation and Social Turmoil." Pages 78–91 in Habel and Wurst, *The Earth Story in Wisdom Traditions,* 2001.

Stowers, Stanley. *A Rereading of Romans: Justice, Jews, and Gentiles.* New Haven: Yale University Press, 1994.

Sweeney, Marvin A. *The Twelve Prophets.* Berit Olam. 2 vols. Collegeville: Liturgical Press, 2000.

———. *Zephaniah.* Hermeneia. Minneapolis: Fortress, 2003.

Talmon, Shemaryahu. "Revelation in Biblical Times." *HS* 26 (1985): 53–70.

Tennant, F. R. "The Teaching of Ecclesiasticus and Wisdom on Sin and Death." *JTS* 2 (1901): 207–23.

Theophrastus. *Enquiry into Plants, Book 9.* Translated by Arthus Hort. Loeb Classical Library. London: Heinemann, 1916.

Tonstad, Sigve "πίστις Χριστοῦ/: Reading Paul in A New Paradigm." *Andrews University Seminary Studies* 40 (2002): 37–59.

Turner, Marie. "God's Design: The Death of Creation? An Ecojustice Reading of Romans 8.18–30 in the Light of Wisdom 1–2." Pages 168–78 in Habel and Wurst, *The Earth Story in Wisdom Traditions,* Sheffield: Sheffield Academic Press, 2001.

Trible, Phyllis. *God and the Rhetoric of Sexuality.* Philadelphia: Fortress, 1978.

———. *Rhetorical Criticism: Context, Method, and the Book of Jonah.* Minneapolis: Fortress, 1994.

Tromp, Nicholas J. *Primitive Conceptions of Death and the Nether World in the Old Testament.* Rome: Pontifical Biblical Institute, 1969.

Van Kooten, George H. *Cosmic Christology in Paul and the Pauline School.* WUNT 171. Tübingen: Mohr Siebeck, 2003.

van Wolde, Ellen. "The Story of Cain and Abel: A Narrative Study." *JSOT* 52 (1991): 25–41.

———. "Facing the Earth: Primaeval History in a New Perspective." Pages 22–47 in *The World of Genesis: Persons, Places, Perspectives.* JSOTSup 257. Sheffield: Sheffield Academic Press, 1998.

Veenker, Ronald A. "That Fabulous Talking Snake." Pages 265–72 in *The Challenge of Bible Translation: Communicating God's Word to the World.* Edited by Glen G. Scorgie, Mark L. Strauss, and Steven M. Voth. Grand Rapids: Zondervan, 2003.

Wade, Nicholas. "Gene That Determines Skin Color Is Discovered, Scientists Report." *New York Times* 155 (2005): A36.

Wainwright, Elaine M. *Towards a Feminist Critical Reading of the Gospel According to Matthew.* BZNW 60. Berlin: de Gruyter, 1991.

———. *Shall We Look for Another: A Feminist Rereading of the Matthean Jesus.* Maryknoll, N.Y.: Orbis, 1998.

———. "The Pouring out of Healing Ointment: Rereading Mark 14:3–9." Pages 157–78 in *Toward a New Heaven and a New Earth: Essays in Honor of Elisabeth Schüssler Fiorenza.* Edited by Fernando F. Segovia. Maryknoll, N.Y.: Orbis, 2003.

———. *Women Healing/Healing Women: The Genderization of Healing in Early Christianity.* London: Equinox, 2006.

Weiss, Hans-Friedrich. *Untersuchungen zur Kosmologie des hellenistischen und palästinischen Judentums.* Texte und Untersuchungen zur Geschichte der altchristlichen Literatur 97. Berlin: Akademie-Verlag, 1966.

Wendland, Ernst R. "The 'Word of the Lord' and the Organisation of Amos: A Dramatic Message of Conflict and Crisis in the Confrontation Between the Prophet and People of Yahweh." *Occasional Papers in Translation and Textlinguistics* 2 (1988): 1–51.

Wengst, Klaus. *Pax Romana and the Peace of Jesus Christ.* Translated by John Bowden. London: SCM Press, 1987.

Wensinck, Arent J. *The Ocean in the Literature of the Western Semites.* Verhandelingen der Koinklijk Akademie van Wetenschappen te Amsterdam; Afdeeling Letterkunde, nieuwe reeks, deel 19/2. Amsterdam: J. Müller, 1918.

Wilckens, Ulrich. *Der Brief an die Römer.* 3 vols. EKKNT. Neukirchen-Vluyn: Benziger Verlag, 1980.

Willey, Patricia. "Sing to God a New Song: Using the Past to Construct a Future." *Reformed World* 46 (1996): 37–46.

Williams, Ronald J. "The Fable in the Ancient Near East." Pages 3–26 in *A Stubborn Faith: Papers on Old Testament and Related Subjects Presented to Honor William Andrew Irwin.* Edited by Edward C. Hobbs. Dallas: Southern Methodist University Press, 1956.

Windsor, Donald A. "Equal Rights for Parasites (Call for Protection of Parasites Against Extinction)." *Perspectives in Biology and Medicine* 40 (1997): 222–29.

Winkler, John J. *The Constraints of Desire: The Anthropology of Sex and Gender in Ancient Greece.* New York: Routledge, 1990.

Wolff, Hans Walter. *Joel and Amos: A Commentary on the Books of the Prophets Joel and Amos.* Philadelphia: Fortress, 1977.

Wood, Joyce Rilett. *Amos in Song and Book Culture.* Sheffield: Sheffield Academic Press. 2002.

Wurst, Shirley. "'Beloved, Come Back to Me': Ground's Theme Song in Genesis 3?" Pages 87–104 in Habel and Wurst, *The Earth Story in Genesis*, 2000.

Würthwein, Ernst. "Der Ursprung der prophetischen Gerichtsrede." *ZTK* 49 (1952): 1–16.

INDEX OF PRIMARY SOURCES

Index of Modern Authors